The Impact of Globalisation on Europe's Firms and Industries

The Impact of Globalisation on Europe's Firms and Industries

Edited by
Marc Humbert

Pinter Publishers
London and New York
Distributed in the United States and Canada
by St. Martin's Press

Pinter Publishers Ltd.
25 Floral Street, London WC2E 9DS, United Kingdom

First published in 1993

Distributed exclusively in the USA and Canada by St. Martin's Press, Inc., Room 400, 175 Fifth Avenue, New York, NY 10010, USA

British Library Cataloguing in Publication Data

A CIP catalogue record for this book is available from the British Library

ISBN 1 85567 113 1

Library of Congress Cataloging-in-Publication Data

The impact of globalisation on Europe's firms and industries / edited
  by Marc Humbert.
     p. cm.
  Includes bibliographical references and index.
  ISBN 1-85567-113-1
    1. International business enterprises--Europe. 2. Competition,
International. 3. Investments, Foreign--Europe. I. Humbert, Marc.
HD2844.155   1993
338.8'894--dc20   93-16879
                                           CIP

Typeset by CERETIM, Rennes, Brittany
Printed and bound in Great Britain by Biddles Ltd., Guildford and King's Lynn

Contents

Preface

The chapters of this book have been selected from papers [1] presented in a preliminary form at an international conference held in St Malo (France) in June 1992. Thirty-five papers by famous expert senior economists from Europe, the United States and Japan - and twenty posters by junior economists - were presented. The theme of this conference "European Firms and Industry coping with Globalisation" permitted active and intense discussion and debate with about 150 people during two full days of work. We convened and organised the meeting with the support of CERETIM [2], a research centre of the University of Rennes I, associated with the CNRS [3] and the sponsorship of many other institutions, especially the European Commission (DG XIII), and the Conseil Régional de Bretagne. The poster session was managed by Maurice Baslé, Director of the Ecole Doctorale de Sciences Economiques et de Gestion de l'Université de Rennes I, and the whole meeting was successfully coordinated by Jean-Louis Perrault with the help of a dynamic team of lecturers, research fellows, Ph.D. candidates ("doctorants") and administrative staff from CERETIM and ADEREM [4]. We would like to thank particularly Fabienne Jégousse who has been working intensively for months, far beyond her usual secretarial work, from the launching of the project for the conference up to the preparation of this book. Most of the papers have been extensively revised for publication, following indications given to the authors after the meeting. We have been helped, in this difficult task of selection and orientation, principally by our scientific committee with Alain Alcouffe, Jacques de Bandt, François Chesnais, Patrick Cohendet, Dominique Foray, David Mowery and also by Maurice Baslé, Michel Marchesnay and Jean-Louis Perrault. We would like to thank them and the authors who suffered our requests for revision and editing of their papers. We would also like to thank John Holstein for his valuable help to ensure that this edition is written in correct English. Finally, we are grateful to our publisher who has handled our material in the most efficient way.

The contributors to this volume, and most of the participants of the conference, are mainly industrial economists who share a common interest in developing an analysis of industry, at the world level, taking into account and combining dimensions that have been omitted by the traditional theory : the technological dimension - creation and diffusion of technology ; the non-market dimension - networks relationships between firms and states not only for trade but also for production of goods and services (knowledge included) ; and the strategic dimension - capacities of vision and of power effects upon structures. Their meeting was a great success allowing a better understanding of what globalisation [5] means for our European industry. However further research is still necessary ; most of the conference delegates have expressed their wish for further meetings, therefore encouraging the authors of the papers to keep in touch and contemplate the possibility of establishing a Network on European Strategy and Technology for Industry where they could exchange and discuss further contributions.

The book is organised in three parts. Part I brings together some of the key questions, implications and challenges which confront Europe - more precisely the EC - and its individual states and firms, in the name of globalisation. Part II considers in detail the EC attempt to maintain a competitive European industry in a global environment. Part III presents an overview of the implications for countries, especially coming from foreign investment. Countries under observation are principally the smaller European economies. Part IV deals with firms' strategies for coping with the globalisation challenge. In all, the book offers an in-depth analysis of European industry in the context of globalisation. To be sure, not all the aspects of such a complex problem are dealt with : for instance there is no direct sectorial entry even though the electronics industry, aircraft industry and car industry are analysed in various chapters. To this first limitation we must add another one : globalisation is still an emerging phenomenon. Therefore the principal objective of our book is to shed more light on what is ongoing in order to help decision-makers at various levels : firms, states, the European commission. The group of authors shares many ideas and analyses but so large a group presents necessarily some differences of opinion, especially when their analyses are still to be completed as the phenomenon is becoming more established. Thus the book does not bring clear-cut and definite conclusions. But the opening chapter, in Part I, outlines some policies and strategies which might be, according to the arguments expressed by the authors within the chapters of the book, most helpful in tackling questions, problems and challenges posed by globalisation to the competitiveness of European industry.

Marc Humbert
CERETIM
CNRS, Université de Rennes I
November 1992

Notes

1 Several papers, presented in French and not selected for this book, have been published in a special issue of *Cahiers d'Economie Mondiale* (7 Place Hoche, 35065 Rennes cedex, France).

2 Centre d'Etudes et de Recherches sur l'Entreprise, la Technologie, les Institutions et la Mondialisation, *Study and Research Centre on Enterprise, Technology, Institutions and Globalisation.*

3 Centre National de la Recherche Scientifique, *National Centre for Scientific Research* (France).

4 ADEREM is a non-profit organisation ; it dealt with all concrete matters involved in the organisation of the meeting.

5 Several authors had previously (1990-1991) contributed to a research programme on globalisation organised by FAST (EC, DGXII) and coordinated by Riccardo Petrella.

Notes on contributors

Fabio Arcangeli	Associate Professor of Economics - DIMEG, Facolta di Ingeneria, Universita di Padova, Via Venezia 1, 35131 Padova - Italy.
François Chesnais	Professor of Economics (non tenure appointment) - UFR de Sciences Economiques, Université de Paris-Nord Villetaneuse, Avenue J.B. Clément, 93430 Villetaneuse - France. Formally - DSTI, OECD, 2 rue André-Pascal, 75775 Paris - France.
Michel Delapierre	Research Fellow (CNRS) - LAREA/CEREM, Université de Paris 10, 200 avenue de la République, 92001 Nanterre cedex - France.
Kenneth Flamm	Senior Fellow - Foreign Policies Studies Program, The Brookings Institution, 1775 Massachusetts Avenue, NW, Washington DC 20036 - USA.
Dominique Foray	Professor of Economics - Ecole Centrale de Paris, Grande voie des Vignes, 92295 Chatenay-Malabry cedex - France.
Colette Fourcade	Senior Lecturer in Economics - ERFI, Faculté de Droit et des Sciences Economiques, Université de Montpellier, 39 rue de l'Université, 34060 Montpellier cedex - France.
Ilaria Galimberti	Ph.D. candidate at Science Policy Research Unit, University of Sussex, UK - Villa il Poggiolino, San Cristoforo, Troghi, Florence - Italy.
Tassos Giannitsis	Professor of Economics - Department of Economics, University of Athens, Pesmazoglou 8, 10559 Athens - Greece.
Françoise Guelle	Research Fellow (EHESS), Fellow at OSI (Observatoire des stratégies industrielles), French Ministry of Industry - OSI, Ministère de l'Industrie et du Commerce extérieur, 68 rue de Bellechasse, 75353 Paris cedex 07 - France.

Peter Holmes	Senior Lecturer in Economics - School of European Studies, University of Sussex, Brighton BN1 9QN - United Kingdom.
Jeremy Howells	Principle Research Investigator - CURDS (Centre for Urban and Regional Development Studies), University of Newcastle upon Tyne, Newcastle upon Tyne NE1 7RU - United Kingdom.
Kirsty S. Hughes	Senior Fellow - Policy Studies Institute, 100 Park Village East, London NW1 3SR - United Kingdom.
Marc Humbert	Professor of Economics at University of Rennes 1, Director of CERETIM (Study and Research Centre on Enterprise, Technology, Institutions and Globalisation) - CERETIM, Université de Rennes 1, 7 place Hoche, 35065 Rennes cedex - France.
Tora C. Lie	Commission of the European Communities, Directorate General XIII, *Telecommunications, Information Industries and Innovation*, Rue de la Loi 200, B1049 Brussels - Belgium.
Paolo Mariti	Professor of Industrial Economics and Policy - Istituto di Economia e Finanza, Facolta' di Scienze Politiche, Universita di Pisa, Via Serafini 3, 56126 Pisa - Italy.
David C. Mowery	Associate Professor of Business and Public Policy - Hass School of Business, University of California at Berkeley, Berkeley, California 94720 - USA.
Lynn Krieger Mytelka	Professor of Political Economy - Carleton University, K1S 5B6 Ottawa - Canada. Senior research associate - LAREA/CEREM, Université de Paris X, 90001 Nanterre - France.
Dermot P. O'Doherty	Manager - Strategic Planning, EOLAS-The Irish Science & Technology Agency, Glasnevin, Dublin 9 - Ireland.
Winfried Ruigrok	Assistant Professor - Department of Strategic Management and Business Environment, Erasmus University of Rotterdam, Burg. Oudlaan 50, P.O. Box 1738, 3000 DR Rotterdam - The Netherlands.

Gérald Santucci

Principal Administrator - Commission of the European Communities, Directorate General XIII, *Telecommunications, Information Industries and Innovation*, Rue de la Loi 200, B1049 Brussels - Belgium.

Vitor Corado Simões

Senior Lecturer in Economics - Instituto Superior de Economia e Gestão, Universidade Técnica de Lisbõa, Rua Miguel Lupi 20, 1200 Lisbõa - Portugal.

Rob van Tulder

Senior Research Fellow - Department of International Relations and Public International Law, Universiteit van Amsterdam, Oudezijds Achterburgwal 237, 1012 DL Amsterdam - The Netherlands.
Assistant Professor in Business Administration, Erasmus University of Rotterdam - The Netherlands.

Jaume Valls

Lecturer in Economics - Economics and Business Administration Department, Facultat d'Informàtica de Barcelona, Universitat Politècnica de Catalunya, Pau Gargallo 5, Apartat de Correus 30.014, 08028 Barcelona - Spain.

Vivien Walsh

Senior Lecturer in Innovation - Manchester School of Management, UMIST, PO Box 88, Manchester M60 1QD - United Kingdom.

Susumu Watanabe

Professor of Economics - Tokyo International University, 1-13-1 Matokakita, Kwagoe, Saitama, Japan 350 - Japan.

Jean-Benoît Zimmermann

Research Fellow (CNRS) - GREQE, Université d'Aix-Marseille, 2 rue de la Charité, 13002 Marseille - France.

John Zysman

Professor of Political Science, co-director BRIE (Berkeley Round Table in International Economics) - BRIE, University of California, 2234 Piedmont Avenue, Berkeley, California 94720 - USA.

Part I

What does globalisation mean ?

1 Introduction : questions, constraints and challenges in the name of globalisation

Marc Humbert

I Introduction

As we observe the real economic world, from various standpoints : a firm, an industry, a nation, a continent, the planet ... we are tempted to use the term **globalisation** to characterise what seems to us a novelty. Globalisation is the name given for lack of a theoretical concept matching more closely observed phenomena. Although we are far from a world integrated economy, which would rationally characterise the completion of a wide globalisation process, we can point out that the evolution of important economic variables, which are necessarily localised and important to the economic future of their location, depends on economic forces that are mainly driven by non-local factors. Global is clearly used as opposed to local and its use reveals local concerns. The growing importance of external factors, of what is abroad, to keep a firm profitable, to support local industries, to ensure nation's competitiveness ... supersedes what was previously known as internationalisation ; therefore designing a strategy or a policy demands a global approach. The purpose of this chapter is first to look into the meaning of the word **globalisation** and identify the key elements of change in the real world that can justify the new term. These elements will shed light on the main characteristics of the global environment in which the EC, its member states, its industries and its firms try to thrive, searching for the best solutions to the questions, constraints and challenges that confront them, and that are studied in detail in the chapters of this book. In the last part of this introduction we will give a tentative synthesis of policies and strategies that seem relevant to this context, according to the arguments developed in the chapters that follow.

II   From internationalisation to globalisation

We have identified four elements in recent economic evolution that call for the use of the term globalisation. We would like to introduce them shortly and then to explore a little further the first three which are directly addressed in this volume. These elements concern the following observed phenomenon : (i) globalisation, in the same manner as internationalisation, is a phenomenon which emerges from within the bloc of the leading industrialised countries. It does not upset the reality of a world of unequal nations with a strong international hierarchy. However the landscape is no longer exactly the same. **The architecture within the bloc of leading countries and the boundaries of this bloc have changed.** It seems difficult to take this change into account under the old meaning of the internationalisation process, therefore it is dubbed globalisation ; (ii) **adequacy between a nation-state economic sovereignty domain and its market is under pressure** from what we can call the globalisation drive (Simões, this volume). Until recently national economic interest lay undoubtedly in its set of national firms acting within its market and this market worked under its national rule. Hence, inter-nation economic relations were defined mainly by relations between these national markets under GATT regulations and the principle of mutual benefits from trade. Before the meaning of inter-nationalisation was obvious but in this new context, it is now becoming more and more blurred ; (iii) **by traditional analysis industry was not given a real international dimension.** It was only taken into consideration through (large) multinationals which were seen as competing for access to markets and to low labour costs in the so-called internationalisation of the production process. The present deep industrial transformation goes along with a series of changes principally driven by a strong focus on quick progress in high-technology. On the one hand, it has put into the picture a technology race where nations are struggling for a competitive edge, and on the other hand, it has made a part of the relationships between (large and small) firms, which are usually market relationships, switch towards worldwide cooperation. Therefore a kind of global networking appears to be organising industry at a world level ; (iv) we must mention a fourth element which facilitates the route from internationalisation to globalisation : thanks to the development of communication infrastructures - airlines and more crucially information networks -, we are witnessing a shrinking world, the planet does not seem so large as it was and, to a certain extent, **the world seems on its way to becoming a global village** (McLuhan, 1960). Moreover consciousness of this evolution is more and more widely spread but this last element does not match the scope of this book, thus we will now only explore the first three to take stock of the analytical and explanatory scope covered by the term globalisation in each case [1].

The global architecture of nations

Standard theory claimed that free trade and International Division of Labour (IDL) between nations according to their existing comparative advantages is the single way to organise an optimal and prosperous world of equal nations. However, during the fifties general opinion became aware of the architecture of the real world, characterised by a hierarchy of wealth between nations. There were Less Developed Countries (LDCs) and the United Nations Organisation launched at the beginning of the sixties a decade programme for development which has been followed by other decade programmes : development is still to come for more populated LDCs. OECD was launched at the same time and formed a bloc of leading countries after the previous organisation (OECE) had successfully achieved the restoration of Western Europe's past economic power. Within this bloc, domination by the United States seemed to be faced with a countervailing power erected by some European countries building up a Common Market. Nevertheless, US domination was obviously extended by growing outward flows of Foreign Direct Investment (FDI) in manufactures. Countries of this bloc were enjoying both hierarchy and rivalry, since American FDI could be interpreted as an American challenge (Servan-Schreiber, 1967) in response to the building of Europe. This was the time for a one-way FDI, which moved, as Vernon (1966) remarked, from the USA to the other advanced countries and then, from the former and the latter to the LDCs. A dominant nation and its firms, several semi-dominant nations and their firms were exercising their economic power upon the rest of the world (ROW). In the seventies this version was undermined, first because Japan who joined OECD in 1964 started to play its part as a leading country, second because of the emergence of a so-called New International Division of Labour (NIDL). According to Froebel *et al.*, 1977, firms from leading countries were intensifying their investments abroad, delocalising massively their production sites from their home countries to LDCs. In fact delocalisation was not so massive and the recipients were only a few LDCs. OECD (1979a) coined the term Newly Industrialising Countries, NICs, to pinpoint on this upsetting fact : some LDCs, partly because they were hosting foreign multinationals, were exporting manufactures to the bloc of old leading countries. This change was taking place in a time of economic crisis and uncertainty after thirty years of growing prosperity for the dominant nations. Incumbent industrial countries were facing the threat of entry by NICs and then from other latecomers today known as Dynamic Asian Economies. All this was reshaping the boundaries of the bloc and the inner structure itself was no longer exactly the same. OECD experts emphasised the growing interdependence between all countries in the world (1979b), however the new architecture of this more interdependent world still has a hierarchical nature. There is still a bloc of leading countries, with a first and a second tier of followers, then, behind them, a little further, LDCs and, still further behind, poor and very poor countries.

Nevertheless the gap between countries within the leading bloc seems to have narrowed and their proximity has been reinforced by a new two-way FDI. European firms are investing in the USA and Japanese firms are also investing in the USA and in Europe as well. The United States have become a principal host country for FDI in industry and Japan is now a major source of FDI in industry. Thus, instead of an internal hierarchy the leading countries have come to form a kind of a "triad" (Ohmae, 1985) : three regions, which together are dominating the rest of the world, are trading openly and exchanging FDI flows, producing and consuming the same high value added and high-tech goods and services. This triad accounts for two thirds of the world domestic product, for half the world's external trade, more than 80 % of the stock of outward FDI and 55 % of the stock of inward FDI with 65 % of the inward flows of FDI for the 1985-1988 average (see UNCTC, 1991). This absence of a clear domination by one of the regions of the triad upon the others does not mean absence of competition ; competition among them in their markets, competition also in the markets of the ROW. Some authors analyse the triad landscape as a set of regional trading blocs in a global world (Zysman, this volume). For Lie and Santucci (this volume) this configuration could be a first and necessary step towards multilateralism. At least tacit competition between regions does exist. Simões (this volume) believes that the single European market is an attempt to keep Europe as a leading region on the world economic scene. Many authors underline the special case of Japan within the triad. Its openness is the narrowest among the triad regions : the trade ratio penetration of Japan in 1988 reaches no more than 5.1 % for manufactured products (coming from 3.6 % in 1973, according to CEPII, 1992), far from 16.6 % for the USA or 13.6 % for the EC (intra-EC trade excluded). Similarly the Japanese economy remains relatively closed to inward investment with no more than 1 % of the world stock (in 1988 as in 1980, see UNCTC, 1991) to compare to 31 % for the USA and 23 % for the EC (intra-EC FDI excluded). Such a situation raises questions about fairness and security (Zysman, this volume), which is an important issue as symmetric access to each region is a necessary condition to sustain politically this new global architecture of nations.

The divergence between *national* and *territorial*

The evolution of economic relations at world level that we have sketched above has given birth to a new distortion for leading countries between what is national and what is territorial. In the time of the old IDL, dominant nations were enjoying national specialisation in manufactured products through their national firms settled on their national territories. They exercised their power upon the ROW via exports and then added one-way FDI. They spread their power across foreign territories ruling perfectly their domestic market and attempting to rule the markets of their national firms abroad. Hence host countries were not always happy with foreign affiliates : even if they were not Trojan horses from their home country policy-makers, the local capacity to impose regulations upon them was weak. More generally, states without multinationals are still weak (see Simões, this volume). Conversely, for leading countries, Multinationals are national champions. Zysman (this volume) gives us a beautiful image of this situation : Multinationals are bees searching for pollen throughout the world but making honey at home. National interest was at stake when put in the framework of the new IDL, it was no longer clear that a multinational pursuing its own interest could contribute to its home country's interest. Producing in a foreign territory to export to the home country, according to the scheme of the NIDL, was like making honey abroad. However many authors considered that these multinationals did no more than use existing comparative advantages abroad : free trade under GATT regulation should not harm any country. This distortion will appear more important as all economies become increasingly open (see O'Doherty, this volume), including the leading ones and above all with the surge of two-way flows of FDI. In many industries, 20 % and more of domestic production comes from local affiliates of foreign firms. At the world level, for the whole industry, CEPII (1992) forecasts 24.8 % by the year 2000. A nation's external trade does not read a nation's specialisation but its territorial specialisation. Many authors in this book emphasise that - in the leading countries - a growing number of domestic firms are foreign producers which could "make honey" in their host territory. Nevertheless, these firms follow their own interests and it is not easy to control them across the world so there is a loss of sovereignty by nation-states (see for instance Chesnais, this volume). The boundaries between national economies are becoming blurred as there is a growing interpenetration of their territorial apparatuses of production. This phenomenon questions the ideas of national - and even regional - differences in supply-bases (see Zysman, this volume) or in national innovation systems and nation-specific regimes of intellectual property rights (see Foray, this volume). Moreover, the idea according to which only trade is international seems obsolete and global issues go beyond trade issues putting into question the world territorial distribution of production.

The global industrial system

The world industrial scene cannot be reduced to a free trade market where imports and exports are exchanged. Countries import goods and technologies to produce, countries export other - and often the same - items to reap economies of scale and to build up-to-date production apparatuses in order to catch up with leading countries. Cross-border exchanges of products, equipment, technologies, FDI are not only driven by a firm's global strategies but also by a state's policies. The new "workfare" state (see Jessop, 1992) is engaged in a high-tech race to enhance "national competitiveness". This race is partly regionalised as the EC commission (see Mytelka, this volume) has attempted to ensure the technological future of Europe (Freeman *et al.*, 1991). Many authors in this book emphasise the R&D spending spree by states (e.g. Flamm) which is partly due to time compression (Howells) and the shortening of the life cycle of technologies. By and large we can write that on the world industrial scene global competition is prevalent : "global competition is much more than rivalry among firms, for it involves "structural competitiveness" of states within the world system" (Stopford and Strange, 1992, p. 63). In this context where governments are subsidising firms for R&D and where many industries are enjoying a rapid technological change with sunk costs, economies of scale, learning curves and external economies as well, perfect competition on markets is the exception rather than the rule. Thus "free trade is not always the best solution" claimed Krugman (1986, p. 12) and the new trade theorists. On the one hand, states are following de facto trade, technological and industrial policies and on the other hand, firms are competing in imperfect markets attempting to gain market power. They still do that in a rather traditional manner building oligopolies through concentration in national markets and internationalisation of their production. However we can also observe a strong concentration process in many industries which is now taking place at the world level building world oligopolies (Chesnais, this volume). But even in such world oligopolies firms are fiercely competing (for instance in cars, see van Tulder and Ruigrok, this volume) while at the same time, the limits to more concentration and uncertainty, provoked by a deep industrial transformation partially parallel to the technological race, are pushing them to search for cooperation (Lie and Santucci, this volume). Alliances between big firms are spreading worldwide, especially in high-tech industries but also in other industries, weaving worldwide private networks. Small firms have resisted provided that they find a way to keep a very specific market, "a niche" or follow the general trend of internationalisation and cooperation : "everyone, it would now seem, is in the race to build positions abroad. Though it used to be thought that internationalism was the preserve of the large, private corporations, today they have been joined by small firms and state enterprises [...] The net result is that enterprises with some form of linkage to the global market now account for the largest part of the global production structure - in raw materials, manufactures and services" (Stopford and Strange, 1992, p. 35). To be sure industry plants and research centres are still localised and they use specific resources which are crucial, like tacit knowledge for learning (see Arcangeli, this volume) but even in this case, particularly in this time of deep industrial transformation, global involvement is needed to have access to strategic resources and to learn about generic technologies (ibid.). Therefore as we expose it in more detail elsewhere (Humbert, forthcoming), the industrial system is driven at world level by global competition between firms and nations. Not only this competition but also, beyond the market, both public institutions and private networks have built up industry, at world level, as a global system, in the sense of the theory of systems, and this system is shaping the future of so-called international trade and the world territorial distribution of industrial production.

III Policies and strategies coping with globalisation

The future of European industry cannot only be drawn by analysing the impact of the Single Market as a lot of studies have attempted to do (e.g. Mayes, 1991 ; Mattson and Stymne, 1991 ; or Bürgenmeier and Mucchielli, 1991) when the strongest shifts fraught with consequences come from the globalisation phenomenon. This is why this book is focused on globalisation. The authors put under scrutiny the questions, constraints and challenges which are confronting Europe, its member states and its firms in order to pave the way for definition of relevant policies and strategies. Although they do not deliver definite conclusions, we will now give a tentative synthesis of the policies and strategies that seem most helpful for the future of European industry in the context of globalisation.

There seems to be a strong consensus about the need for a European answer to the questions posed by globalisation. Smaller European economies cannot imagine improving their industry and firm's situation (O'Doherty [2]), without the help of the EC. A country without multinationals of its own (Simões), a country technologically weak (Giannitsis) can only benefit from globalisation if Europe serves as a mediator. Neither are big European economies in a very safe position since the competition struggle within the triad is harsh, thus they also need Europe. All of them have to deal with two main constraints : flows of inward investment and abnormal levels of trade penetration. As for inflows of FDI, many authors (Delapierre and Zimmermann, Lie and Santucci, Zysman, etc.) are claiming : what difference does it make if high value added goods are produced by local affiliates of foreign firms and not by national firms ? The policy indication is quite clear : if these affiliates are efficient - but it is not always sure (Hughes) - , if they fit into the local industrial fabric, what can be translated by a sufficient local content level of their inputs (Guelle) and if they bring resources from abroad, opening to local producers global advantages (Giannitsis), they could be "naturalized" (Delapierre and Zimmermann) and considered as good citizens, contributing to common welfare. As for abnormal trade penetration it appears that states and the EC itself are in a weak position facing this constraint with the traditional policy instrument. Anti-dumping measures do not provide the country victim of unfair practices with a solution restoring it to a situation it would have enjoyed without the damages that have been caused (Holmes). The ideal solution is to prevent unfair practices by settling a level playing field (Lie and Santucci, for example) and ensuring a real market access. To be sure, qualifying import penetration as abnormal is not easy since unfair practices are not always demonstrated (as in cars according to Holmes). The issue that would guide policy-makers for this case and that of inflows of FDI is national interest (Delapierre and Zimmermann). Therefore many authors have stressed the importance of defining a political project. We need a full public debate (Holmes) since the future depends on the EC's future political structure (Mowery). Analysis of some industries in this book show how their future is linked to the implementation of policies clearly conceived and targeted. Mytelka claims that Esprit cannot do the job of maintaining the competitiveness of the European Information Technology industry, that is to say that so-called pre-competitive programmes too far from the market and without strong involvement of European and national industrial policies are inefficient. In contrast Airbus Industrie in which state subsidies were used in a market minded orientation appears to be a success (Mowery). From our point of view, faced with a global industrial system, Europe should prepare a strategic industrial policy (Humbert, 1992). However this means explicit involvement in a costly and harsh global competition. In some cases the battle could appear to be already lost : Holmes is not confident that Europe could be a 3rd player in high-tech integrated circuits, after the USA and Japan. If we wish to keep a world of economic peace we must build up new international institutions for which Europe's inner organisation can be seen as a model by some outside observers (Flamm). D'Andrea Tyson who is expected to be a close adviser of the newly elected president of the United States claimed : "deep interdependence requires deep integration - the harmonization of significant structural differences among nations and the development of comprehensive rules in a variety of 'non-border' policy areas, both backed by multilateral institutions of dispute settlement and enforcement. The blueprint for Europe 1992 provides a model of what will ultimately be required at the international level" (in Caldwell and Moore, 1992, p. 92 ; and also D'Andrea, 1992). If needed institutions are GATT body like (Flamm), they must encompass other fields than trade : competition (Flamm, Holmes) and also, beyond the market, the management of science and technology (Zysman) not to mention the central issue, the world territorial distribution of industrial production.

What can firms do in this challenging context ? Certainly they often have to make do with globalisation without any help from state policies still to be designed ; biggest firms seem to be in the best position to become global whether or not they are yet and to benefit from this context. Van Tulder and Ruigrok, in their conclusion, underline the weak situation of European car producers : although they are big firms in a world oligopoly they are not really global and their future is at stake because of this lack of globalisation. Thus it is clearly recommended for big firms to go global (Howells) although this assertion needs to be interpreted. Global firms, in a certain sense, must be local - or "glocal" - and for example, they should employ local management staff (Watanabe) and they should avoid inside centralisation : heterarchy (Howells), that is to say some kind of interdependence between affiliates and headquarters, is better than hierarchy. Similarly, in the process of radical technological change, big chemical, pharmaceutical and agribusiness firms have acted in a way that can hardly be seen as global. They have launched small R&D groups and have tried to learn from small firms dedicated to biotechnology before attempting any entry into this new field by usual means and M&A (Walsh). Thus small firms have still a part to play. They still have advantages on global firms remarks Mariti and must exploit them with shrewd niche strategies. However small firms can and must be linked to global evolution, especially in R&D (Valls) and more generally, according to Fourcade, they have no choice but to develop, as big firms and also with them, global networking strategies. This is also the only way for European Industry as a whole to cope with globalisation.

Notes

1 Detailed analysis and telling illustrations are provided in the different chapters of this volume.

2 All authors mentioned below are cited for their contribution to this volume.

2 Globalisation, world oligopoly and some of their implications

François Chesnais

I Introduction

Globalisation is largely a term coined by journalists and politicians. It has been thrust on the academic community. Some economists have rejected it, characterising it simply as a catchword (which is partly true of course), and others have adopted it, but only using it to characterise certain types of corporate strategy. Others again have attempted to give the term scientific meaning by relating it to certain objective processes underway in the world economy (see OECD, 1992, chap. 10). In contrast with other contributions in this volume we would argue that in the present context globalisation *is* a state of fact. It expresses the increased **advantages** and opportunities for value- and profit-creating production, that are now open to certain types of firms (the restricted group of large multinational enterprises (MNEs) belonging to the principal world oligopolies), but also the severe **constraints** placed on smaller firms, governments outside the G7 and non-corporate social interests in all countries : for all of the latter, today globalisation and all its consequences **are** facts, and only fairly determined policy enacted simultaneously in at least several large countries could reverse this trend.

Globalisation refers to **two** intimately related processes. One has to do with the emergence of global oligopoly as the most significant type of supply structure coupled with important changes in the scope and effects of international production, technology sourcing and marketing by MNEs. This dimension is fairly well recognised by the recent OECD study concluding the TEP programme. It defines globalisation as "the stage now reached and the forms taken today by international production [...] in which an increasing fraction of value and wealth is produced and distributed world wide through a system of inter-linking private networks. Large multinational firms (MNEs) operating within concentrated supply structures and capable of taking full advantage of financial globalisation are at the centre of this process" (OECD, 1992, pp. 210-211). The other dimension (regarding which the OECD study remains extremely discrete) concerns the loss of many of the attributes of economic and political sovereignty suffered by an increasing number of countries even within OECD (probably all save Japan, Germany and the United States).

II   The factors behind the transition to globalisation

A common set of identifiable factors have been driving the two processes above. Perhaps the most decisive of these has been the sustained accumulation of capital both in the form of **productive capacity** and of **liquid assets**. This accumulation has been implemented by the particularly high rates of growth of the "Golden decades", but also by the inflationary policies adopted by most governments and more specifically still by the funding of the huge US federal deficit. One result has been the onset of financial globalisation, which has led especially to the formation of totally internationalised financial and monetary markets, placing governments under the sway of the level of interest rates established in the strongest countries. But large-scale capital accumulation has also set the scene for the spectacular growth of foreign direct investment despite the context of economic turbulence and/or outright recession which has prevailed since the end of the 1970s. Nor can the development of transnational mergers and acquisitions as the main form taken by FDI be dissociated from the part now played by financial globalisation. FDI's dynamism can best be illustrated by comparisons with trade, gross fixed capital formulation (GFCF) and gross domestic product (GDP). From 1983 to 1989, FDI by OECD countries grew at an annual average growth rate of 31.4 %, nearly three times faster than trade (11.0 %) and GFCF (11.9 %) within OECD and over three times as fast as GDP (10.4 %). Since 1985, the gap between the growth rate of FDI and that of trade has widened drastically, leading one author to suggest that "as a means of international economic integration, FDI is in its take-off phase : perhaps in a position comparable to world trade at the end of the 1940s" (Julius, 1990, p. 36).

As the technological basis for financial globalisation, the growth of FDI has been insured by telematics as well as the facilities it offers multinational banks and MNEs for establishing world-based intracorporate IT networks. The progress made in international telecommunication technologies and networks, the convergence of previously separate functions and the rapid drop in telecommunications and computing costs, have all provided a strong and extremely efficient technological foundation for the worldwide deployment of resources within global corporate structures and the international banking system. In this respect, globalisation corresponds to a qualitative step in the opportunity offered to large and very large firms to distribute their R&D, manufacturing and marketing facilities worldwide in a number of different national locations, to source key technological and intermediate product inputs internationally and to manage their value- and profit-creating activities in real time on a global basis. The advent of a new type or "style" of the transnational firm, the "network firm" (Antonelli, 1988 ; Dunning, 1988a and b) embodies a number of these changes. The adoption of new forms of corporate organisation has been fed by Japanese competition and the Japanese Keiretsu which demonstrates that a new approach can be taken to management and control of the manufacturing process with the extensive use of subcontracting and "just-in-time" delivery.

The third set of factors behind globalisation are political. They concern, of course, the enactment in GATT and OEEC/OECD of numerous codes, agreements and treaties for the liberalisation of international trade, FDI and services, further consolidated in Europe by the Common Market and its subsequent developments now leading up to 1993 and the new treaties now under ratification within the EC. But they also concern all the policies associated with the triumph of Reaganism and Thatcherism since the beginning of the 1980s. Taken in conjunction with the factors just discussed privatisation, deregulation, trade and investment liberalisation have seriously impaired the capacity of governments to encourage structural competitiveness and social cohesion through industrial policy.

III   International concentration and world oligopoly

The combination of these factors has laid the foundations for the development of industrial concentration as an international process, distinct from that taking place on a national basis, and hence for the onset of world oligopoly. World oligopoly is not, of course, in any way a totally **new** form of supply structure. In petroleum and in several non-ferrous metal mining and processing industries (for instance aluminium), world oligopoly has long been a key feature of supply. What is new is the **extension** of global oligopoly and the fact that it now constitutes the dominant form of supply structure in most R&D intensive or "high technology" industries as well as in many scale-intensive manufacturing industries according to Pavitt (1984) terminology. In R&D intensive industries, the only exceptions are those industries where supply structures are even more highly concentrated with only two (as for instance in the case of space launchers) or three (as for instance in the case of long range civil aircraft) manufacturers competing in the market.

World oligopoly and the "global competition" which goes with it, is the outcome of two related but none the less distinct processes, that of

internationalisation and that of **industrial concentration** supported by financial centralisation. It occurs at the point when in a given industry : (i) industrial and technological development has both created opportunities and imposed constraints on firms (notably in the form of large R&D costs which must be recouped) to make them produce for world markets distinct from even the largest domestic markets and also to source key inputs to production, notably in the form of scientific and technological advances made in foreign countries on a worldwide basis ; and (ii) when concentration, after having developed principally on a domestic basis, has evolved as an international process involving transnational cross-investment occurring in the form of acquisitions and mergers. The scale of FDI channelled to acquisitions instead of ex-novo investment gives an indication to what degree international cross-investment into the US has taken the form of integration of US firms into global hierarchies of Japanese and European origin associated with rising concentration in the 1980s.

Table 2.1 Sources of growth of foreign control of US firms, 1982 to 1990

Mode of entry	Total investment ($ billions)								
	1982	1983	1984	1985	1986	1987	1988	1989	1990
Acquisitions	4.8	11.8	20.1	31.5	25.6	33.9	64.9	59.7	56.8
New establishments	3.2	3.4	3.0	7.7	4.9	6.4	7.8	11.5	7.7

Source : Graham (1991) based on US Commerce Department data

As noted already by R. Newfarmer (1985) work on concentration at an international level has fallen seriously behind the deep changes in the world economy resulting from the overall process of internationalisation. Measures of concentration (e.g. market shares by the first 4, 8 and 20 firms) are still being carried out **mostly on a purely domestic basis** at a time when the most significant indicator of concentration now pertains to **global, e.g. world market shares**. In our opinion, the only relevant measure of concentration in an industry is now the share of the largest 5, 10, or 20 firms in total **world** assets or sales. This provides an initial significant index of the power of a selected group of firms in a given industry to influence business decisions, build collective entry barriers **inter alia** through the individual **and** collective **protection of their technological progress**, and also, when conditions permit, to limit price-competition around the world (as has been the case for certain pharmaceutical products). Figures showing this concentration have begun to be collected in the context of industrial sector studies carried out over the last few years at OECD, the EC (FAST) and the United Nations. They have been put together in the OECD study (see OECD, 1992, tables 46,

47 and 48) and show that in a wide range of industries and product groups the world market is shared by 10-12 firms, and often fewer.

IV   International oligopolistic reaction as a determinant of FDI

Currently global concentration and international or world oligopoly are not attracting the attention they deserve. There has been, however, some earlier research, explicitly treating such issues, on which to build, as well as a great deal of apparently unconnected work which could prove worthy of purposeful analysis.

The single most important proposition established regarding oligopoly is that not only is it marked by fewness, but more decisively by **interdependence** and **mutual recognition**. Oligopolists "respond not to impersonal market forces, but personally and directly to their rivals" (Pickering, 1972). Or again, "the key distinguishing feature [...] is that oligopolists are strategically linked to one another. The best policy for one firm depends on the policies of each rival firm in the market" (Friedman, 1983). Applying this proposition to the study of outward FDI by large US firms in the 1950s and 1960s, S. Hymer and his associates and friends at Harvard (in particular P. Caves and Knickerbocker), established that foreign investment for US firms "involved market conduct that extended the recognition of mutual market dependence - the essence of oligopoly - beyond national boundaries" (Caves, 1974). We owe it to Graham to have started extending this approach to international cross-investment (sometimes also called "intra-industry foreign direct investment"), thus bringing analytical substance and supporting data to the prediction made by Hymer in his last essay before his death, regarding the transition from US-dominated international oligopoly to truly global oligopoly (Hymer and Rowthorn, 1970). He noted that the European FDI fed into the US economy in the 1970s went mainly to industries which had previously attracted US investment in Europe and suggested that three factors were acting in combination to stimulate this investment. The first of these were the advantages classically associated with the capacity to serve a large market on the basis of production proximity to consumers. The second concerned the capacity "to replicate the cost and benefit trade off experienced by US rivals in the development of new product technologies". The third was directly related to oligopolistic rivalry and concerned the "capacity of European firms to pose a threat to US rivals on their 'home turf'", countering for instance their US rivals' cross-subsidisation to increase market shares in Europe by initiating similar behaviour in the United States (Graham, 1985).

Cars, tyres and parts of the chemical industry were sectors where the capacity to counter severe rivalry in one market area with retaliation in another began to shape the conduct of international oligopolists from the early 1970s onwards. European MNEs tended however to remain cautious and not provoke the US leaders too strongly. The entry of the Japanese Keiretsu as major global oligopolistic rivals in the late 1970s and their large-scale penetration through investment into the US economy modified this situation radically. It gave the onset of global oligopoly its irreversible character and made international cross-investment an imperative strategy for the survival of large firms. Increasingly the fate of "national champions" is sealed by their capacity to become what Ohmae (1985) has called "global insiders". Given that the collective ability to pose a counter-threat now depends on the extent to which all rivals can actually operate in one another's markets via cross-investment, the capacity that large Japanese groups have demonstrated in cooperation with their government, by **limiting** (in all but a very few industries) inward FDI to an **almost negligible level** gives them an important, perhaps even a decisive, advantage over their rivals.

In the late 1970s, it appeared that MNEs, in order to maintain their firm specific advantages, in particular their technological advantages, could use their competitive strength and market power to eliminate some of their effective or potential rivals through **acquisition and merger**. These arguments were generally dismissed at the time and evidence was collected dating back to the **1950s and 1960s** to show that in most cases US MNEs in Europe had not been powerful enough to eliminate local rivals and that their entry had generally provoked the larger indigenous firms, often helped by their governments, to accelerate their efforts to generate new technologies. However, most studies underplayed the fact that the resistance of European firms had evolved at the time very significant processes of domestic concentration, again aided by many governments in the context of building "national champions". Nor did they consider the role of **overall demand conditions**. The type of corporate behaviour which may prevail when there is **room** in the market for many rivals to develop is likely to change as soon as slow or very slow growth sets in. This, of course, is what has occurred since the 1980s. Corporate growth and multinational expansion must now take place at the expense of other firms and thus FDIs occur principally in the form of mergers and acquisitions ; technologically dynamic firms are specially being targeted.

V   Sunk costs, technological appropriability and cumulativeness, and transaction cost economies

The discussion of international concentration calls for a new look at entry barriers, the factors (in certain types of technology) now shaping the competitiveness of firms and those affecting the relationship between size and management. Even if concentration occurs through capital accumulation coupled with international mergers and acquisitions, and if oligopolistic interdependence, especially in the form of exclusive inter-firm alliance between major oligopolists, also acts to consolidate their position, concentration must also rest on other objective factors relating to R&D, production and corporate governance.

Bain's classical, and in many ways still unparalleled, work on entry barriers has been strengthened by research on the contestability of markets in relation to **asset specificity** and **sunk cost** (e.g. costs that cannot be recovered if a particular activity is abandoned). The perfectly contestable market is one where sunk costs are negligible, so that firms can enter or exit an industry with ease and therefore new entrants can enter, undercut the price of existing firms and exit before these have a chance to react. As sunk costs increase, so does the risk assumed by entrants. Thus barriers to exit in the form of tangible and intangible sunk costs that make exit unattractive and costly even when profits fall and possibly become negative also serve to discourage entry (Schmalensee, 1988). In the context of high technology, and of course as well as scale and capital intensive industries, sunk costs have become astronomical. The generic features of the most important contemporary technology have not done away with the very strong industry or indeed the **firm specific character of a large part of corporate R&D**, or of intangible investment or even of much tangible investment related to production. Work by K. Flamm (1990) on the semiconductor industry concludes that the level of R&D (circa 20 % of value added) plus the highly specific nature of much fixed capital has seriously reduced the credible threat of lateral entry by non-specialised MNEs or entry by newcomers. Data may even reveal the situation where a collective hold on output by four or five Japanese groups, which might follow the incapability of existing US firms to continue meeting the requirements of successful rivalry, could give the Japanese the opportunity of "starving" user firms in other countries and certainly of fixing prices as they wished.

The semiconductor industry is also the classical example of an industry where high technological opportunities and high degrees of private appropriation based mostly on dynamic learning curves and the cumulativeness of technology-based advantages, lead among other things to big firms and high degrees of concentration. The notion of the "dynamic learning curve" was initially borrowed from managerial economics, and generally includes a) learning effects stricto sensu ; b) economies of scale ; and c) technical progress. They create the basis for market pre-emption (Dosi, 1984), leading rapidly to concentration even in very young industries. But broader generalisation can also be made.

Both industrial case studies and evolutionary planning (see in particular Nelson and Winters, 1982) indicate today most modern industries are subject to processes where the existence of big firms and high degrees of concentration are directly related to a history of technological opportunity, of a sufficient degree of appropriation of innovation (i.e. legal and **ad hoc** measures to protect innovation and slow down imitation by rivals) as well as high sunk costs. Market structure and technological performance are **generated endogenously** with two-way connections between innovation and market structure thus producing self-feeding mechanisms which lead inherently to the consolidation of concentrated market structure. This is why it is now the rule rather than the exception that concentrated market structures are **further consolidated** by "reverse causation" in the form of existing oligopolists in their capacity to assimilate and domesticate new technology (as in the case of biotechnology, Chesnais, 1986).

The spectacular progress made in technology permitting the management of large global corporations, coupled by the **inherently imperfect character of contemporary markets**, notably those where technology is a key factor in competition, to act simultaneously while driving the process of concentration, is where one can use effectively the Coase-Williamson theory of industrial organisation. This argues that the organisation of the economic activity (within or outside the boundaries of a given firm) may depend as much or **more** on the relative balance between hierarchical coordination costs and market transaction costs, as on the technical factors of production commanding the size of plant. According to the contemporary approach on industrial organisation inspired by Williamson, it is essentially "transaction costs and the set of techniques available to govern transactions within the firm which determines the size of firms" (Antonelli, 1988). These implications are important. As markets grow (if more imperfect only as a result of the role now played by technology, of the general transition to oligopolistic supply structures and of the high transaction costs incurred by all firms who attempt to go transnational) and as the techniques of corporate management **improve**, large or very large firms of "minimum efficient size" will tend to consolidate. **Minimum size for effective oligopolistic rivalry** will become tantamount to that of the world's largest firms adopting the "network" form of organisation which now maximises the "information capability" required for effective corporate management in an environment marked by turbulence and high uncertainty. The opportunity for corporations to "internalise externalities" through a wide variety of non-equity interfirm relationships and contractual agreements in addition to classical vertical integration, adds to their "global reach", serving in particular their need to obtain complementary technical assets through external sourcing and cooperation (Chesnais, 1988a and b).

VI   National production systems in the context of global industries

In the limits of this very short essay, I have endeavoured to suggest why highly concentrated global supply structures may depend on very strong objective processes, thus establishing world oligopoly as a permanent phenomenon which poses a whole set of new problems for industrial and technological policy. In another paper (Chesnais, 1992), I have argued that the inter-firm technological alliances (Mytelka, 1991b) established among the world's leading corporations (see in particular Hagedoorn and Schakenraad, 1990a) can only be properly analysed and interpreted in the context of these concentrated global supply structures and of global oligopoly. I have discussed some of the implications for smaller firms and for policies on technology in different countries, in particular small ones. Here I will conclude with a few remarks relating to the restructuring of industries.

This process must be studied, not only in Europe but also in the United States, in terms of oligopolistic interaction, international cross-investment and the opportunities now open to MNEs for centralising at the "regional" (e.g. continental or sub-continental) level their whole chain of activities. Cross-entry into rivals' home markets is now a major factor behind the progressive restructuring of domestic industries in the context of globalisation. Alongside cross-entry, the shift from multi-domestic to global industry involves a simultaneous process of **focusing** and **switching** of activities by the MNE between its numerous production sites. "Replica" subsidiaries previously set up to cater to domestic markets are being closed down. Production is being organised on the basis of **internationally interdependent** production facilities which are becoming increasingly centralised into a small number of affiliates to which world or "regional" product mandates have been assigned. This leads to the closure of plants in many countries and the upgrading or downgrading of facilities remaining open in others. Of course such restructuring has been strongly facilitated by trade liberalisation and the creation of large "regional" markets (EC 1992, North American trade area, the Far East zone organised and structured by Japanese MNEs).

Home and host countries to MNEs are also progressively locked into an increasingly **tightly knit set of trading relationships**, at the basis of which are **intra-firm flows of parts and intermediate goods** between MNE subsidiaries. Countries which are not host to MNEs will, on the other hand, only be involved in such trade **to the extent that they supply** raw materials or act as second or third tier subcontractors. An exclusion process is at work alongside the increasing interdependency of the major agents. Intra-firm trade represents one measure of these flows ; another indication, which reflects these intra-group exchanges is the level of imports in intermediate goods.

Country specific location advantages (Dunning, 1981) still exist from the standpoint of MNEs, but their foundations are significantly different from those of earlier periods. In the phase of classical multinationalisation, access to large and/or high-income markets partially protected by trade barriers, occupied a major place in MNE strategies even within the OECD area. Now FDI location is almost exclusively determined by specific supply-side features of countries, in particular their potential for certain types of technological skill on which MNEs can build. For MNEs, the yardstick for measuring location advantages of a country will concern local knowledge-intensiveness, certain skill qualifications required for the production of technology and the possession of agglomeration economies which bring together the complementary assets needed for successful innovation, production and exportation. **A totally new set of cards are being distributed**, but most countries remain to be invited to have their say although many of them are aware that a new type of distribution is underway.

3 Regionalisation, globalisation or glocalisation : the case of the world car industry

Rob van Tulder and Winfried Ruigrok

I   Introduction : globalisation, an overstatement ?

Writing on the growth and spread of transnational corporations (TNCs), Peter Dicken has argued that "one of the most common features of much of the writing on TNCs (is) the tendency towards overstatement" (1986, p. 65). In the 1980s, a new term entered the jargon of international business and decision-making : **globalisation**. Since the mid-1980s, most large firms and governments have included this word in their vocabulary, pointing at the demands of international competition or stating that globalisation is the ultimate objective for the years to come. In this chapter we argue that Dicken's cynicism should be applied to the discussion on the concept of globalisation without major modifications. Globalisation seems to be as much an overstatement as it is an ideology and an analytical concept. For the aim of this article we concentrate primarily on the second deficiency. The notion of rival internationalisation strategies in the car industry will be elaborated. More specifically, the concept of globalisation will be confronted with another rival concept : glocalisation.

II   Internationalisation : expansion and retreat

Michael Porter distinguishes two key dimensions in a firm's internationalisation strategy : the **configuration** of its activities - or the location in the world where an activity is performed - and the **coordination** of these activities (1986a, pp. 23-29). Together these two dimensions lead to a simple four-by-four figure (Figure 3.1).

High	High foreign investment with extensive coordination among subsidiaries	Simple global strategy
Coordination of *activities*		
	Country-centred strategy by multinationals or domestic firms operating in only	Export-based strategy with decentralised
Low	one country	marketing

Geographically dispersed   Geographically concentrated

Configuration of activities

Figure 3.1 Types of internationalisation strategies according to Porter

A **global** industry, according to Porter, is an industry in which a firm's competitive position in one country is significantly affected by its position in other countries. High levels of coordination, thereby, automatically produce a global strategy. There are many different kinds of global strategies, depending on a firm's choices about configuration and coordination throughout the value chain. Porter identifies two extremes : a **simple global strategy** (based on a concentration of activities) and one of **high foreign investments with extensive coordination among subsidiaries**. A "simple global strategy" would differ from an "export-oriented strategy" in that the latter presupposes decentralised marketing with low levels of coordination by the exporting firms [1].

Porter, however, does not really operationalise the dimension of coordination because he does not analyse the production process. Porter's framework does not take into account the possibility of **rival models of the organisation of production** and subsequent **rival and mutually excluding models of corporate internationalisation**. Secondly, Porter tends to analyse internationalisation strategies mainly in terms of **corporate expansion**. Thus he simply states for instance that Toyota moves from a simple global strategy towards one of high foreign investment and extensive coordination among subsidiaries. But how does Toyota implement this shift ? Given Toyota's heavy reliance on domestic suppliers, does Toyota take these suppliers with it when establishing production abroad ? In fact, was Toyota's "simple global strategy" in the mid-1980s as "simple" as Porter suggests ? Porter's model, like most models on internationalisation, presents an almost **linear expansionist view of internationalisation** and does not take into account possible contradictory tendencies. Corporations can expand abroad but also **retreat** [2].

Finally, Porter's model tells little about the company's strategic objectives to operate abroad, nor about the effects of its investments on actors in the country of establishment. With the vast majority concentrated in the three major trade blocs, the logic that guided earlier periods of corporate internationalisation, such as of the product life cycle (Vernon, 1971), or of the tendency towards a New International Division of Labour (Fröbel *et al.*, 1977) has changed radically. Any theory on the rise and meaning of "globalisation" should provide an integral explanation of how these Japanese strategies may have contributed to the "triadisation" of the world economy over the 1980s.

III   Rival global strategies and trajectories

This section shortly distinguishes two rival global strategies (glo*b*alisation versus glo*c*alisation) as a further elaboration of Porter's dimension of "coordination". **Globalisation**, thereby, aims at a **worldwide intra-firm division of labour**. A firm striving for globalisation aims to secure the supply of strategic inputs by producing them itself and locating their production according to specific location requirements. A global strategy will lead to continued growth of trade volumes. Companies aiming for globalisation tend to make senior management positions accessible on the basis of personal merit (Table 3.1).

The alternative "global" strategy is that of **global localisation** or **glo*c*alisation** [3]. The objective of glo*c*alisation is to establish a **geographically-concentrated inter-firm division of labour** in the three major trading blocs. Firms which strive for glo*c*alisation build their competitive advantage on close interaction with suppliers and dealers, as well as with other relevant actors, such as trade unions and governments. As glo*c*alisation aims at production close to the major markets, international trade may gradually decline. Two essential elements stand out in a firm's glo*c*alisation strategy : (i) the **decentralisation of production** to hierarchical networks of local subcontracting ; (ii) but at the same time a high degree of **control** over the supply and distribution chain.

Table 3.1   Comparison between globalisation and glocalisation
at the firm level

Internal firm organisation	Globalisation	Glocalisation
Organisation of value chain	Worldwide intra-firm division of labour	Geographically concentrated inter-firm division of labour
Location strategy of activities based on	Comparative advantage and economies of scale : progression of international division of labour	Introduction of integrated supply, production and distribution chain in depressed regions of major international trade blocs
Nationality of management	More inclined to promote "foreign" managers to senior ranks	Very difficult for foreign managers to reach senior ranks
Approach to data- and telecommunication	Used for coordination of globally spread activities	Used to control local supply and distribution chain
Production focus	Production for world markets and tastes (research facilities spread more around the world)	Production for local and/or regional markets and tastes (basic research not spread, applied research spread)

The strategy of global localisation implies that a firm will strive to become accepted as a "local citizen" in a foreign community, yet relinquish as little control as possible over its strategic activities. Glocalisation is **first of all a political and only in the second place a business location strategy.** A firm aiming for glocalisation will only localise activities abroad to the extent that host governments will become or remain more dependent on this firm (plus its surrounding network) and not vice versa.

The difference between globalisation and glocalisation results from different coordination mechanisms based on different ways of organising the production process :

(i)   **high levels of coordination** imply that the end producer faces an utmost effort to organise the production process efficiently, due to its logistical complexity. Activities are scattered over the entire world, and dependency on other firms, such as suppliers, is high. High levels of coordination presuppose a strategy of globalisation or glocalisation ;

(ii)   **medium levels of coordination** can represent a transitory stage from low coordination to high coordination. Medium levels of coordination often imply forced expansion from a traditional export-oriented strategy, involving the establishment of screwdriver facilities abroad to circumvent import barriers. However, medium levels of coordination can also represent retreat from an earlier strategy of globalisation ;

(iii) **low levels of coordination** imply that the required logistical effort is relatively simple, as most of the production is concentrated in one country, or because activities are dispersed over many countries to meet local demands independently.

Combining the dimensions of configuration and coordination leads to a representation of international strategies and trajectories as shown in Figure 3.2. This figure in the first place, presents two alternative, in fact **rival**, internationalisation trajectories. This means that the choice for one internationalisation trajectory makes it very difficult to change to the other trajectory. Secondly, unlike mechanistic (and evolutionary) internationalisation models, the figure also takes into account the possibility of a company's retreat.

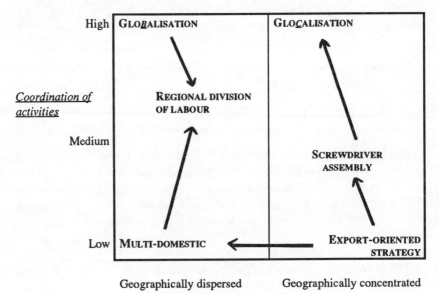

Figure 3.2   Internationalisation strategies and trajectories

The separation line in Figure 3.2 indicates that companies start from a relatively fixed organisation of production, and are likely to stick to the logic of this organisation when expanding or retreating along the dimension of coordination.

For most companies and in many industries, the **export-based strategy** represents the starting position in formulating an internationalisation strategy. The category of **multi-domestic** firms represents the traditional multinational company which in the 1960s and 1970s expanded its production to other countries. Over the 1980s, an alternative to the multi-domestic expansion trajectory became popular, i.e. **screwdriver assembly**. Screwdriver assembly aims to circumvent existing trade barriers by setting up a local facility. Screwdriver assembly is meant as a transitory stage from an export orientation to a glocalisation strategy, provided that a minimum "local content" is required. The strategy to create a **regional division of labour** strategy will represent more often a **retreat from a strategy of globalisation rather than a corporate growth strategy**. A firm aiming for a regional division of labour (in one or two of the Triad regions) is seeking the shelter provided by trade barriers or industrial policies. The strategy towards a regional division of labour represents a reaction to the growth trajectory of export-orientation - screwdriver assembly - glocalisation. On the other hand, however, the rise of a regional division of labour will reinforce the strategy of glocalisation. Both strategies towards glocalisation and towards a regional division of labour will therefore contribute to the further rise of the three large trade blocs. To what extent is the car industry globalised and what does this imply for the coming decade ?

IV Regionalisation, globalisation and glocalisation in the car industry [4]

The internationalisation of car production at the end of the 1980s was relatively limited. The two large US car producers, Ford and GM, had made most of their progress in internationalising their production by 1988. Except for Volvo, all large European car makers had contracted over 60 % of their production in their domestic market, and over 80 % in Europe. The Japanese car complexes with the exception of Honda, also produced most of their cars in Japan and in the rest of the Asian region. Japanese car makers Toyota and Nissan, however, are making rapid progress in this respect.

The openness of each national complex regarding import penetration ratios in the 1980s has been strongly affected by the national regulatory environment. Many governments (Italy, France) have tried to find primarily political answers to the threat of the Japanese exporters, which affected the import penetration ratios of Japanese cars and resulted in very different and artificial import penetration ratios. The Japanese car industry has grown heavily dependent on the world market for its exports but hardly for its imports. Simply on the basis of these observations, it is easy to understand the Japanese government's trade policy strategy : promote a liberal international trade regime, yet avoid that such a regime leads to a dramatic rise of imports.

Table 3.2 summarises the international position of the sixteen most important car manufacturers at the end of the 1980s along two strategic dimensions: marketing and production. The **vertical axis** considers the relative spread of production, along five categories (with somewhat arbitrary lines of division) in which the region represents one (region I) or two (region II) of the triad regions. It can be seen in fact that the so-called global car firms in the car industry have at the moment production sites in basically only two out of three regions. The **horizontal axis** looks at the control producers exercise over the distribution of their products. When a company gets more control over the dealers and importers within its own region, but is still faced with a large number of independent distribution channels in one or both of the other Triad regions, the company has a regional orientation. A further distinction is made between companies having extensive distribution networks in only one Triad region and those having them in two regions at the same time. When the company has established at least fully-owned or dependent importers in all three regions (or has established production in the most important market), the distribution channel can be called global. When the company is able not only to control/own the importers but also the dealers (exclusive dealers) we should call this distribution network glocal since it gives the assembler the possibility to coordinate the network to the maximum extent.

At the end of the 1980s no car maker was entirely global or glocal. European volume producers such as Renault and Volkswagen even chose a retreat strategy and removed all production facilities from the United States (something which Fiat had already done before World War II). In 1991 Peugeot (PSA) and Rover even decided to stop selling their cars in the United States. In 1992, on the other hand, BMW decided to plan a considerable production site in the United States. Now most European car manufacturers appear to be concentrating on their own region. A company like Volkswagen which could be called a "global player" stuck to its own region. This regionalisation includes a continued campaign *vis-à-vis* Japanese companies for Voluntary Export Restraints, and a simultaneous reduction of production capacity in Europe. US companies at most are maintaining their long established facilities in Europe. At the end of the 1980s, the car industry as a whole was clearly not yet globalised and the degree to which this will happen depends, therefore, largely on the **future strategies** chosen by the actors, in particular of some of the Japanese firms.

Table 3.2   Relative positions of the sixteen complexes in marketing
and production : 1988

		Marketing/distribution				
P R O D U C T I O N		**Local** (primarily national organisa-tion)	**Regional I** (present primarily in one region)	**Regional II** (present in 2 of 3 major regions)	**Global** (high pro-portion of indepen-dent dea-lers and importers)	**Glocal** (fully con-trolled local dea-lers)
	Local (> 80 % domestic)	Rover Chrysler	PSA Fiat	Mitsubishi	Mercedes BMW Toyota Mazda Nissan	
	Regional I (< 70 % local ; > 80 % regional)		Renault		Volvo VW	
	Regional II (produc-tion in 2 regions ; > 70 % in one region)					
	Global (< 70 % regional)			GM Ford	Honda	
	Glocal (major presence in each Triad region)					

V   Globalisation or glocalisation of the Japanese car complexes ?

The rise of **Japanese transplants in the US** has been impressive. The large and medium-sized Japanese players have each set up a manufacturing operation in the US, either fully-owned or as a joint venture, or both.

Japanese transplants in the US, including joint ventures, accounted for 21 % of total US car output in the first half of 1990, compared with less than 15 % a year earlier. During this period US car production fell by almost 17 %, while Japanese transplant output rose by nearly 18 %.

Toyota arrived relatively late in the US. Obviously, the problems related to the introduction of production and supply systems in the US similar to the **Just-In-Time** production system it had developed in Japan would be enormous. Moreover, Toyota's stable domestic coalition with workers did not demand any internationalisation at all, in fact internationalisation could easily destabilise this coalition. Nissan set up its first US operation in the early 1980s, partly because Nissan's domestic coalition with workers served less as a hindrance to the internationalisation of production. Some would even argue that Nissan's troubled relations with its workers caused an early internationalisation. The impetus for Honda to internationalise its operations has been stronger than for Nissan and Toyota. Until the beginning of the 1960s, Honda produced only motorcycles. Honda sold its first car in 1963. This made the company a latecomer with far less control over its distribution and suppliers' network, and latest in the row for quota allocation by MITI. Given Honda's overwhelming reliance on exports and its vulnerability to currency shifts, it obviously needed to internationalise operations at an early stage. Honda's inclination to a more global strategy is, for instance, reflected in its new management team. Honda is in the process of establishing a world headquarters system that should be finished by March 1993. Under this system, overseas subsidiaries will have much greater decision-making power, based on unified sales, production and development. In establishing **transplants in Europe**, Honda and Nissan took the lead. As the establishment of Japanese operations in the EC started at a later stage than in the US, production volumes are still limited.

VI   Eastern Europe : the low end of the European car complexes

For Western European volume producers the Eastern European countries in the first place started to constitute a cheap production base after the opening of their economies. The inclusion of Eastern Europe in the European car makers' "regional" or "global" strategy is to offer improved economies of scale and a better intra-company division of labour, not a marketing objective. In this division of labour the Eastern European countries, situated at close distance to the EC, would supply cheap labour and assemble cars for the lower market segments. Component production in Eastern Europe has rapidly become dominated by European end producers and their captive suppliers. To find an answer to glocal competition, therefore, European volume producers are continuing to improve their internal (regional) division of labour. Except for Suzuki, no major Japanese car company has decided to set up an operation in Eastern Europe. As the first priority of the large Japanese car makers is to become glo*c*al players in the EC, they are not likely to start large-scale production in Eastern Europe until they have become full "insiders" in the EC.

VII Conclusion : The international position of the car complexes in the year 2000

The discussion on **globalisation** in the car industry has largely to be denounced as **ideology**. The most staunch prophets of the globalisation concept (the Japanese firms in particular, but not all and not exclusively) do mean something quite different than what is publicly stated. The respective company strategies put into a long-term perspective leads to Table 3.3 that extrapolates trends based on strategic choices which have already been made.

Table 3.3 Assessment of the relative position of the sixteen complexes for the year 2000

		Marketing/distribution				
P R O D U C T I O N		Local	Regional I	Regional II	Glo*b*al	Glo*c*al
	Local	Chrysler	PSA	Rover (in coope- ration with Honda)		
	Regional I		Renault Fiat (incl. Lada)	Volvo	VAG (Volkswag en Audi, Seat, Skoda)	Daimler-Benz (Incl. Eastern European strategy)
	Regional II					BMW
	Glo*b*al			GM (incl. Saab)	Ford (incl. Jaguar) Mitsubishi	Mazda Honda
	Glo*c*al					Toyota Nissan

With regard to the internationalisation of the **production structure**, the only actors to change their degree of internationalisation in the Triad regions will be the Japanese. Most American and European car firms only plan to add some production capacity in Eastern Europe, without the guarantee that efficiency and coordination will also be increased. In two years, however, this strategy has almost destroyed an independent Eastern European car complex.

The two firms aiming for the most ideal type of glocal international production structure are Toyota and Nissan. The regional orientation of **almost all** European producers in their production structure not only affects their pattern of strategic alliances, but also makes good bargaining structures at the European level with the European Commission, mandatory. This is also true for dealers, subcontractors as well as consumers. Failing such relations, American and Japanese firms could easily play off one European firm/government/union against another.

The important question with regard to the internationalisation of **marketing**, i.e. of the dealer-assembler relationship, is whether manufacturers are willing or are forced to take into consideration the heterogeneity of the dealer network as it has developed, or whether they will be able to remodel it into a structure they are more able to control. By departing from existing structures, manufacturers, especially in the USA and the UK, are bound to accept higher levels of "interdependence" with their (mega) dealers. Working towards "dependence" of the dealers on assemblers leads to restructuring the dealership and marketing structure into more hierarchically controlled networks. European luxury car producers like BMW and Daimler-Benz have also come to the conclusion that control over their dealership networks in each of the Triad regions is of the utmost importance.

When we finally review the relative position of the European car firms, both in terms of production and marketing, the strategic positions of Peugeot, Renault, Rover, Volvo, and also Fiat look very vulnerable. The EC-Japan trade agreement on car imports will hardly relieve these relatively weak positions. The large Japanese car assemblers' strategy of glocalisation and most European car makers' strategy of regionalisation will reinforce each other. A European Automobile System (de Banville, Chanaron, 1990) in strategic terms is thereby non-existent. The strategy of regionalisation is unlikely to mend the structural weaknesses of Peugeot, Renault, Rover, Volvo and Fiat. In the long term, the establishment of Japanese manufacturing facilities in Europe only but lead to further restructuring in the European car industry. Until the year 2000, changes in the world car industry will therefore also continue to have major political consequences. The European Commission thereby, will have to mediate between the primarily regional orientation of the EC assemblers, the global orientation of the US assemblers and the glocal orientation of at least two major Japanese assemblers. The diversity in the strategic landscape in Europe is reinforced by the relative independence and strength of the component suppliers. However, they are not well represented within the EC Commission (Boston Consulting, 1990). It is **virtually impossible** to find a balance between these diverse strategic objectives and we do not anticipate a stable and coherent trade regime in the EC for the coming decade.

Notes

1 Prahalad & Doz (1987) have implicitly criticised Porter's equation of high levels of coordination and global strategy. In their words, "(t)he essence of global competition ... is the *management of international cash flows and strategic coordination*, even when global coordination across subsidiaries in terms of product flows does not take place" (1987, p. 40, original italics). We fully acknowledge the importance of managing cash flows successfully at an international level. However, we believe this element should be analysed not only at the level of corporate internationalisation strategies, but at the level of corporate restructuring strategies as such.

2 Taking the phrasing of the debate on the international division of labour, we could dub both strategies the (1) runaway, and (2) the *re* runaway strategy (cf. Junne, 1987).

3 The word glocalisation is not a self-invented combination of global localisation, but appears in several official Japanese documents.

4 This section summarises a more extensive research report written for the FAST project on globalisation. See Ruigrok and Van Tulder (1991).

4 Local and global features of the learning process

Fabio Arcangeli

I Introduction

Rosenberg (1982, chap. 5) argued that there is something peculiar about learning how to use complex system technologies, and that similar problems might develop with the penetration of information technology. This chapter deals with the "locational" consequences of this key hypothesis, with a view to the implications for the debate on globalisation.

The literature on innovations and their diffusion supplies new insights for the classical topics in location analysis. After a brief review of some selected issues on location, we will analyse the changing environment of the firm, when : (i) new industrial complexes relate to specific user and/or producer industries on the basis of the development and applications of new information technology (IT) systems ; (ii) such industrial complexes evolve across time and in space, due to the diversity of generations along a technological trajectory, and the spatial diffusion of their use ; (iii) the extent of markets and competitiveness is driven towards "globality", although localised externalities are still relevant, even for the performance of a global firm and particularly for the location of its R&D activity.

A relevant duality in this respect is the one between the global and local factors in the firm-environment learning interaction. A joint view of the learning process and the new location forces might provide some insights about : (i) the likely effects of tacit knowledge (TK) on some segments of IT-based industrial complexes ; (ii) the optimal location of IT-producer and IT-user firms ; (iii) some consequent spatial features of IT-based industrial restructuring and growth ; (iv) the local and regional elements (innovative centres, technology flows), connected through the systems of cities and of industrial centres into a national system of innovation ; (v) some policy guidelines for a world peripheral area or for a NIC (New Industrialising

Country) aiming to define a catching-up strategy of technology transfer and accumulation.

Section II will focus on the location issue, and Section III will relate to the location analysis with an interpretation of the learning process already proposed elsewhere (Arcangeli 1992).

II   A regional system of innovation

Location theories have evolved from a cost-minimising approach for the location of a perfectly competitive industry (Weber), to a demand-led location in the case of imperfect competition (Chamberlin and Loesch), and to a strategic interdependence approach for a duopoly or an oligopoly (Hotelling).

In his first introduction to contemporary industrial location analysis, Alfred Weber (1909) identified three basic forces : the minimisation of transport costs and labour costs, and the cost-saving effects of agglomeration (reduced by the extra costs of land use within agglomerations). He did not deal in depth with the third force, agglomeration, but many other authors have, starting from the contemporary analysis of the industrial district made by Marshall and ending up with current models of strategic interdependence.

In an extreme synthesis, the historical evolution of industrial locations might be summarised as follows. During the First Industrial Revolution, immobile energy sources and high transport costs for raw materials forced the new industries to locate very close to localised pools of primary resources.

What happened during and after the Second Industrial Revolution (electrification) fits in with contemporary analysis and, in part, even with some long-run forecasts attempted by Weber. According to him, the new world centres of gravity would have been the manufacturing labour pools, or the well-endowed and organised labour markets ; even less developed countries, through the modernisation of their labour markets, should have attracted, due to their cheap labour, a share of the "foot-loose" or light industries (Weber 1911). In his forecasts, he had assumed that technical change in transport systems and the decreasing cost of energy transmission (finally, its ubiquity) would have transformed most manufacturing into foot-loose and dispersed activities. This did not happen because labour, the second factor in his scheme, became such a key location factor in the "Fordist era", as to overcome the "Diaspora" effects of energy and transport trends. In fact, Weber, at this time, could not foresee in detail the forthcoming effects of Fordism and dedicated automation, putting at the centre of the location game the concentrations of unskilled labour ("operaio massa"). But, at least, in his 1911 paper he caught this major trend at its beginning.

The current Third Industrial Revolution might follow Weber's unwritten instructions and resort to what is left, his third factor : pure agglomeration, unconstrained by transport or labour costs. One might object that the new resources and the requirements of innovative activities, in the creative phase of the Revolution, have been establishing new location constraints, at least for IT-based industrial complexes and industries (Arcangeli and Camagni, 1990). This is true, but the analysis can not draw just on cost factors and market forces as it does in Weber's theory.

We must identify which are the characteristics of technology creation and appropriation, and how they might shape a typical regional economy and intra-regional locations, beyond Weber's predictions. A key distinction is the one between : generic knowledge, which actually might be considered a public good as it is in standard economic theory ; and application specific knowledge, to which Schumpeter's theory must be applied : at least for some time, it is kept proprietary knowledge.

A further distinction is the one between formal and tacit knowledge. Generic knowledge is formal in some degree by definition, in order to be codified, transmitted and taught. A specific technology has mutual exchanges with the closer areas of generic technology (or with science as well, in some cases of radical innovations) ; its generic fall-outs will assume a formal shape after some delay, but the bulk of it will always keep the nature of tacit knowledge (TK).

Definition : *Tacit knowledge is practical (that is, drawn from direct experience) and action-oriented knowledge about relevant empirical facts and situations ; its accumulation by a subject has a very high use-value for his technical and economic activity. Although this gives him a potential exchange value, this value can hardly be realised through market exchanges, and this difficulty is not only due to economic or strategic reasons (e.g. for free-riding problems and related disclosure routines). It is also due to the very nature of this type of knowledge, which is idiosyncratic, cooperative, informal and only partially "codifiable".*

Idiosyncrasy comes from the roots of TK in direct and cumulated experience : it can hardly be produced by an individual alone, therefore it is cooperative, and it is usually created and appropriated by an institution or a part of it. Any formal language will only partially codify the information contained in a set of TK, mainly because it does not articulate functional relations among objects in such a way as to be represented by a formal model ; moreover, even names to codify new facts might be missing in some of the creative phases of technological (or new markets) exploration.

Coming back to a spatial view of the economy, let us assume that TK, not necessarily only about technology but also about financial and other markets, is relevant for most activities, ranging from manufacturing to services. It will be one of the agglomerating forces : therefore, this spatial effect can not be interpreted just in terms of exchange values, as it is in the regional science tradition, since the early works by Weber and Isard. A stylisation of an economic region of the Third Industrial Revolution might include the following type of centres (see Table 4.1). First of all, most agglomerations assume the generic shape of an industrial (or central services) district, once we define it "as a socio-territorial entity which is characterized by the active presence of both a community of people and a population of firms in one naturally and historically bounded area. In a district - and unlike in other environments, such as the manufacturing town - the community and the firms tend, as it were, to merge" (Becattini, 1990)[1]. With a generic "district" we refer to a subset of the characteristics of a Marshallian District (MD), that **mutatis mutandis** can be found also in other, different areas. We extend here Becattini's definition of an industrial district into a much more general form, including both a MD with many independent small firms, and a CBD (Central Business District). In fact, most empirical findings on the latter subject stressed the importance of the frequent, face-to-face and informal contacts within the business community. Moreover, the importance of the interpenetration between firms and the community for the circulation of TK in high-tech districts is well known, and is also confirmed by empirical research. Therefore, High-tech and Automation districts are new forms of a generic district. Finally, the only agglomeration not sharing the generic district characteristic, is the "growth pole" (GP), i.e. the outcome of Fordist regional policies and of late Fordist delocations of industries from the manufacturing town : it is now the weak point of the regional innovation system, although it is still important for employment, production and diffusion (Charbit et al., 1991).

The financial, R&D, and applied engineering communities create distinct environments, respectively, in the CBD, in the High-Tech (HT) and in the Automation Districts (AD) ; as one can see in Table 4.1, all districts or poles have a range of specialisation including both manufacturing and services, although with different measures of importance and alternative specialisation. But let us now concentrate on the flows of technological services, either embodied in marketable commodities or disembodied.

Table 4.1   Main forms of spatial agglomeration of activities

Location	Manufacturing	Services
CBD = Central Business District	Demand-led products, fads and innovations	Contact-intensive services Standard-setting bodies Industrial, S&T policy
HT = High-Tech District	Science-based products and processes Information technology-based innovations Use of new material	University, Polytechnic Basic and applied research Venture capital
AD = Automation District	Machinery, manufacturing processes Engineering-intensive, and skilled L-intensive products or parts System-related learning-by-doing	Process development Cross-technology applied research System integration
GP = Growth Pole	K-intensive and/or large scale production Deverticalisation from large plants (indotto) Learning-by-using and by interaction	Product development Manufacturing-led services General services indirectly induced by the growth pole (local attraction of global effects induced via macro and I-0 multipliers)
MD - Marshallian District	Small-medium enterprises and/or L-intensive production	Networks and services for SME (small-medium enter.) Regional and local banks Professional schools

What creates a regional system of innovation, out of a geographical pattern of more or less dispersed or concentrated locations, is the existence of a network of exchanges of technological services. Being located in the right node of the network gives the opportunity, on the one hand, to exploit the "pollution" of TK dispersed in the atmosphere of the selected district (a chance which is scarce in the growth pole) ; and on the other hand, to enter the regional exchange network with the other districts (and interregional networks as well, but this is out of the explicit focus of this paper). Many flows go through this network, namely : (i) public services, or other services subject to political exchange, such as industrial policy, science and technology (S&T) policy, basic education and training, the setting of technical standards ; (ii) a variety of forms of public-private or private-private technological cooperation ; (iii) mixed, market and non-market flows, such as the trade of capital-embodied technical change, and the related user-producer interactions ; (iv) pure market interactions, such as private financing of research projects, licensing and sales of technological services.

The intensity and reciprocity of these flows generate a hierarchy of districts within the region. The Fordist region had a location centre of gravity somewhere in between the CBD, the manufacturing town, the Growth Pole and the Marshallian Districts (usually in this hierarchical order).

The Post-Fordist region always sees the CBD and the state or regional capital city as the centre of political and financial events. But manufacturing, related services and technological flows have created a new barycentre in between the High-Tech district, the Automation District and the Growth Pole. This is the new hierarchy : the High-Tech district attracted by relevant resources and institutions in the areas of formal knowledge and generic technology ; the Automation District that, once generated from an old manufacturing town or growth pole, starts its own independent trajectory and draws on the accumulation of tacit knowledge about specific process technologies ; and finally those Growth Poles that avoid decline, succeed in the process of restructuring, and take advantage of being linked to the regional assets located in higher-level nodes.

The technological flows are both upward and downward in the hierarchy : as HT and AD in the region are a location advantage for the traditional mass production in the GP, for example, the latter is also an important local market for R&D and engineering outputs from the higher level nodes which are receiving inputs of learning-by-using from the GP. These inputs or upward flows are very important, particularly in the early phases of an innovation cycle, before a new product or process enters national and international markets.

Finally, the manufacturing town and some growth poles are declining or have disappeared already ; Marshallian Districts, for being confined into supplier-dominated industries, are excluded from most benefices of the regional innovation system, although they maintain their traditional linkages with an AD pole located very often outside the region.

In conclusion, a regional system of innovation characterises an ideal regional production and location system that is coping with IT in an active way, as a user and/or as a producer region. It is made up of specialised districts, each one focusing upon a range of activities sharing some common resources and interacting very frequently with each other. But the degree of coherence of the system consists in the quality of cross-district market and non-market exchanges. As for the exchange of technological flows, a hierarchy emerges with HT and AD nodes as dominant producers, and GP nodes as users.

III   Is learning local, regional or global ?

In the previous section we have analysed from a new viewpoint the impact of an increasing role of tacit knowledge in creative technological activities, an issue dealt with from a diffusive and learning perspective also, in a previous paper (Arcangeli 1992). Let us now draw these two views together.

My previous analysis of learning by-products from innovative activity led to the identification of two components. First, learning related to specific technologies is continuous, incremental and local in its nature, although a large firm or a multinational (MNE) might be able to transfer it, at least partially, across regions and nations. Learning about generic technologies is global in its nature, because its outcome is transferable, but it has a much higher local potential closer to (or in efficient communication with) relevant scientific and technological institutions. Therefore the globalisation of competition would not stop the creation of "new agglomeration economies in specific nodes of the global networks, based upon the externalities arising from imperfectly transferable learning" (Arcangeli, 1992). Now we can add a new, intermediate regional dimension to the analysis of the externalities arising from interactive or cooperative learning. It follows that : (i) national systems of innovation can not arise from market forces (Chesnais, 1990a), also because they are composed of a hierarchy of similar regional systems, which are themselves a web of flows of services and communications across specialised districts, a large part of these district-to-nation relations escape both market and intra-organisational boundaries ; (ii) tacit knowledge, its generation and mutual exchange without any monetary value (i.e. the barter of use values) is the cement between old and new districts. Its idiosyncratic nature excludes its commercialisation and precludes even a partial transmission at distance in many ways. Therefore only appropriate social and cultural environments can increase the strictly local circulation of some vital elements of tacit knowledge, much before they become formal and are eventually read and interpreted by the abstract models of generic science and technology ; (iii) finally, a regionally-based catching up strategy might help to solve at least one side of the problem for a Newly Industrialising Country : the cumulative ability of technical change, even in its tacit aspects and with reference to the specificity of technological and professional resources ; although it will not entirely solve the other side of the problem (Foray 1990), i.e. the capability to abandon an old trajectory for a new one, which will always require a combination of tacit and formal knowledge (in training and research). This will often imply an access to some strategic resources located abroad or within MNEs. In fact, in the global web of international-to-local networks, the degree of access to and control of **interregional** flows of technological services is a key source for the reversibility of a path or a trajectory, when it turns out to be wrong or saturated. In fact the necessity of reversing trajectories from time to time gives some advantages to a MNE compared to a specialised regional innovation system (RIS). This is an area of conflict and perhaps a major issue for the industrial policy of the 90s : the contradiction, increasing with "globality", between efficiency within a regional innovation system (innovative production **per se**) and power-related communication in national and global networks connecting many regional innovation systems (innovative processes assumed under the command of global capital).

Notes

1   "The Marshallian Industrial District as a Socioeconomic Concept", in Pyke *et al.*, op. cit.

Part II

Questions about a European answer

5 Does Airbus Industrie yield lessons for EC collaborative research programmes ?

David C. Mowery *

I   Introduction

Airbus Industrie is an important (and relatively rare) example of successful public funding for the collaborative development and manufacture of a high-technology product in Western Europe. The characterization of Airbus as a "success" refers mainly to its ability to survive and to remain an important competitor in a global, high-technology industry ; Airbus does not yet appear to have evolved from an "infant" to a financially viable enterprise. Nevertheless, Airbus's achievement is noteworthy when contrasted with the achievements of more recent EC programs of support for strategic technologies, especially ESPRIT. Does Airbus provide guidelines for the design of Western European programs for the support of high-technology industry ?

This issue is important as well for other high-technology industries in which Western European firms face high levels of supplier concentration. Flamm (this volume) argues that in such cases, a "cartel insurance" policy, including public support for entry, may be warranted. Flamm's characterization of the incipient cartelization of the DRAM and other semiconductor product markets is open to debate. None the less, Airbus is a good example of an "insurance policy" in another industry characterized by

* An earlier version of this paper was presented at the conference on "European Firms and Industries coping with Globalization", Saint-Malo (France), 25-26 June, 1992. I am grateful to conference participants, especially Prof. Marc Humbert, for useful comments and discussion. Preparation of this paper was aided by support from the Alfred P. Sloan Foundation through the Consortium on Competitiveness and Cooperation

high fixed costs and high levels of producer concentration. As such, any "lessons" from its recent history are doubly relevant.

Although the apparent success of Airbus Industrie makes this consortium a logical source of lessons, little else about the program commends it as a model for government support of high-technology industry. In sharp contrast to the prescriptive conclusions of most economic analyses of government high-technology programs (Nelson, 1982, 1984 ; Eads and Nelson, 1971 ; Cohen and Noll, 1991), Airbus has not devoted its efforts to "precommercial collaboration," but has focused on the development of commercial products. Similar government-sponsored efforts in the development of new civil aircraft have failed in the US (the SST) and Western Europe (the Concorde). The product focus of Airbus also distinguishes it from many of the activities supported by ESPRIT and other EC strategic technology development programs, most of which support precommercial research in specific technologies. The lack of inter-firm competition in developing a new high-technology product that characterizes Airbus also contradicts much of the received wisdom about the strengths of Japanese strategic technology programs, in which precommercial collaboration is followed by competition among firms in the development of commercial applications.

ESPRIT's modest impact thus far on the competitive strength of European electronics and IT firms (see Mytelka, this volume, for a similar assessment) has led to considerable criticism of the program's structure and content. In this comparative context, such criticism may strain credulity - after all, Airbus required a number of years to develop into a competitive global producer of commercial aircraft (the United Kingdom government rejoined Airbus and initiated its participation in the development of the A320 only in 1979, by which time Airbus had been operating for a dozen years). None the less, contrasts in the structure, aims and (apparent) effects of these programs raise serious questions about more than just the design of technology policy for international competitiveness. They also suggest some reason for concern about the ability of the "federalist" EC political structure to design and manage programs of industrial support without succumbing to the redistributive politics that have plagued many such undertakings in the United States.

Space constraints, as well as the necessarily preliminary character of any conclusions about the "success" or "failure" of EC regional technology policies, mean that this discussion is speculative, rather than definitive. None the less, it may suggest some guidelines for future program design. I will briefly summarize the development of the Airbus and ESPRIT programs below, and follow up this discussion with some suggestions as to why Airbus appears to have had more significant competitive effects.

II   An overview of the development and impact of Airbus Industrie

The development of Airbus Industrie has been extensively discussed (see Hayward, 1986 ; Mowery, 1987, 1990). In 1966 the West German, British and French governments began discussions on the design and production of a wide-body aircraft. A 1967 agreement among the three governments outlined a joint venture in the development of both an airframe and an engine. The British government elected to withdraw from Airbus in 1969, an action that precipitated important organizational and policy changes in the consortium. The German and French governments invited Spain and the Netherlands to participate in the project, and abandoned the attempt to jointly develop engines and an airframe. Along with less ambitious technological goals, the Airbus project modified its economic goals considerably. Rather than maximizing European content in the aircraft, project members elected to pursue low-cost components from any source, which necessarily meant US suppliers in many instances [1].

Great Britain's decision to rejoin the consortium in 1979 coincided with Airbus's emergence as a serious competitor in the global commercial aircraft industry. Two new aircraft, the A310 and the A320, were introduced during the 1980s, and development of two additional aircraft (the A330 and A340) is well advanced.

With the development of a "family" of aircraft that have different operating characteristics and are best-suited to different routes, yet utilize some common design principles and components, Airbus has achieved a goal that has eluded all commercial airframe producers save Boeing. Along with the innovative technological characteristics of its aircraft (on occasion, as in the case of the A320's advanced "fly-by-wire" system, these have proven to be a mixed blessing), Airbus's development of a global product-support network has also increased its credibility as a supplier of advanced commercial aircraft. Partly because of its commercial "success" (which is defined largely in terms of market share, rather than financial returns to the consortium's investors) and its maturation, the management of Airbus Industrie and its member firms has gained increasing autonomy from direct political control [2].

Is Airbus a success ? Airbus Industrie's market share in large commercial transports has grown during the 1980s. Airbus gained 11 % of new aircraft orders in 1985, and 19 % during 1986-90, surpassing McDonnell Douglas in the share of new aircraft orders by 1989 (Congressional Research Service, 1992 ; Moran and Mowery, 1991). By 1990 Airbus accounted for 30 % of the backlog of orders for new aircraft (a market share indicator that is less reliable than deliveries, since airlines' orders can be cancelled). Moreover, as Airbus has matured, its European content has increased, supporting growth within the broader European aerospace sector. The EC Commission estimated that total turnover in European civil aerospace (which obviously includes firms not engaged as prime contractors or as suppliers to Airbus) grew from 2.6 billion ECU in 1978 to almost 11 billion ECU in 1988, and exports expanded from 2.8 billion ECU in 1981 to 6 billion ECU in 1987 (Commission of European Communities, 1990a).

In addition to its market share achievements and the (possibly coincidental) growth of the European aerospace industry since its establishment, the mere survival of Airbus Industrie is a significant accomplishment, in view of the unhappy history of trans-European collaboration in high-technology industries in general and in commercial aircraft in particular (see Sharp and Shearman, 1987, for a brief review of this history). None the less, Airbus has not met any conventional financial tests of success and the consortium has required significant investments of public funds. The 1990 Gellman Research Associates study commissioned by the US Commerce Department estimated that the British, French and German governments contributed more than $13 billion to Airbus, most of which (nearly 59 %) supported the development of aircraft; a portion of the remainder took the form of production subsidies (Gellman Research Associates, 1990). Less than $500 million has been returned to the "investor" governments, according to the Gellman study.

III　ESPRIT and the EC information technology sector

The ESPRIT program is but one of a number of regional EC programs for the support of technology development and diffusion within Western Europe. None the less, its relative maturity (by comparison with other EC programs), its visibility, its focus on a broad "generic technology" (information technology) and its broad structural similarity to other EC programs make it an interesting case for comparison with Airbus.

ESPRIT (European Strategic Programme for Research in Information Technology) was established in 1983-84 in response to concern within member state governments, the EC Commission and leading European electronics firms that European competitiveness in this sector was lagging because of too little R&D investment and because of the fragmented distribution of this investment. The program's establishment was also influenced by the widespread perception that public financing for R&D cooperation among firms had been an important factor in growing Japanese competitiveness in this sector, and by the establishment of the "Fifth Generation" program in the Japanese computer industry in 1982. According to Mytelka, the program had three objectives : "(i) to promote intra-European industrial cooperation in R&D in five main IT areas - advanced microelectronics, software technology, advanced information processing, office systems and computer integrated manufacture ; (ii) to furnish European industry with the basic technologies that it needs to bolster its competitiveness through the 1990s; and (iii) to develop European standards..." (Mytelka, 1991b, p. 184). By emphasizing standards, the architects of ESPRIT hoped to encourage collaboration among firms in different EC member states [3], providing a technological complement to the economic integration codified in the Single Act that followed ESPRIT's foundation. Although it "targeted" the information technology sector, ESPRIT in fact has not specified detailed performance goals or research priorities. In order to qualify for ESPRIT funds, projects involving industrial firms must receive 50 % of their funds from industrial sources, thus saddling industry with a considerable share of the risk and providing incentives for cost minimization. The results of ESPRIT research projects must be shared among the participants in a given project, although they may be patented. ESPRIT participants in any single project or group of projects have preferential access to the results of all ESPRIT projects (see Sharp, 1991).

The costs of ESPRIT are substantially lower and its funds are far more dispersed than those of Airbus. The EC Commission's contribution to what came to be known as "Phase I" of ESPRIT, originally intended to last for 10 years (1984-93), amounted to 750 million ECU, roughly $1.5 billion. These funds were to be matched by industrial contributions within individual projects. The EC funds were exhausted by 1987, and a second phase of ESPRIT was begun, to which the EC Commission has been slated to more than double its contribution, to 1.6 billion ECU. Phase II also has narrowed its technological focus to microelectronics and computer systems and related technologies (Sharp, 1991). According to Mytelka (1991b), whose data differ slightly from those of Sharp (1991), Phase I of ESPRIT funded 225 projects, which involved firms or "research organizations" from all 12 EC member states (Sharp counts 204 projects). During Phase I, according to Sharp (1991), 57 % of ESPRIT projects involved firms with fewer than 500 employees, and 75 % involved academic research institutions. Mytelka concluded that participation in ESPRIT projects was far more intense among the large, northern member states - firms from Britain, West Germany and France were involved in more than 55 % of the total number of ESPRIT projects under Phase I, and accounted for an even higher share of ESPRIT projects during Phase II (more than 70 %). Firms from Ireland, Portugal and Greece, however, participated in a larger share of ESPRIT projects in Phase II (respectively, 20.2 %, 18.2 % and 27.3 %) than was true of Phase I (3 %, 6 % and 22 %).

ESPRIT was established to support "precommercial" research, which meant that financing for the development of technologies for commercialization was to be excluded. Partly in response to criticism of Phase I's research for being "too far removed from the market to provide the basis from which European firms could compete internationally" (Mytelka, 1991b, p. 189), Phase II adopted a more aggressive approach to "near-market" research, with the share of projects classified as "precompetitive R&D" dropping to 52.3 % from a Phase I share of 64.9 %. The share of "application specific" projects, on the other hand, has increased from 23.1 % in Phase I to 34.6 % in Phase II (Mytelka, 1991b).

Has ESPRIT achieved its objectives ? Since this program had multiple objectives, some of which were more oriented towards European economic integration than to enhanced competitiveness, a definitive answer is difficult. In addition, the ultimate effects of ESPRIT, positive or negative, on the EC information technology sector may not be realized for some time. None the less, ESPRIT and other EC and related programs (e.g. Eureka and JESSI) have failed to stem further declines in the competitive fortunes of Western Europe's major producers of computer systems and microelectronic components. Numerous journalistic accounts have noted these difficulties [4], and the EC Commission concluded in a March 1991 report that : "An analysis of the situation of the Community [electronics] industry indicates a limited presence in certain key sectors : semiconductors, peripherals, consumer electronics, and a precarious situation in computers. Apart from the consequences for the balance of trade, this situation obliges European companies to obtain supplies of certain vital components from their competitors, which impedes their decision-making ability" (Commission of European Communities, 1991b, p. 4).

The perceived importance of the information technology sector, as well as the political salience conferred on this sector by the EC's investment through ESPRIT and other technology development programs, mean that trade policy has played a significant role in supporting Western Europe's information technology industry. As in the US, anti-dumping actions have become a popular instrument for selective EC intervention against imports from other industrial and industrializing economies. These actions have had important consequences for the regional adoption of this technology. Commenting on the recent EC Commission paper on information technology, *The Financial Times* noted that : "... as IT becomes more deeply-embedded throughout economies, its benefits increasingly accrue from its application rather than from its production ... European demand [for advanced IT equipment] is depressed by artificially high prices. Many types of computer equipment and consumer electronics products cost twice as much as in the US - a difference which cannot be explained simply by higher distribution overheads. In some cases, product prices have been increased as a result of EC anti-dumping actions" (*The Financial Times*, "Europe and Electronics", 27 March 1991, p. 16).

IV　Lessons from a comparison of Airbus and ESPRIT ?

Airbus and ESPRIT and its related programs are very different in aims and structure. Nevertheless, the implications of some of these structural differences merit attention. Airbus's success (recalling the qualifications inherent in such a characterization), by comparison with precursory ventures in aerospace and other sectors, can be attributed to several factors : (i) the relative (by comparison with earlier programs) and growing freedom of Airbus Industrie's administrative structure from political interference [5] ; (ii) the willingness of Airbus and its political sponsors to sacrifice its ambitious goal of an all-European technology leader for a more commercially palatable design that incorporated higher non-European content ; and (iii) the substantial financial commitment of sponsor governments to the consortium.

Among the most unusual features of Airbus Industrie was the responsiveness of this publicly funded consortium to the preferences of its commercial customers (reflected, for example, in the sweeping redesign of what became the A300). In contrast to most cases of this type, this example of "picking winners" with public funds relied heavily on market signals in the choice of design and product features. In this respect, Airbus contrasts sharply with such celebrated failures as the Concorde, the SST, or the US liquid metal fast breeder nuclear reactor.

The contrast between the ambitious technological goals of the Airbus consortium in 1967 and the more modest goals pursued with the A300 project is striking, and differs as well from the EC Commission's focus on retaining a high European content in the products of European IT firms. Paradoxically, the commercial focus of the publicly supported Airbus consortium may have enforced greater clarity and discipline in its economic goals than is true of the "precommercial" ESPRIT program. Such "market discipline" is exceedingly unusual in projects like Airbus, however, and this took time to develop.

ESPRIT, for all its decentralized project structure and "precommercial" focus, appears to have less political autonomy. This contrast between Airbus and ESPRIT, reflected in the far broader dispersion of funding and projects within the latter program, underscores the complexity of program design and operation within a political entity as large and heterogeneous as the European Communities. The sheer complexity of ESPRIT's structure, as well as the relatively small size of its average project, may have contributed to its modest near-term impact on technology commercialization and EC competitiveness in information technology.

Redistributive motives inevitably figure much more prominently in the operations of a "federalist" political system such as the EC, in the same manner as these influences often shape the structure and operations of military and civil science and technology programs in the US (see Cohen and

Noll, 1991 ; Mowery, 1992a). Paradoxically Airbus's far more hazardous "eggs in one basket" approach, which was reflected in its control by a small group of member states, each of which had a single "national champion" firm that depended on Airbus's success, may have contributed to its success. It is difficult to conceive a comparably centralized, costly, focused program being developed under the sponsorship of the EC Commission. The political environment that gave rise to Airbus may be a thing of the past in Western Europe.

Another very important influence on the contrasting fortunes of Airbus and ESPRIT is the difference between their technological returns and the competitive structure of the industries "targeted" by each program. Commercial aircraft is an industry in which public intervention has lasting competitive effects [6]. The very high fixed costs, long product lives, steep learning curves and significant economies of scope associated with aircraft "families" mean that the effects of technological or commercial success in one generation of one product may persist in other generations of products. Public subsidies for the introduction of new commercial aircraft thus may have lasting competitive effects that are stronger and more pervasive in this industry than in almost any other.

By contrast (and despite frequent assertions to the contrary), information technology appears to exhibit fewer of these characteristics. The ability of nations such as South Korea or Taiwan to enter into the production of microelectronic components and computer systems suggests that "first mover advantages" are surprisingly weak in this sector. Moreover, the competitive behavior of firms in the US and East Asia further indicates that the advantages of vertical integration into the production of both components and systems, cited approvingly in the 1991 EC Commission paper, may be overstated. The enduring competitive effects of public subsidies in the IT industry thus may be less pronounced than is true of commercial aircraft. ESPRIT, after all, is not the first program of public support for information technology in Western Europe. The substantial sums expended by member state governments on their information technology industries have yielded modest competitive results. Contrasting characteristics of structure and underlying technologies in the information technology and commercial aircraft industries may tend to undercut the competitive effects of programs like ESPRIT.

A final important point of contrast between these two industries is their importance to other commercial users in industrial economies. The economic consequences for users of an inefficient commercial aircraft industry may be less harmful than those associated with an inefficient information technology industry, because of the far more pervasive utilization of information technology in a broad array of other service and manufacturing industries. Support for the adoption of "strategic technologies," rather than intervention to protect the producers of such goods, may be economically justified in a sector like information technology.

The growing use of trade policy to support the goals of the ESPRIT program has been facilitated by the need to preserve the results of the large public R&D investment in European IT, and illustrates the inability to clearly separate trade and technology policy instruments in modern industrial economies. Similar intervention to support Airbus may impose smaller economic costs on EC consumers and firms, since these costs consist largely of the direct expenditures on export and development subsidies, rather than require differences in both the price and quality of a key capital input to European manufacturing and non-manufacturing industry [7]. Moreover, the economic costs of Airbus subsidies are further reduced, as Baldwin and Krugman (1988b) have noted, by the reductions in the price of commercial aircraft that result from the greater competition in the industry created by the entry of Airbus (as was noted earlier, this effect reflects the unusual market structure and dynamics of this industry).

V   Conclusion

The tentative nature of verdicts on the success or failure of either ESPRIT or Airbus must be re-emphasized - it is too early, and these industries are too dynamic, to render a verdict. Nevertheless, the contrasting near-term effects and structure of these programs suggest that the specific dynamics and structure of a given high-technology industry may be just as important as the point on the continuum from basic research to commercial development at which public agencies intervene. In this respect, commercial aircraft may be a more easily justified and ultimately less costly industry for intervention than is IT. Certainly, the contrasting structure and linkages associated with these two industries suggest that the economic costs associated with focusing ESPRIT more intensively on commercial development could be very high indeed. At the same time, however, the very high direct costs and lengthy gestation period associated with the "cartel insurance" program of Airbus Industrie surely will give pause to the most determined and/or **dirigiste** government.

The future of strategic technology programs like ESPRIT is further clouded by the potent redistributive forces that are likely to operate within the EC in the future. As and if a "federalist" EC political structure is overlaid with a "separation of powers" system of government (e.g. a stronger, independently elected European Parliament with committees for investigation, resource allocation and program oversight), the resemblances with the US political system will increase. If recent US experience is any guide, the resulting European political structure will face difficulties in designing and managing regional policies for the promotion of selected "strategic" technologies.

Notes

1 "The original Franco-German MoU of 1969 specified that Airbus Industrie had to build an aircraft according to strict commercial criteria, and consequently, to choose components and equipment from the cheapest source, qualified only by user preferences." (Hayward, 1986, p. 75).

2 "Compared with earlier cooperative ventures, Airbus Industrie has achieved a high degree of decision making independence. The growing integration, or at least the common feeling of commercial and technological commitment on the part of Airbus Industrie's members, has generated an increasingly formidable industrial momentum capable of applying considerable pressure on national governments." (Hayward, 1986, p. 71 ; see also Mowery, 1987).

3 ESPRIT requires that each of its projects involve at least two firms from different EC member states (Mytelka, 1991b).

4 See *Business Week*, "It's Crunch Time for Europe's High-Tech Giants", 23 July 1990, p. 41, or *The Economist*, "Second Thoughts : a Survey of Business in Europe", 8 June 1991, which concluded that "... Europe has a high-tech headache. The EC's trade deficit in electronics has doubled over the past four years to 31 billion ecus in 1990. Computer firms and chipmakers blame their dire performance on a crisis similar to the one which hit Europe's steel industry in the 1980s. Overcapacity in the world semiconductor business has forced down prices. At the same time, the cost of developing new generations of microchips has soared. European firms have been caught napping. As a result, they now control barely one-tenth of the world market for semiconductors, while fast-moving Japanese firms control nearly half of it. European computer-makers are also in a fix. Sales have plunged and profits have followed suit. Though American and Japanese companies have suffered too, European manufacturers have been the hardest hit ..." (p. 18).

5 This independence should not be overstated. The debates over the site of final assembly operations for the A321, which now appear to have been resolved in favor of Hamburg, suggest that politically motivated redistributive concern, which implies some efficiency costs, continue to loom large within the consortium.

6 Baldwin and Krugman (1988b) note that "The international market for large commercial jet aircraft is about as far as one can get from the standard trade theory paradigm of static constant returns and price-taking competition" (p. 45).

7 In other words, the major beneficiaries of innovation in information technology are users, who benefit from "spillovers" associated with declines in the price-performance ratio. These spillovers are much greater in an "intermediate-goods" technology like IT than in commercial aircraft. Bresnahan (1986) estimates that these spillovers in the US financial services industry during 1958-86 amounted to 1.5-2 times the very large investments in computers made by this industry. To the extent that ESPRIT and associated EC trade policies in IT prevent comparable reductions in the price-performance ratios faced by European users, severe economic costs result.

6 Strengthening the relevance of European science and technology programmes to industrial competitiveness : the case of ESPRIT

Lynn Krieger Mytelka

I   Introduction

During the 1970s, as large, diversified Japanese information technology firms accelerated their investment in product and process development and began to move from technological catch-up towards the frontier through collaborative R&D projects, their relatively smaller European rivals, cloistered within national markets, lacking economies of scale and slow to move towards economies of scope, steadily lost competitiveness. In response to this deteriorating situation, the European Communities launched the European Strategic Programme for Research and Development in Information Technology (ESPRIT).

ESPRIT 1 began with a pilot year in 1983 and ran through 1987. It was renewed as ESPRIT 2, for an additional four-year period in 1988. By 1992 a total of 561 projects were underway or had been completed. Nearly 800 firms and 500 research laboratories in universities and research institutes across the EC's 12 countries had participated in the ESPRIT programme. Despite this high level of participation and the large number of projects that have been undertaken, Europe's Information Technology (IT) firms continue to lose market share and through acquisitions, many have ceased to exist as independent companies [1].

Clearly ESPRIT alone has not been able to arrest this decline. Three interrelated factors, it will be argued, account for the limited role that

ESPRIT has thus far played in bolstering European competitiveness. These are : initial design failures for which both business and government share responsibility ; the vacillations of Europe's major information technology firms with regard to the importance of a strong home base from which to penetrate world markets ; and the absence of complementary policies at the national level.

II Designing ESPRIT

From the outset the design for ESPRIT was heavily influenced by macroeconomic growth models of the 1960s and 1970s. These assumed an automatic and linear link between R&D expenditures, innovation and competitiveness[2]. Adopting a linear research to market approach oriented the ESPRIT programme towards a focus on research and development as the engine of innovation, rather than on the process of innovation and the wider incentive system through which it is stimulated. That incentive system, as we shall see in section III, critically depended upon the existence of complementary policies at the national level.

Underlying the design of ESPRIT was also the strong antipathy to state intervention in the economy that constituted the reigning ideology of the day. Administrative guidance of the sort that MITI has made famous, industrial policy and even the type of indicative planning practised in France were spurned and market forces enshrined. This was also the period in which governments in Europe and North America equated partnerships with collusion and anti-competitive behaviour. Combined, these two ideological predilections led to an initial emphasis on pre-competitive R&D projects within ESPRIT 1. Of the 225 ESPRIT 1 projects, 65 % were thus 'precompetitive' and only 23 % were designed to produce working prototypes with immediate market application[3]. Many of these projects, moreover, had four- to five-year terms. As a result, four years after their start-up only 37 projects had been completed.

Despite their long terms, much of the R&D undertaken during the first phase of ESPRIT consisted of efforts to catch-up rather than move beyond the existing frontier. Although, as Mike Hobday (1992) has argued, Europe's IT firms were particularly weak because they specialized in older less dynamic technologies, ESPRIT 1 did not encourage a faster movement away from traditional technologies such as bipolar integrated circuits and silicon substrates and into CMOS technology and galium arsenide or indium phosphide substrates which are particularly important in optoelectronic applications. Not until ESPRIT 2, did a concerted drive to develop design and production technologies for Application Specific Integrated Circuits (ASICs) begin.

The emphasis on pre-competitive research also influenced the process of project selection by diminishing the importance of a strategic positioning approach that stressed coherence among projects. Thus few integrated project clusters were developed in ESPRIT 1 despite the stress in much of the recent economic literature on the dynamic impact of innovation clusters as opposed to single innovations (Freeman, 1982).

Midway through ESPRIT 1, European decision-makers became less concerned about the potential for anti-competitive behaviour within ESPRIT and more concerned about the competitiveness of European enterprises. The EUREKA programme, which aimed at joint development with a view to producing products for the market was already underway and criticisms were being raised with regard to programmes that did not directly contribute to improving the competitiveness of European industry. ESPRIT 2 responded to such criticism by moving somewhat closer to the market. Projects were now consciously selected for their commercial potential (Commission, 1990), integrated project clusters that shared a number of partners together and undertook different aspects of a related technological problem were developed and projects completed under ESPRIT 1 were extended so as to move project results closer to the market. Although ESPRIT 2 thus had a more pronounced market-orientation, much time had already been lost in Europe's attempts to catch-up to the industry's leaders.

III   ESPRIT and the strategy of firms

Conceptualized as a user-oriented collaborative R&D programme, both the design and subsequent functioning of ESPRIT have been heavily influenced by Europe's IT majors - 12 firms brought together in Brussels by Etienne Davignon, then Commissioner of Industry, to develop the work programme for ESPRIT. These same 12 firms subsequently constituted the ESPRIT round table that continues to advise the ESPRIT secretariat on work programmes and choice of projects. Yet these firms are hardly unified in the vision they have of Europe, particularly those that had played the role of national champions, as Thomson and Bull did in France or Siemens in Germany. Several, moreover, have been ambivalent about the role that a strong European base should play in developing the global competitiveness of Europe's IT industry.

Two major consequences flow from this. First, levels of participation by the Big-12 firms have varied across companies and over time. Figure 6.1 illustrates the large gap in participation rates between major players such as Thomson, Siemens, Bull and Philips, and firms such as AEG, ICL, Plessey, Stet and Nixdorf whose level of participation is significantly below the average. In the case of several Big-12 firms, notably, GEC, Olivetti, AEG and ICL, the level of participation has declined over time.

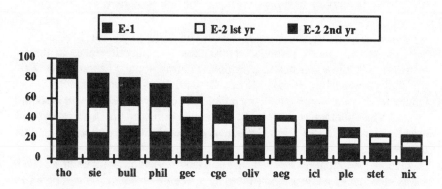

Source : Mytelka data set

Figure 6.1   Participation Rates of Europe's Major IT Firms
in ESPRIT 1 and 2 (number of projects)

Second, Figure 6.1 also points to the abrupt changes in firm strategies that have tended to weaken the potential contribution of ESPRIT to the competitiveness of Europe's IT industry. The case of Philips is illustrative of these shifts and their impact on efforts to strengthen Europe's flagging semiconductor capability.

Initially one of ESPRIT's foremost supporters, Philips participated in 10 % of the ESPRIT projects formed during the pilot year 1983 and 13 % of the projects in each of the following two years. Then in 1986/87 its participation rate fell to 5 % as its attention turned to the US market through its absorption of North American Philips and its alliance with AT&T. Juggling both commitments with difficulty led to reductions on both fronts. The failure of its alliance with AT&T subsequently contributed to a shift away from telecommunications towards semiconductors [4] and a renewal of its interest in the ESPRIT programme. This was reflected in a dramatic rise in Philips' participation in ESPRIT 2 when it participated in 17 % of all projects accepted under the first call for projects in 1988/89 and 28 % of the projects in 1990. It was also reflected in a reinforcement of its ties in the semiconductor field to Siemens with which it now engaged in 22 collaborative projects and with Thomson-SGS, a partner in 20 ESPRIT 2 projects. In addition, Philips entered into new collaborative R&D projects with Bosch and with the European ASIC Joint Venture, E2S. Dramatic deficits, however, would provoke yet another attempt by Philips to refocus its activities, this time by withdrawing from many of the very same semiconductor R&D activities in which it had only recently become involved.

IV   The interplay between national policy and firm strategies

While shifts in participation rates and in commitment by the Big-12 firms have limited ESPRIT's potential contribution to competitiveness in the IT industry, it is important not to overlook the structuring effects of policy on the choices available to these firms. Of particular importance here is the failure to develop complementary policies at either the EC or the national levels. The interactive effect of national policies on the pattern of participation in ESPRIT by German and French firms is notable in this regard.

Overall participation by German firms and research institutes in ESPRIT 1 was considerably lower than should have been the case when compared to French participation. Although, as Figure 6.2 reveals, German participation rose in ESPRIT 2, it still lagged behind what one might expect given the size of the German IT industry.

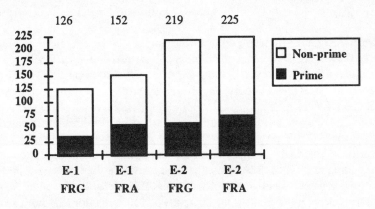

Source : Mytelka data set

Figure 6.2   A comparison of German and French participation in ESPRIT

Moreover, if we compare German and French involvement in ESPRIT as prime contractors - a role with considerable influence both in the shaping of projects and in the networking that such consortia promote, then significant differences again emerge. From Figure 6.2 it is clear that not only has overall German participation been lower than French participation, but German participants play the role of prime contractor less frequently than do the French. This is particularly true of the German Big-12 firms, Nixdorf, AEG and Siemens as compared with the trio of French Big-12 firms, Thomson, Bull and CGE.

As Figure 6.3, moreover, illustrates, in ESPRIT 2, not only was the number of projects with German prime contractors well below the French (59 to 74) but the share of total projects involving a German participant in which the German Big-12 firms are prime contractors has fallen from 44 % to 32 %. What has changed rather dramatically is the involvement of non-Big-12 firms from Germany in ESPRIT 2, particularly as prime contractors.

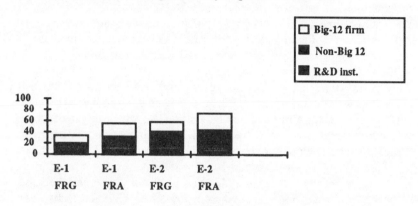

Source : Mytelka data set

Figure 6.3   A comparison of German and French prime contractors
in ESPRIT 1 and 2

To explain these differences requires an understanding both of the traditional networking practices of German firms and of the role of the state particularly in so far as the creation of incentives for participation in transeuropean R&D is concerned. The contrast between the French and German experiences is quite revealing.

Prior to ESPRIT, in the French, as in the German case, few firms had established partnerships with other European firms. Many had participated in national programmes that involved joint research and development activities, but in Germany both large and small firms maintained close ties to local universities and research institutions and a well-developed pattern of close supplier-client relationships frequently based on geographical proximity, existed.

To draw firms towards making the extra effort needed to form transeuropean partnerships, the state's role became crucial in both the French and German cases. Under President Mitterand a very pro-European policy was pursued. Working through a number of ministries, the government actively encouraged French firms to participate in European programmes and considerable support to projects involving French participants was given by French representatives, both state officials and French big-12 firms members of the ESPRIT Roundtable and other Community consultative bodies, such as the industrial working groups that structure the work programmes. When parliamentary elections failed to return a socialist majority midway through

President Mitterand's first seven-year term, the centre-right coalition led by Jacques Chirac initiated major cuts in the R&D budget. From an annual average growth of over 17 % between 1982 and 1985, the Civil R&D budget was cut to 2.5 % growth per annum 1986-88 (Delapierre *et al.*, 1988, p. 16). This spurred French firms, which by this time had become sensitized to the opportunities for funding offered by the Communities, to increase their participation in ESPRIT and in the newer EUREKA programme.

Quite the reverse process seems to have taken place in Germany. For many years no centralized German agency existed to defend the interests of German firms and institutes in ESPRIT consultative bodies. At the same time, larger German firms such as Bosch or SEL, which might conceivably have led consortia in ESPRIT 1 participated little in the ESPRIT programme. Participation by two of Germany's three big-12 firms, AEG and Nixdorf also remained low or declined, in part because their narrower range of interests did not coincide with the ESPRIT work programme but also because of rationalization following their takeover by other German firms. Larger German firms, moreover, seem to have been more attracted to EUREKA than to ESPRIT and in this they were supported by the German government which praised EUREKA's "pramatischen Ansatz under seiner flexiblen Organisationsstruktur" (BMFT, 1990, p. 245).

Reducing R&D costs through participation in ESPRIT was also not as much of an incentive for German as for French firms. Again this is partly a function of government policies which made a wide range of domestic incentives available precisely at the time that ESPRIT was getting under way. German small and medium-sized enterprises (SMEs), for example, had significantly more opportunities to obtain R&D financing from the BMFT and from "Länd" governments, especially "indirect" funds that were quasi-automatic because they were based on past investment costs or past levels of research personnel. This had an overall effect of reducing the interest of SMEs in participating in European programmes where the costs of developing proposals and the difficulties of working in English, of finding European partners and of meeting reporting requirements were far greater than looking towards traditional partners within their regions[5].

V   Conclusion

In sum, what the above analysis suggests is that policies such as ESPRIT alone cannot do the job of maintaining the competitiveness of Europe's IT industry. They are not sufficiently oriented to the market and to the key technologies needed to get there. They do not provide the coherence and the focus on longer term strategic objectives that rival Japanese firms although the projects in which they are involved do, and they have yet to build the kind of consensus upon and commitment to a vision of Europe that is needed to sustain a drive for European excellence.

Developing such a vision and harmonizing EC and national innovation policies to give effect to it is a task for the longer term. To strengthen the European information technology industry in the medium term, however, there are a number of changes that could be implemented within the ESPRIT programme itself. First, enhancing the role that SMEs play in inter-firm networks is the key to stimulating productivity enhancing changes in SMEs and the more rapid development of new product and process applications by SMEs. Second, there is a critical need to build a more coherent structure through integrated project clusters and to orient collaboration towards problem-solving forms of innovation-led research and application specific technological development. Lastly, greater efforts must be made to promote inter-sectorial collaborative R&D aimed at stimulating a more rapid and continuous process of technology diffusion.

Notes

1   In Germany, Siemens took over Nixdorf, Daimler-Benz acquired AEG and Alcatel-Alsthom of France purchased ITT's European telecommunications operations including its large German subsidiary, Standard Electrik Lorenz (SEL). In the UK, a Siemens-GEC joint venture took over Plessey, Fujitsu acquired ICL and Northern Telecom purchased STC.

2   These models have since been seriously challenged both empirically and theoretically. See, for example, Fagerberg (1988a), Kline and Rosenberg (1986) and Nelson (1981). For a discussion of ESPRIT in this context see Mytelka (1992).

3   A further 12 % involved the development of standards as a means to overcome the deficiencies of small size that limited the range of products produced by European IT firms when compared to their larger American and Japanese rivals. This taxonomy was developed in Lynn K. Mytelka, "States, Strategic Alliances and International Oligopolies : The European ESPRIT Program", in Mytelka (ed.) (1991a).

4   Philips is Europe's largest manufacturer of integrated circuits .

5   These data are based on interviews with German SMEs in May 1991 and with officials at the BMFT.

7 Coping with strategic competition in semiconductors : the EC model as an international framework

Kenneth Flamm *

I   Introduction

In the 1980s, the global semiconductor industry was the scene of a bitter struggle between American and Japanese high-technology companies. The role of government and national policy was a central issue in the battle, as activist trade and technology policies were mustered to support the interests of national firms on both sides of the Pacific. A watershed of sorts was reached in September 1986, when the US and Japan formally approved a Semiconductor Trade Arrangement (STA). The STA, renewed in modified form in 1991, represented a radical departure from the liberal trading system put into place after the Second World War : it set up a system for "monitoring" chip prices which in principle could be applied to virtually all semiconductors, and in a side letter, the STA specified a 20 % quantitative market share target for foreign company sales in the Japanese market.

The idea of "managed trade" had suddenly become an operational reality. Perhaps more importantly, the arguments - intellectual and emotional - which had so altered the landscape of the semiconductor industry were applicable to a broad range of high-technology industries. This chapter argues that structural changes in the semiconductor industry have made **strategic** issues - those predicting how the actions of others may be influenced by one's own

* The views expressed in this paper are those of the author alone, and do not represent those of other staff members, administrators, or Trustees of the Brookings Institution. I thank Yuko Iida Frost for her valuable research assistance.

choices, and vice versa - central to an understanding of these conflicts [1].

Seen in this context, the European Community's recent policies affecting the semiconductor industry must be analysed as a reaction to events and policies which have transformed the nature of international competition in this and other high-technology industries. One defensible line of analysis is that the EC is proceeding to build a protective barrier around its high-technology markets in general, and semiconductors in particular, and that steps taken by the EC down this path represent a further push toward global protectionism in high-tech products. A more optimistic analysis, however, is that the EC has put into place within its boundaries the basic ingredients needed to maintain an open trading system in high-technology goods : the free flow of products, uniform anti-trust standards to guard anti-competitive exploitation of monopoly power, the gradual regionalization of R&D subsidies and vigorous advocacy of the reciprocity principle concerning access to R&D programmes in order to neutralise investment in technology as a tool of rent-seeking nationalistic industrial policy. If the EC experiment with these principles opens up to wider international participation, in a new sort of high-tech trading regime, Europe may be blazing a path that will offer a way out of the rapidly increasing trade friction troubling global flows of technology-intensive products.

II   Structural change in the semiconductor industry

Until the late 1970s, the international semiconductor trade was dominated by a relatively large and fluid group of relatively young and entrepreneurial American companies, so-called merchant chip producers [2]. These firms specialised in the production of leading edge ICs, which were then sold at arms-length to an entirely different set of firms, that is, electronic equipment producers.

The development of this distinctive semiconductor industry structure in the United States was linked to a number of factors : on the demand side, much was due to the willingness of the military, the largest consumer of leading-edge components in the 1950s and 1960s, to buy expensive products from brand-new firms which offered the ultimate in performance in lieu of an established track record ; and the rise of a highly competitive commercial computer industry [3] willing and able to buy the most advanced component technology from whomever offered it for sale. Other factors at work included the high degree of mobility within American industry, which made it easy for engineers to leave established firms and start new firms if an existing company was slow to commercialise new developments, the ready availability of venture capital to fund such new spin-off companies, huge federal investments in R&D in the underlying technology base from which companies drew to develop their commercial products and a first-class educational and scientific university infrastructure which fed research and manpower into the electronics industry (again built with a great deal of federal support, and disposed to cooperate with industry as a consequence of the conditions tied to that federal funding).

The semiconductor industry developed quite differently in Europe and Japan. Established electrical equipment manufacturers were the primary force driving investment in semiconductor electronics, as they sought to produce cheaper components for use in their electrical product lines. For the most part, semiconductors were developed and produced within existing electrical equipment companies and semiconductor production took place within **vertically integrated** electronics producers.

At first driven largely by demand for use in consumer and industrial products, cost rather than the highest possible performance was the primary criterion behind semiconductor technology in Japan, which lacked a significant military demand. However, Japan embarked on a program to catch up in computer technology in the 1960s, and the development of high-performance components became a prerequisite for success in this area. Since the 1960s, both MITI and NTT have invested substantial resources towards the promotion of semiconductor research and development. The focus of these programs has almost always been on technology to be used in producing high-performance components for use in computer systems. By the end of the 1970s, it became clear that - combined with large private investments by companies - these support programs had paid off, and that Japanese companies had reached the technological frontier in semiconductors.

From 1980 to 1984, Japanese-based producers made significant inroads into global chip markets, at the expense of both European and American firms' market shares. Trade friction in semiconductors gradually began to increase during this period. After the deep semiconductor industry recession of 1985, a particularly large decline in the US industry's share of world markets was registered, as American firms dropped out of some segments of the semiconductor market. It is probably fair to say that a very sharp increase in trade friction also occurred. This period of friction culminated in the signing of the US-Japan Semiconductor Trade Arrangement in September 1986. However, instead of ending, trade problems in semiconductors entered a new - and potentially more difficult - stage.

The rise in Japanese semiconductor producers coincided with some important changes within the global industry, ultimately driven by technology. The semiconductor business in general was becoming much more capital intensive. Packing the maximum amount of circuitry onto a state-of-the-art chip required increasingly expensive manufacturing equipment and facilities. The capital costs of a fabrication line for leading-edge chips had risen from about 15 % of the total fabrication cost in the mid-1970s to about half the cost by the mid-1980s, and was projected to pass

60 % of total cost by the early 1990s. Since much of this equipment was highly specialised - had little or no scrap value outside of the semiconductor business - and, due to the continuing rapid pace of technological change, it had a relatively short economic life span. Investments in semiconductor manufacturing facilities, therefore, were often difficult to liquidate for more than a fraction of their acquisition cost. Such investments took on the character of a sunk cost. The increasing share of such sunk costs in total manufacturing cost made entry and exit from the industry more expensive and difficult. Even having made the decision to undertake this investment, it typically took a year or more to carry out such a project, adding a further element of risk in a notoriously cyclical market [4].

Another change within the industry was also largely driven by technological forces. As the level of integration (the number of circuit elements packed onto the surface of an IC) increased, it became possible to put more and more of the circuitry for an electronic system onto a single IC. Today, in fact, virtually all the circuitry of a complex system, like a computer, can be packed onto one or two chips.

This has led to an important change in the relationship between systems producers and chip manufacturers. In the past, when only relatively small numbers of circuit elements could fit within a single IC, chip manufacturers developed "standard" parts which performed general, "generic" functions that could be designed into more complex - and proprietary - systems. Today, however, when an entire system can be integrated onto a single chip, it is no longer economic to take standard "building block" chips and wire them together into a more complex system, since the cost of wiring together the standard components and testing such a system is prohibitively expensive [5].

Both of these factors - increasing capital intensity, and the requirement for greater proprietary information transfer between chip producer and systems designer - may have played some role in the rapid rise of the Japanese chip industry in the early 1980s. Japanese chip production has been dominated by large, vertically integrated systems houses, and both size and integration may have been increasingly advantageous elements in the changing environment for the semiconductor industry.

III   The growing importance of strategic concerns

Throughout the 1970s, European systems companies grew increasingly reliant on chips produced by American semiconductor companies, however this posed no threat to their systems business because these merchant chip companies were not in direct competition with their systems products, downstream. Indeed, the intense technological competition among American merchant semiconductor manufacturers led to a continuous stream of new, leading-edge products, with prices dropping rapidly as the result of aggressive imitation and competition from the many other merchant chip producers fighting for the same markets. While they may not have been happy about the poor showing of European-based producers (often components divisions within the same companies), this posed no threat to their downstream systems business. Indeed, cheaper components may even have decreased costs and prices, and increased the overall size of systems markets.

In the early 1980s, competition entered a new phase as Japanese companies reached the technological frontier in semiconductors, and entered international markets in force. Initially, this led to even more intense competition in the semiconductor market, and put further downward pressure on chip prices, to the apparent benefit of systems producers. During this period, however, as the chip divisions of some vertically-integrated Japanese companies became the industry's technological leaders in some areas, the first inklings of a new concern appears to have become evident among some European and American systems producers. Because Japanese chip producers were part of larger systems houses, some foreign competitors began to suspect that systems divisions belonging to the same Japanese companies were getting access to leading-edge products ahead of their foreign competitors. While this may have been perfectly natural, in so far as systems divisions and chip-making divisions collaborated in the design of new products, and were therefore able to design them into new systems earlier because of their privileged access to the development process, it put foreign systems houses at a competitive disadvantage in getting timely access to the new part. The resurgence of European support for semiconductors in the mid-1980s, in frameworks like the so-called "Megaproject," and the Esprit program, in some measure reflected these mounting concerns. Similar worries had also begun to take root in the United States.

After 1985, and the exit of many American merchant chip producers from the commodity DRAM (dynamic random access memory) market, trade frictions in semiconductors entered a new phase. For the first time, the important commodity memory market (a cost-sensitive input important to a large number of downstream systems products) was dominated by a handful of integrated Japanese companies. At first, such worries seemed to be a highly academic concern. The Japanese companies producing these products competed ruthlessly against one another, and prices for DRAMs continued to plummet throughout 1985.

In the Fall of 1986, the US and Japan signed the Semiconductor Trade Arrangement (STA), which fixed price floors for DRAMs and erasable programmable read-only memories (EPROMs), which accounted for a large share of the commodity memory market, and introduced a price monitoring mechanism for Japanese exports of many other ICs. At first, the STA seemed ineffective, as systems producers shopped for chips outside the US in order to avoid the minimum price floors, the so-called Fair Market Values (FMVs).

Bowing to US pressure to end sales at less than FMV prices in so-called third country markets, however, MITI issued "guidance" to Japanese firms in 1987 thereby cutting down production of DRAMs to drive prices above the FMVs. MITI also used the export control system to eliminate free access by foreign firms to the Japanese chip "grey market" and to fix a higher price level for memory chip exports [6].

Memory chip prices subsequently rose far above the FMVs, and stayed well above them throughout 1988 and 1989. This created immediate and severe impacts on chip users outside Japan (users inside Japan appear to have suffered somewhat less, and a significant price differential between the Japanese and other markets apparently opened up in 1988). For the first time, strategic concerns of user industries became part of the trade friction environment, and remain a significant issue today. These strategic concerns have two dimensions: coordination within an oligopolistic supplier industry used to increase collections of monopoly rents from users, and vertically integrated chip producers using their monopoly power to increase their market share in downstream systems products.

Rent collection by coordinated suppliers. The main strategic concern troubling chip users was that a small group of suppliers might use their market power to coordinate production or pricing in order to maximise profits collected on sales to outside customers, rather than compete as aggressively against one another as had been the case in the past. That this was more than a theoretical argument was proven when MITI's 1987 production guidelines successfully reduced DRAM production on a scale large enough to significantly boost DRAM prices. To be sure, this measure was a response to external foreign pressure, but it succeeded in greatly improving the profitability of Japanese DRAM producers, and showed that coordinated action by Japanese producers was feasible and profitable.

Though the subsequent rise in DRAM prices to levels far above FMV levels was undoubtedly in part due to other factors, including a recovery in semiconductor demand, restraint in expanding supply and production capacity by Japanese producers was also notable through mid-1988. By 1989, the concept of "bubble money" - super-normal profits due to abnormal scarcities of product - was widely used in Japanese industry circles to describe the profits being made on DRAMs, and estimates of "bubble money" being collected in DRAMs by early 1989 hovered around 3 to 4 billion US dollars per year. This was quite a significant sum in an industry whose global sales in 1988 were only a little over 30 billion dollars. Some evidence of the extreme profitability of DRAM sales was apparent in Toshiba's balance sheets. Toshiba, the largest producer of 1 megabit DRAMs, received only 20 % of company sales revenues from semiconductor components, yet was estimated to have received half of its FY 1988 operating profit on semiconductors !

More troubling were indications that Japanese companies were determined to put a permanent end to the "excessive competition" that had triggered rapid price declines in periods of slack semiconductor demand in the past. Despite price levels that by all accounts remained vastly higher than average (or marginal) costs of production, producers began to reduce production in order to stabilise prices, rather than cut prices in order to continue to sell more chips, as would occur in a competitive industry operating with prices well above (an essentially constant) marginal cost. By late 1989 and early 1990, continued production cutbacks by leading Japanese producers appeared to have slowed down price declines in a seriously depressed chip market, and rampant price cutting had not broken out despite prices remaining well above the average cost of production for leading Japanese producers.

Diminished systems industry profits and growth is not the worst possible scenario for downstream chip users, however. What should trouble them more is the possibility that differential access to chips could leave them disadvantaged relative to their vertically integrated competitors. It is well known that in the case of an intermediate input, like ICs, rent collection by a producer with monopoly power is maximised by integrating forward into the downstream industry (like computers) and collecting the rent in the downstream industry [7].

IV   Implications for policy

The main point of the above analysis is that trade friction in semiconductors has entered a new stage. Prior to the mid-1980s, sufficient competition within the industry prevented fears of strategic behavior by keeping vertically integrated chip suppliers from being a major worry for systems companies lacking a large, vertically-integrated chip-making capability. Trade friction in semiconductors was largely a series of disputes among chip makers based in different regions.

Since 1985, however, increasing industrial concentration in the production of key products, and the need to transfer increasing flows of proprietary information between chip producers and users, has been coupled with the growing domination of merchant semiconductor markets by vertically integrated Japanese chip suppliers. This has created strategic concerns for other systems companies which, in my view, will play a new and increasingly prominent role in semiconductor trade issues.

Whether or not monopoly power in chip supply is currently being exercised, and whether this hypothetical exercise of monopoly power is undertaken by private firms on their own, or under government guidance in order to avoid trade friction which might result from falling prices in an excessively competitive free market, the potential exercise of such monopoly power creates an economic argument for coordinated defensive action by user industries.

The essentials of this argument are spelled out in Figure 7.1. For the sake of simplicity, I have assumed constant returns to scale in chip production, and have assumed that technological investments and past learning have created a cost advantage for Japanese chip producers, so that their constant cost of production is J dollars (and their marginal and average cost schedule represented by line JJ'). Foreign companies have higher unit costs of U dollars (and their cost schedule given by line UU'). Foreign demand is given by demand curve DD', and marginal revenue by line MR-MR'. If Japanese producers were then able to act as a profit-maximising cartel, without fear of foreign entry, they would produce output Q0, charge price P0, and collect monopoly profit P0AEJ. If entry and exit in the industry were without cost, however, foreign producers could effectively contest the market, and put a cap at U placed on price by the threat of entry into a contestable market. I have argued that sunk costs - in the form of specialised and short-lived capital investments - are substantial in this industry, however. No individual foreign firm then is going to be willing to invest in a high cost production facility, because in the event of a price war the cartel can lower its price below U and still fully cover costs, while the high cost foreign producer will be forced to produce at a loss or to shut down and lose an amount equal to its sunk costs.

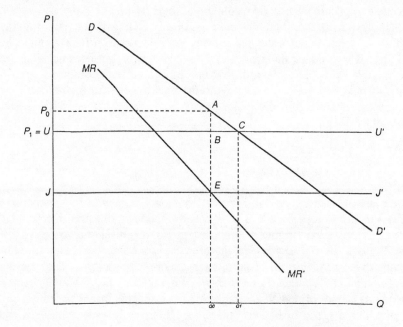

Figure 7.1   Theoretical case for domestic production

If the alternative is to face a cartel charging price P0, however, it is clearly advantageous from the viewpoint of the foreign country to subsidise high cost domestic production of output Q1 at cost level UU'. Monopoly profits equal to P0ABP1 which would otherwise have been paid to the cartel are thus saved, and in addition, consumer surplus equal to triangle CBA is gained. Subsidy of high cost domestic production proves superior to passive acceptance of uncontested, "cartelized" imports.

Viewing trade friction in semiconductors from the perspective of a user industry which believes it is facing a foreign cartel supplying it with needed chips (whether or not this is true), leads one to a very different prescription than has thus far been adopted in American and European semiconductor trade policy. Floor prices which raise costs above those faced by overseas competitors, and might even facilitate coordination among foreign suppliers, are not welcomed. Direct subsidization of entry by domestic producers, while maintaining imports of chips at competitive international price levels, is welcomed. This would seem to be a solution acceptable to both domestic producers and users.

Unfortunately, the introduction of subsidies raises a whole set of new types of difficulties, given the general trend toward reducing the role of direct subsidies for traded goods. If this is not practical, this sets the stage for further trade friction in semiconductors : a new stage in which user concerns greatly complicate the orderly resolution of trade frictions.

On the other hand, if the objective of subsidy is to facilitate entry into the industry, a creatively formulated subsidy - one focused on R&D - might be set up in a way that stimulates entry into the industry, yet does not grant an advantage to national firms at the expense of foreign competitors. Some such policy would be a welcome addition to the trade regime for high-technology industries, where future discussion of the rules for R&D subsidies seems inevitable.

V   The European model

There are alternatives to subsidies. International standards for competitive behavior, if enforced by a GATT-like body - perhaps like the International Trade Organisation originally proposed as an organisational sister to the GATT back in the 1940s - might alleviate some of the fears of anti-competitive behavior in concentrated high-tech sectors. The further development of a single Community competition policy would seem a promising model of demonstrating how such standards might be ironed out, even within a group of nations where very different historical attitudes and institutions regulate market behavior.

Indeed, further European moves toward regional technological integration might even become the first step toward a more functional trade regime for high-technology goods, a regime with two distinguishing characteristics. First, it would attempt to encourage investment in new technology by creating the widest possible market for high-tech goods (increasing the returns on fixed costs of R&D projects). The single EC market provides an obvious model here.

Second, it would encourage the greatest possible social return on collective international investment in technology (within the group of nations pledged to the new regime). Presumably this would mean that instead of investing resources in the national or regional production of **every** high-tech good, it would specialise in particular market segments (because of the economies of scale created by high fixed R&D costs).

Technological specialisation would be endangered if many would-be specialist firms feared that other members of the global community could manipulate this deliberate dependence on others, in order to increase the collection of rents at their expense. Minimal safeguards against anti-competitive behavior by groups of firms within the boundaries of the regime would be needed. In this respect, emulation of the EC-wide competition policy would seem to be just the ticket.

Another danger would be the use of public subsidies to boost selectively national firms in world markets. Subsidies to production are already illegal, but subsidies to R&D are permitted by the GATT. In high-tech industry, where R&D costs are high, research subsidies are an easy and GATT-legal way to help the local team. Putting an end to R&D subsidies would be much more complicated than stopping subsidies to production.

Subsidies to high-technology industries have been advocated for two quite different reasons. One argument applies even in an economy cut off from international trade ; it might be labelled the domestic social case for policy intervention. Government support for research is desirable if it prevents market failures which lead private return to investment in technology therefore falling short of being a full benefit to society. The principal cause for market failure is thought to be the difficulty an investor encounters in trying to reap the full fruits of his R&D investment for his exclusive financial benefit.

The possibility of collecting or shifting technological rents from foreigners (or avoiding payment of such a rent) provides a second reason for government intervention. If national policy creates a situation where technology-based rents can be secured for national producers, then national income and the standard of living will increase. This may be called the strategic trade rationale for intervention in high-technology industries.

The upshot is that, for several reasons, it seems inevitable that governments will be highly involved in national investment in technology, and technology-intensive industries. The multiplicity of motives means that such involvement can not be internationally regulated - in any operational way - by rules that strike at "forbidden" motives, and tolerate "acceptable" motives.

The challenge, then, is to propose some way of neutralising subsidies to R&D as a tool of rent-shifting strategic trade policy, yet preserve a government's ability to engage in socially beneficial public investment in R&D. The concept of reciprocity in R&D - permitting firms from other countries to join domestic subsidised research programs in exchange for reciprocal access by home firms into the foreign country's R&D projects - would seem an important step in that direction. Exploration of how such bilateral or multilateral reciprocity in industrial R&D subsidies might be negotiated could be an important subject for those interested in preserving an open international trading system. Here, again, the EC seems to offer one lead, with its de-emphasis of national technical programs in favor of EC-wide technical links, and its championing of the idea of reciprocity in access to research programs in its talks with the United States.

To conclude, the EC model of technological integration seems to be moving toward further development of community-wide standards of competition, coupled with a regionalization of access to R&D funded out of the public purse. Fortress Europe - building walls against the outside - is one concept of this idea. Some Europeans seem to view it this way.

But another way to look at it is as a model for the sort of arrangement that might work in high-technology industries on an even grander international scale. The same two EC principles could serve as ground rules for a technological community including the United States, Japan and any other country that wished to join. The wider the net, of course, the more difficult rule-making becomes, as economies with very different institutions are included. Some method to apportion the costs of public R&D investments would clearly have to be worked out. As public expenditure on technology becomes a truly international public good, equitably sharing the burden among nations and firms becomes that much more important.

The EC 1992 phenomenon tells us that the notion of an open international trading community is not hopelessly utopian. Reasonable nations can make reasonable compromises in their collective common interest. Nowhere is the common interest in an open trading system more threatened than in high-tech industries, particularly in semiconductors, where the world seems to be sliding rapidly toward a collection of balkanised regional markets. Will others be able to seek refuge within the same common walls that the EC is building, if an acceptable set of rules can be worked out ? Will Europe cooperate in such an effort ? For high-technology industries, this is the key question for the 1990s

Notes

1　See Kenneth Flamm, "Semiconductors," in G. Hufbauer (ed.), *Europe 1992 : An American Perspective*, Washington : The Brookings Institution, 1990 ; Kenneth Flamm, *Mismanaged Trade ? Strategic Policy in Semiconductors*, The Brookings Institution, forthcoming.

2　The standard source for this history is John Tilton, *International Diffusion of Technology*, Washington : Brookings Institution, 1971.

3　Whose main customer, in turn, for the most technologically advanced products in the 1950s and early 1960s was the US military. See Kenneth Flamm, *Targeting the Computer*, Washington : The Brookings Institution, 1987, chapter 4 ; *Creating the Computer*, Washington : The Brookings Institution, 1988, pp. 13-19.

4　The world record for bringing up a new plant appears to be held by NMB Semiconductor, which claims that it took only nine months to go from initial groundbreaking on a new fabrication facility to initial production of 256K DRAMs in 1985. See Larry Waller, "DRAM Users and Makers : Shotgun Marriages Kick In", *Electronics*, November 1988, p. 30.

5　It is uneconomic because lower density parts are more expensive per circuit element than higher density parts, and because physically making and testing connections between circuit elements mounted on a circuit board is much more expensive than making such connections within the internal microcircuitry of a single IC.

6　This is essentially the conclusion of a GATT panel report on a European complaint against MITI controls on export prices for chips shipped to markets other than the US.

7　See John M. Vernon and Daniel A. Graham, "Profitability of Monopolization by Vertical Integration," *Journal of Political Economy*, vol. 79, July-August 1971, pp. 924-5. This is because the user would normally substitute other inputs for the monopolized input as price is raised.

8 From scale to network effects in the computer industry : implications for an industrial policy

M. Delapierre and J.B. Zimmermann

I Introduction

Nowadays the computer and data-processing industry is going through a drastic transformation. The earnings of the big main suppliers, including IBM, are rapidly deteriorating. They suffer from a growing lag between their organisational rationale and the new rules that are presently shaping the industry. For European firms their weakness is all the more disquieting that their slow progress on external markets doesn't balance their loss of influence on the European ones.

From the 1950s and 1960s up to now, the computer industry has experienced a complete collapse of the principles on which were founded the power and the growth of the big North American and European firms. Subsequently, the foundations of the industrial policies that warranted, in Europe, the building and the support of "national champions" have broken down.

Today, at least for the computer industry, globalisation is all but homogenisation, i.e. similarity of manufacturers, products and usage characteristics. Furthermore, globalisation cannot be equated with its territorial acceptation, the fading away of national boundaries. It generates complex competitive and complementary stratagems that radically affect the business environment. Due to the universality of the computer, as a versatile tool opening a wide area of applications, and also to the combinative nature of the relevant industrial and technological activities, firms' strategies have gradually revealed a definite pattern of globalisation.

Isolated, the individual firm doesn't represent any more the relevant level to analyse competition, hence industrial policy. Built on the combinative rationale of the industry, networks which enhance industrial and technological complementariness, form the operational level for the constitution of an offer of system-goods (Imai, 1990). In that sense, an industrial policy can no longer be firm oriented, but a global project built on the ability to exploit the possible "network effects" that can be realised.

II   The essence of globalisation : from world market to global networks

At the very beginning it was possible to characterise the computer industry as being homogeneous in three ways. Big computers, built by big enterprises, for big users. Economies of scale were the common law of computer production as well as of data-processing investments ("Grosch Law"). There was consequently a general propensity to seek increasing returns which has resulted in the concentration of producers as well as of installed bases. The industry presented an oligopolistic structure, dominated by an uncontested leader, IBM. Market partition was organised, based on artificial variety, resulting from incompatibility with the proprietary systems of main suppliers. This constituted an effective market growth mechanism, which contributed exclusively to IBM's ultimate profit (Perrault, 1984). The leader established prices and technological orientations, for the others to follow, thus promoting a relatively stable environment.

Since that era, through the late 1970s and the 1980s, the computer industry has been marked by an outburst of small machines, manufactured by newcomers for small users, SMEs as well as individual departments of large groups. The data-processing function was then split and distributed throughout industrial and administrative organisations. The transition has led today to a very high degree of differentiation, resulting from entirely new principles. By way of integration skills, users can now have access to an extreme variety of systems, built from a highly diversified offer of constituents (hardware and software) that can be combined into information systems, provided that the adoption of common standards allows their interconnection within a given architecture. The world of the computer industry has been atomised into a multiplicity of industrial actors involved in very acrid competition through prices and innovations. The search for scale effects has been displaced from computers to standardised constituents, particularly the semiconductor components, while the actual effectiveness of the industry, in a general sense, arises from the existence of coordination procedures and architectures, that allow "network effects". Thus standardisation has a new part to play, not to reduce variety but to help it to emerge, making it possible to implement effectively technical and productive complementariness. Formerly used as a hierarchical tool within vertical structures, standards have become a harmonising mechanism within the networking structures generated by such complementariness.

From the very beginning, every big computer manufacturer was a multinational corporation or had to become one rapidly in order to benefit from strong scale effects on the worldwide market (Brock, 1975).

Presently firms, keeping to the peculiarities and competitive advantages of their country of origin, have to make use of the different advantages of their multinational plant locations. This includes the access to growing diversified markets as well as to contrasted productive conditions, technological resources, innovation dynamics, financing capacities or relationships with downstream users. The resulting industrial circuits are set at the world level. **The competitive and cooperative game is undeniably global, in the sense that it sees the conjunction of a variety of patterns of competition.**

In such a context, the main change has been the transition from a homogeneous market to a complex field ruled by combinative practices. The apparent paradox between the diversity of activities involved and the industry's unity has to be analysed taking into account the combinative nature of the data-processing products. First of all, a plurality of goods has to be combined in order to constitute computers or more complex information systems. Secondly, the assembly of a given set of goods according to their complementary functions into systems is made in order to provide appropriate solutions to utilisation characteristics, which is ultimately the objective of the data-processing industry. As a consequence, both organisation and competition within the data-processing industry have to be analysed at these three levels : goods ; systems-performance ; characteristics of utilisation, and their inter-relationships (Zimmermann, 1991). What has been supplied, for a long time, by integrated manufacturers is hereafter furnished by a multiplicity of agents. Within the data-processing industry the offer is reduced to a supply of solutions to usage problems as well as of systems performance and data-processing goods which are themselves sets of parts that have subsequently to be articulated into data-processing systems.

The very significance of the data-processing industry, itself based on the traditional concept of industry, is put into question here (Delapierre and Zimmermann, 1991a). The market segments still used to describe the computer industry have become less and less relevant. The cumulated computing power of microcomputers and workstations has today overcome mainframes and minicomputers. The wide diffusion of RISC architectures will probably reinforce this trend in the near future. This movement will be strengthened by the development of distributed operating systems architecture, that allows the interconnected stations to share power, resources and skills through a common network.

Systematising the combinative nature of data-processing, globalisation doesn't mean the melding of the computer industry within a wide undifferentiated field that could be labelled as the "information industry". Moreover, within the combination, functions, thus technologies and industrial activities, have to be specified, but also combined. Therefore globalisation implies a growing complexity of the industrial system, as products and activities become more and more interrelated and can only be implemented in a coordinated manner. This leads one to consider the computer and data-processing industry not only by itself but also through its connections to other activities. Therefore networks effects are also to be understood in a wider sense, including inter-industrial relationships.

Technological progress can no longer be assessed by the continuous speed of quantitative improvements in terms of performance or power (treatment, storage, display). It depends more and more on the ability to build information systems adapted to the needs of economic and social organisations, from the smallest to the largest and most complex ones. Skills related to systems architecture and integration have a strategic role to play here.

The generation of a new industrial structure cannot stem from the success of individual agents, who would thus provide recipes and targets for their followers. Firms entering new, systemic and combinative activities have to find a place within a coherent industrial system and, from the very beginning, must therefore get involved in coordination procedures. They cannot be left to chance or "small historical events" (Arthur, 1988). They have to take their stance within a comprehensive coordination, in convergence with collective preoccupations, which implies a political project.

The design and guidance of a comprehensive project however, cannot be based solely on the search for scale effects, or the concentration of industrial capacities and market shares that have been the groundwork for national champions' policies. On the contrary it is necessary to emphasise "network effects", that will constitute the basis for the coordination and operation of the industrial system. Actors atomisation, which doesn't mean autonomy, has progressively replaced a hierarchical integration of functions under one single agent's control. But the viability of an enterprise depends on its ability to operate within a **global combine**, on which hinges the cohesion of the entire system including interrelationships between agents.

III   The need for a European policy : from hierarchy to coherence

Industrial policy is in most instances conceived as an unavoidable disorder, aimed mainly at restoring straight and fair market conditions. Within worldwide competition, every state finds a justification of its industrial policy in the policies implemented by the other states (*Business Week*, 6 April 1992). Similarly, a tight competition policy is legitimised by market failures or by a non-proper mode of market operations in foreign countries. We do think, however, that a European industrial policy should positively contribute to the structure of the global computer industry, rather than only provide a cure for its malfunctioning (Jacquemin and Marchipont, 1992).

As a direct consequence of the vertical hierarchical structure of the worldwide computer industry in its early years, industrial policies at that time focused on the promotion of national champions, principally within the framework of protected markets, in accordance with structures of nations, firms and industries. What was good for Bull or ICL was good for France or the UK. Nowadays, doubts cast upon this overlapping hierarchy have led to two consequences. On the one hand, the space of the firm is disassociated from that of the states. Firms are more and more independent from conditions prevailing in their country of origin. It is, henceforth, less and less possible to match the interests of the nation with the interests of its enterprises (Petrella, 1989b). This establishes the necessity to define explicitly what the national interest is. It also leads to evidence of the present inanity of national champions' policies.

The nation state, on the other hand, can no longer be described as a semi-closed system, formed by a set of activities, themselves organised into a vertical structure, linked by supplier-customer, upstream-downstream, relationships. The spreading of transverse relationships within the framework of combinative architectures, tends to emphasise coherence more than hierarchy, in the analysis of the firm as well as of the State.

The main issue for the nation state today is to design its own project, that is a goal which will establish it as a nation, and a policy that will direct it toward that objective. The control of the computer industry has largely escaped from the realm of the USA, IBM and the large systems. Nation states have subsequently appeared in direct competition in order to determine new forms of organisation and operation of the industry. National economies do not represent undifferentiated territories, but are the outcome as well as the shaping ground of the new structures of the data-processing industry.

Market forces can constitute an efficient selection mechanism in a world where rules are stable, and largely independent from the influence of the actors themselves. Today we are undergoing a transition process. The main features of this new system, often categorised as global or technoglobal (OECD, 1992), are still in the making. Leaving the building of a new economic and social organisation to market mechanisms equates admitting an evolutionist approach of social transformation. This would have at least two drawbacks. First it considers only actors and not structures, new products and new firms would emerge through a selection process of the fittest, as if the system within which these newcomers appear were a purely external environment. The world economic system is at the same time, a constraining framework for the implementation of firms' strategies and states' policies and the result of these actions (Michalet, 1985). This, secondly, justifies that the orientation of the system's evolution should be left neither to historical determinism leading mankind down the path of a supposed universal progress nor to the compliance to an imported model.

In this transition process, the data-processing industry deserves particular attention reaching beyond its situation as an industry still in the making, but moreover as an activity which strongly contributes to the structuring of society. Data processing plays a critical role in the shaping of new infrastructures (EC Commission, 1991b), therefore it calls for explicit political intervention, in order to control its implications on lifestyle, work organisation as well as consumption habits. Furthermore, one must consider that the immaterial nature of these new infrastructures, by contrast with the traditional ones like harbours, roads or bridges, are much more flexible. They free economic activities from their territorial embodiment, and the lessening of these constraints widens the choice of possibility therefore reinforcing the need for society to have a clear vision of the most desirable orientation of its development.

Two general consequences can be drawn from our approach concerning the coherence of a computer industry policy for Europe. The first one is the need to clearly differentiate between domains pertaining to the firms and those pertaining to the states. All too often, industrial policy has only put civil servants in the place of private executives. Every firm is solely responsible for the way it produces value from the specific assets it owns and masters. Meanwhile, governments are responsible for structuring a nation's comparative advantages that are the main condition of efficiency for national industrial systems. It is concerned more by the development or the maintenance of activities, than by the survival of any given individual corporation. The State, nevertheless, has to take into account the social effects of business failures, but this must be done under social solidarity policies not to be confused with industrial ones.

The need to take a full part in the shaping and structuring of the industrial and social national systems, secondly, raises the issue of the nationality of firms (Reich, 1991c). The relevant distinction should not be the nationality of the firms' shareholders, but instead their degree of involvement in the local industrial fabric. In other words, industrial policies should tend to a naturalisation rather than a nationalisation of foreign companies operating in the country. This means that some kind of assessment of firms' contribution to the coherence of the national industrial system must be designed - localisation of R&D, use of local subcontractors, proximity to customers requirements, etc. Such a criterion has already found some applications in the opening up of the European cooperative programmes to groups like IBM and Fujitsu. It should be defined more precisely in order to help multinationals set their international strategies accordingly.

IV   Some lines of definition for a European data-processing industrial policy

As far as an industrial policy specifically devoted to the computer industry is concerned, two main lines of action can be taken aiming at the development and control of knowledge, and system architecture.

Control of knowledge related to the computer industry is a key issue concerning the position of European industry in worldwide competition. Europe should have its own scientific and technological capacity in order to ensure its ability to design technologies and goods that are best suited to its own needs. There should obviously be circulation of information, i.e. knowledge, to and from Europe, but Europe will only get access to technologies developed outside if it can trade them against some knowledge it has produced. Moreover, without any capacity of its own to produce knowledge, it would be particularly difficult to assimilate efficiently foreign ones.

Furthermore, it should not be forgotten that we are in a period of industrial transformation. There is no stable acquired position anymore ; even such a large, dominant, group like IBM appears to be in trouble. Industrial policy should then provide a more flexible structure to the European computer industry in order to give European manufacturers themselves a better capacity to adapt to the changing situation, and more, to influence the direction of the transformation itself (Delapierre and Mytelka, 1988). The State could play an inducing rather than a slowing down role here, in the sense that traditional European manufacturers, locked into their old strategic mould, supplying large systems on narrow, protected, national markets, often do not earn the amount of resources necessary to finance rapid, drastic restructuring. Our perception, contrary to the well-received assumption that short term pertains to the firm while the State must take care of the long term (Delmas, 1991), is that the responsibility attributed to the State could act as a remote time horizon for its vision and with immediacy for its action.

The second line of action is directly related to the characteristics of a new structure for the computer industry. The new forms of architecture emphasise the modular and combinatory nature of data-processing goods. Computers are systems built as networks of components and activities. This network aspect calls for a good interoperability of the constituting devices, which implies more their coherence rather than their identity, as mentioned in the first part of this chapter. This constraint of interoperability is clearly in tune with the development of partnership strategies. The European Commission has stated in its diagnosis of the European computer manufacturers that there is a lack of relationship between their European and worldwide counterparts (EC Commission, 1991b). The establishment of European cooperative programmes appears necessary to help European producers catch up with their foreign competitors. The rationale of these programmes however, goes further than a mere defensive gathering, it is directly related to the systemic and combinative nature of data-processing goods and industry.

In any case, to avoid the danger of bureaucratic government substituting itself to private management, one should insist on the need to innovate the overall policy design process and not just the measures themselves. It should not be forgotten that many industrial policy decisions are taken, at the European level, by civil servants who do not report to any elected instance. Such a deficiency in democracy is rightly pointed out by people who want to see a real political stance taken in Brussels.

Partnerships and the multiplication of linkages in order to establish coherent industrial structures should be promoted. To advocate cooperation does not mean to favour cartelisation. The cooperation we have in view is aiming at interoperability, not homogeneity. In that respect, partnerships between suppliers and final users should be induced, as well as between manufacturers and specialised subcontractors. In both cases the rationale of such policies goes towards the development of a supply well adapted to users characteristics and buttressed by compatible devices and components (Delapierre and Zimmermann, 1991b).

The network effect would then allow the appearance of coherent structures. Some specific features of the European industry would be left free to emerge from the interplay of the various actors. By substituting the network relationship to the previous structure based on scale and size, in other words coherence to hierarchy, it would be possible to maintain flexibility and the opening of a wide array of possible outcome solutions for the European computer industry. The promotion of its own specificity would then reinforce its worldwide competitiveness, as it would therefore be easier for European suppliers to introduce diversified goods to new customers, than to emulate the catalogues of well-established competitors.

A general application of the above arguments can be made in the case of the component industry. It is considered vital for the computer industry, and many advocates of a data-processing industry policy insist on building an autonomous European semiconductor industry. From the sole rationale of manufacturing, as long as there are suppliers engaged in cut throat competition, selling components at no profit if not at a loss, there is no need to manufacture them in Europe at higher costs. However, the strategic point of view shows that in such a situation the European computer industry could be put in jeopardy if foreign component manufacturers, being either themselves, or linked to, computer manufacturers, stopped or slowed down the flow of components into Europe. The issue is then a strategic one : how to prevent such a threat from materialising. A first step could be to maintain European capacity, in R&D and manufacturing, without any ambition to reach autonomy of supply, but guaranteeing the possibility to start large-scale production on very short notice in case of emergency. A second one would be to seek ways to promote European naturalisation of some of the leading foreign manufacturers, through their integration, for instance, into some European cooperative programmes. Obviously both proposals can be implemented by the states, most probably even at the European level for obvious scale reasons. It could not be executed by a firm or a group of firms, the sheer cost would deter any single state from doing it, and there would be a danger of cartelisation if several of them engaged in such a move.

To conclude, it must be clear that we are neither proposing the dismantling of the State, nor the curbing down of the firm, but rather the assessment of their own specificities. It appears, in particular, that firms have engaged themselves in a drastic reorganisation of their structures. They have gone a long way, striking down purely hierarchical, pyramidal lines of command, to build networks of interrelated and coordinated functions. In that sense, there is an innovative imbalance in the social system. What is needed is forceful innovation in the social and economic spheres, matching that which prevails in the field of enterprise.

9 Feasibility of a single regime of intellectual property rights

Dominique Foray

I Introduction

The institution of a unique regime of intellectual property rights (IPR) at the European and global levels appears ex ante to induce many significant economic advantages. In particular, it would allow more effective organisation of the international diffusion of science and technology, according to rules accepted in all countries, including relations between the North and the South as well as between industrial countries. However, the inconveniences of such a single regime of IPR must also be considered. In our view, they would be so significant that they would eventually undermine the bases of the potential benefits of the IPR regime's unification ; those benefits which a superficial analysis of this question seems to predict (Foray, 1992).

Indeed, it is clear that the national regimes of IPR (and of patents in particular) are the results of historical processes of institutional change. These processes have allowed distinct societies to design progressively specific forms of compromise between individual incentive to innovations and collective organisation of diffusion [1]. These forms of compromise allow the protection of the "informational virtues" of the patent system. Therefore, they preserve the role of general coordination of the activities of research and innovation that the patent system may assume (Kitch, 1977) [2].

These forms of compromise, however, are only viable when they are linked to specific characteristics of the innovation systems of the societies under consideration. Thus, a regime of IPR, defined as "weak" (diffusion-rather than exclusion-oriented) will also ensure incentives for a certain model of innovation. Similarly, a "strong" regime (focusing on the individual incentive) will also ensure collective diffusion if appropriate legal and administrative conventions exist to encourage the dynamic management of the industrial property. In other words, the spirit of concrete IPR regimes cannot be correctly captured outside the coherent relationships linking them to the other components of national innovation systems. Thus, the specificities of the innovation systems, to which each IPR regime is linked, are an obstacle to the standardization of these regimes. To achieve a single-global regime would thus require a reduction in the diversity of the innovation systems themselves. But, as suggested by Rosenberg (1992), this kind of diversity is a key feature of the process of scientific and technological change : "The historical outcome of this long-term freedom to conduct experiments which, as I have argued, has been the central feature of western capitalism, has been an economy characterized by a truly extraordinary pattern of organizational diversity." It is inconceivable that this diversity be altered [3].

II   The economics of incentive to innovation

The economics of research and innovation is currently the scene of an intense debate : what are the characteristics of the outputs of this activity, and what can be deduced from these characteristics in terms of a scheme of incentives and organisation ? Answers to the above questions will vary greatly according to whether the research activity is considered only as producing codified and perfectly transferable knowledge, or if it is viewed as including a great part of tacit knowledge. Some theoretical elements therefore need to be specified.

Codes and tacit knowledge

The characteristic of public good externality or the characteristic of non-rivalry, as is commonly said today, can be attributed to any form of knowledge. This is a purely technical characteristic : the utilisation of goods by an agent does not physically exclude their utilisation by others. A component of knowledge thus defined does not possess the physical pre-conditions of appropriability. This is clearly a question of major incentive failure since this characteristic determines the "natural" inferiority of the private benefits of research activities, according to the benefits that the society as a whole may expect to reap.

This incentive failure can then be either reinforced or attenuated, according to the transferability of knowledge : certain forms of knowledge are codified and thus easily transferable (at duplication costs) : "Codification of knowledge is a step in the process of reduction and conversion which renders the transmission, verification, storage and reproduction of information especially easy. Codified information typically, has been organized and expressed in a format that is compact and standardized to facilitate and reduce the cost of such operations" (David, 1992). The codification of knowledge slightly increases the problem of incentive : each firm can make a choice between committing resources to its own research effort or profiting from the efforts of others via spillover effects. It is remarkable that in this view the choice is therefore only a matter of cost and is not a question of quality or of the applicability of the knowledge ultimately available within the firm. The level of quality, which in essence is only that of the photocopy (of a manual or a scientific paper) is assured no matter which option is retained, since the knowledge sought is codified and transferable (Foray and Mowery, 1990 ; Foray, 1991a ; and 1991b).

However, a great part of knowledge cannot be codified. Here we encounter the concept of tacit knowledge, that is to say, knowledge which is inseparable from the collective work practices from which it comes : "These forms of knowledge are acquired experientially, and transferred by demonstration, rather than being reduced immediately or even eventually to conscious and codified methods and procedures" (David, 1992). The producer of tacit knowledge is thus naturally protected by the fact that this knowledge cannot be expressed outside the research context in which it is produced.

Regarding the functioning of new products and processes, codified and tacit knowledge are inseparable. Some tacit knowledge is always required in order to use new codified knowledge. However, the latter has clear self-sufficient value associated with its role of information and learning : the competitors, who are able to appropriate the codified part of knowledge will be able to appropriate and elaborate the tacit part of knowledge more quickly, and then use these new processes and products more quickly as well. It is thus relevant to study appropriation problems regarding codified knowledge [4]. We can reproduce some results of the microeconomics of information to apply them to the problems of incentives and resource allocation in the R&D field. This perspective is that of Arrow (1962). How can incentive failures be corrected so that the society does not suffer too much from the weakness of the private initiative in research activities ? Three institutional solutions have been identified by David (1992) as *"the three P's"*, i.e. "patronage, procurement and property" [5]. The last "P" serves to create private incentives for research, either by setting up property rights (ex-post cooperation) or by supporting cooperative research (ex-ante cooperation) (Katz and Ordover, 1990 ; Metcalfe, 1991 ; Antonelli and Foray, 1992). Setting up property rights results then in a market for knowledge, whose main instruments, in the case of industries, are patents.

Patents and public welfare

The organization of a patent system can be broken down into three steps : first, compared with trade secrecy, the patent system increases output from the resources used for technological innovation : "A legal system which has trade secrecy and a patent system will better serve the public welfare than a legal system with only trade secrecy" (Kitch, 1977). This superiority from the public welfare viewpoint is based on the informational properties of the patent. Indeed, patents impose some forms of disclosure, which can be considered the counterpart of property rights [6]. Secondly, firms must be encouraged to employ this particular appropriation mechanism. Accordingly, it is possible to either reduce the costs of the patent process or to ensure strong property rights. Third, the system must be designed so that the informational properties are maintained. It is thus necessary to elaborate forms of compromise between individual protection (exclusion) and collective diffusion of information.

Informational virtues and the patent's role in coordination. According to Kitch (1977), innovation processes may be considered as a set of "prospects", that is to say a particular opportunity to develop a known technological possibility. Each "prospect" can be pursued by any number of firms, the activities of which need not be disclosed to the others. Thus a system allocating efficient resource among the different "prospects", at an effective rate and in sufficient amounts, must be established. Efficiency will only be assured if : (i) management of each prospect lies in the hands of the entity best equipped to manage it ; and (ii) if information found by one entity is communicated to other firms at an efficient rate. Kitch demonstrates then that a legal system with patents will fulfil these conditions better than a system using only trade secrecy. Seven arguments are presented, each one dealing with the informational properties of patents and thus with the possibility of coordinating research activities, which the patent system provides. This set of arguments suggests to what degree the informational properties of patents may be useful in the general coordination of research and innovations activities.

Exclusion versus diffusion in the patent system. Therefore, firms must be encouraged to use patent as a leading mechanism of appropriation. The problem for the policy-maker then is to reduce the costs of patenting or to ensure that the patent will provide strong protection. However, the crucial problem is maintaining conditions conducive to the quick disclosure of strategic information. Otherwise, the relative superiority of the patent system (in terms of increased efficiency in resource allocation for research) would be threatened : a patent system incapable of diffusion is not superior to a legal system based only on trade secrecy.

Herein lies the main problem of the modern economics of patents : how can one solve the conflict between the social goal of using information efficiently, once it has been produced, and the need to provide optimal incentives to the potential producer of this information ? "Some protection to inventors is traded off against protection to users of invention" (Hirshleifer and Riley, 1979). This standard economics of intellectual property rights is developed in Besen and Raskind (1991) : the principal problem lies in arriving at a compromise between protection and dissemination of intellectual property. By providing incentives to innovators, the system can be adjusted towards innovative activities. If, however, the innovations derived from these incentives are not widely used, this system will be less beneficial than another, having less creativity, but with a broader dissemination of innovations. How can one balance these two contradictory requirements; that is, on the one hand, the necessary protection of the inventor, and on the other, the social need for broad diffusion of knowledge ?

Argument

First, the trade off between the need to protect and the need to diffuse must not be considered as a pre-existent binary choice before political and legal decisions of a society that would opt to support innovation. Anyone who wants to support strongly innovation is necessarily against diffusion. Conversely, anyone who supports wide propagation is necessarily a weak supporter of innovation. This double argument merits further discussion. It leaves aside a set of modalities and arrangements that would ultimately allow for the reconciliation of both goals. As suggested by Ordover (1991), "weak patent protection need not be inimical to economic growth and, conversely, strong patent protection need not be an enemy of diffusion". Thus, both terms of the trade off are not mutually exclusive. Forms of compromise can be set up between the individual incentive requirement and the need for collective diffusion. Two forms are of particular importance. They include individual incentives to innovate while maintaining the informational property of the patent system. In other words, these forms of compromise maintain the role of coordinating innovative activity which should be assumed by the patent system.

Indeed, protection and diffusion can be carried out at the same time. This will depend upon the coordination between the incentive system and the innovation system, that is, between the incentive system and a given model of innovation on the one hand [7] ; and between the incentive system and a set of legal and administrative conventions, more or less open to effective management of intellectual property, on the other [8]. Thus, we will see that in a certain model of innovation ("techne pull"), a patent system which is diffusion-oriented can also support individual incentives to innovation.

Similarly, because intellectual property can be managed efficiently, a strong protective patent system can also support diffusion. "Historically there has been much experimentation - both unintentional and deliberate - to establish an optimal balance between invention and diffusion" (MacLeod, 1991).

Each society adjusts the setting up of IPR according to its own visions and interests, granting these rights specific attention. A society will invent a specific regime of IPR and then transform it, according to the needs of the moment either as a means of enforcing strong protection or as an option for more rapid diffusion. For example, if the French legal system gave up the notion of absolute novelty in the eighteenth century, it was as a result of technological advances in Great Britain (Gille, 1978). As suggested by David (1992) : "the protections accorded intellectual property by nation have not manifested any great consistency in adherence to pure principle. Intellectual property rights have been pragmatically altered over time in response i) to changing perceptions of the way that the creation and dissemination of information and information products affect national interest and ii) to remedy unanticipated problems".

So, the diversity of IPR systems reflects the diversity of innovation systems. Thus, any policy concerning international standardisation of IPRs should be based on the standardisation of innovation systems (this is another, perhaps even more crucial, question) ; otherwise the uniform and global incentive system might be poorly matched to the procedures and conditions of innovation in certain countries.

III   Intellectual property rights and systems of innovation

As an incentive mechanism, the patent system possesses a certain flexibility, which allows for the elaboration of specific patterns of incentives, adjusted to given historical situations. This flexibility allows for the design of many concrete systems while taking into account different components of the innovation system in order to elaborate the compromise between protection and diffusion.

D-system : diffusion, model of innovation and incentives

Thus, according to Ordover (1991), the Japanese system combines low cost and the obligation to disclose strategic information quickly. Low costs are linked to factors, including the mandatory demonstration and examination of prior art. In Japan, this task is carried out by the opposing parties, not by the applicant, so that the latter can economise significant resources. In most systems, demonstration and prior art investigation are carried out by the applicant. Some characteristics of the system push innovators into the Patent

Office as soon as possible, indirectly allowing a more rapid diffusion : the "first to file" priority rule (versus "first to invent") ; the ability to modify the project, during the first 15 months after the filing, (versus prohibition of any modification after the filing). A last characteristic directly influences the speed of information diffusion : the "pre-grant disclosure" rule, i.e. the requirement to lay open the application for 18 months after filing. In most systems, disclosure occurs only after the patent is granted and not before. Early disclosure is an effective device for diffusion, whenever the conditions of exercising property rights (the patent scope) are weak and the novelty requirements are low. According to Ordover (1991), "potential competitors who have 'reverse engineered' the invention during the laying-open and opposition phases can file their own patent applications, thanks to the narrow scope of patent coverage and very relaxed novelty requirements". As a result, the Japanese patent system is a concrete form of the D-system, designed to drive innovators to disclose strategic information early, but only where the property rights are weak.

However, this is not the end of the story. My main goal is to show that particular forms of the D-system are not necessarily ineffective in matters of protection. The D-System is not a system which does not protect innovators. It is a system which allows for the protection of a certain category of innovators : "it rewards those who reverse engineer and modify often in minor ways the existing inventions and penalizes those who wish to protect their major technological breakthrough" (Ordover, 1991). The D-system is, thus, capable of fulfilling simultaneously both protection and diffusion requirements, in the case of a given model of innovation. Therefore, there is a necessary coherence between the incentive system and the innovation model. The Ordover argument brings to mind Aoki's thesis regarding the ways in which R&D and innovations are organised in the Japanese firm : "At the J-firm, the motivation to make the best economic use of accumulated stock of in-house engineering knowledge (what the Greeks called techne) exercises a 'pull' upon the R&D agendas rather than new scientific knowledge (what the Greeks called episteme) 'pushing' the development of new products or processes" (Aoki, 1984). In other words, the production of new industrial knowledge within the Japanese firm is not organised according to hierarchical principles, i.e. proceeding through sequential applications from scientific discovery to engineering problems and ultimately to the elaboration of a marketable product. Aoki's observations support our argument that in the case of the Japanese firm a strong coherence exists between the patent system and the innovation model. This coherence renders the incentive system effective, both for protection and diffusion. It is applicable, however, only to a particular category of innovation. D-system and "pull by techne" models are strongly linked. This coherence is reinforced by an additional element which is the absence of legal rules on trade secrecy. As a consequence of strong laws for trade secrecy, firms tend to abandon the patent system (particularly if that system only provides weak protection) and to opt for secrecy as a more attractive mechanism. This is close to the case of the less efficient system, described by Kitch.

In summary, the incentive system of the Japanese firm is a complex set of institutional elements - including (i) a specific patent system, and (ii) the absence of laws for trade secrecy. Moreover, the viability of the system is highly dependent upon the predominance of a given model of innovation, supporting in this case incremental innovations. The system is designed to meet the intellectual property requirements of an economy oriented towards imitation and minor innovations. On the other hand, it does not favour radical innovation.

P-system : incentive, exploitation and diffusion

In contrast, the P-system provides strong protection to innovators but penalises the rapid disclosure of information. Indeed, it emphasises the novelty requirement and enlarges the scope of the patent, while it decreases the constraint of disclosure, and creates a number of "barriers to entry" to the Patent Office. However, this system is not necessarily an enemy to diffusion. In some circumstances, it may even prove efficient by supporting both goals at the same time.

First, according to Ordover (1991), one advantage of a strong protection system is that firms are not tempted to rely on secrecy to achieve appropriability, this is even worse for the diffusion of ideas, but not for patents. Therefore, laws for trade secrecy ("the Uniform Trade Secret Act") in the US call for the establishment of a strong patent regime. Second, a strong patent regime reduces the risks of licensing. For example, "Take the worst-case scenario when the potential licensor demands to see the information before taking the license and then simply appropriates it without any compensation to the innovator. In a case like this, a strong patent regime improves the licensor's ability to preclude the potential licensee from utilizing the leaked information" (Ordover, 1991). In other words, a strong patent system supports commercial exploitation and thus, ultimately, diffusion.

Thus, the factors which render the P-system favourable to diffusion are the legal and public policy arrangements that allow for a dynamic management of intellectual property (licensing).

In summary, in the D-system models of innovation make protection and diffusion compatible, while legal and administrative arrangements (open to effective management of intellectual property) play this role in the P-system. We have then two opposing groups of incentive systems. The opposition of these groups stems from the fact that they draw their efficiency from their particular interpretation and usage of the innovation systems. They differ in their modes of coordination in diffusion, which is defined as a collective process : in the case of the P-system, the market (licensing) ensures coordination. In the case of the D-system, coordination of diffusion is based on a set of non-market rules guaranteeing limitations in the exercise of property rights and a certain suppleness in the modalities of patent application.

IV   P-system and anti-trust laws : when coherence lessens

The coherence of the P-system is based on a certain form of good will on the part of legal and administrative powers towards the patent applicant. This condition was fulfilled in the nineteenth century by the US as well as France. In both countries, the system allows for dynamic management of intellectual property and, thus, supports both protection and diffusion. Therefore, it preserves its role of macroeconomic coordination. In France, the key element of coherence depends upon the role of the state (Perez, 1991), according to a model that would certainly not be politically acceptable in Great Britain or the US (MacLeod, 1991). In the US, the key element of coherence lies with a legal system which favours the patenter in the licensing process : "The compatibility of wide diffusion through 'the front door' of the patent system with financial success for the individual patentee has been consummately demonstrated by Carolyn C. Cooper's study of Thomas Blanchard's adroit management of his U.S. patents for woodworking machinery [...] Blanchard decided that the way to fortune lay in widely disseminating his inventions, not only by manufacturing them for sale himself, but also through extensive licensing and assignment of rights" (MacLeod, 1991). Mowery (1992b) also stresses the positive role of the legal system in licensing for firms such as General Electric and Du Pont at the beginning of the twentieth century.

This coherence is then decreased, under the American anti-trust laws, "designed to confine the operation of patent system to its proper sphere" (Kitch, 1977). Legal actions against patent infringement usually go against the patent holder, while the penalty for "patent misuse", which nullifies the patent, breaks the original agreement between licensor and licensee. Because it supports protection exclusively the P-system is incapable of preserving both goals of protection and diffusion. This diminishes the efficiency superiority of a patent system compared to a system exclusively based on trade secrecy.

V   Conclusion

The diversity of national regimes of IPR is linked to other elements of diversity which concern models of innovation and the legal and administrative arrangements governing commercial exploitation of intellectual property. The viability of the national regimes (that is, their ability to reconcile both protection and diffusion, and thus to assume the role of general coordination of the innovative activities) is dependent upon their ability to fit with specific innovation.

The main conclusion to be derived from our argument is clear : "Proposals to establish a uniform international regime of intellectual property are not practical" (David, 1992). The diversity of national innovation systems remains an obstacle to international efforts (in particular those of the World Intellectual Property Organisation, GATT and the EC [9]) in standardising IPRs. This is why international conventions remain of little use, since they do not overcome the necessary simplification of procedures, which retain their national character. But is it worth getting beyond this step, when this could only be accomplished through altering the diversity of innovation systems ?

Finally, let us not forget the link between intellectual property and tacit knowledge. The most recent works, by Nelson (1987) and Von Hippel (1988), have demonstrated that some forms of coordination, such as "technology sharing" do exist in the case of tacit knowledge. However, these forms necessarily have a local character. Thus, despite different conditions due to the difficulties of expressing tacit knowledge (i.e. its inseparability from the people who use it), the problem is of a similar nature : to identify the informational channels which allow for the general coordination of research activities, in order to avoid duplication, to benefit from the cumulative nature of technical change and, finally, to increase the efficiency of resource allocation in research and innovation.

Notes

[1] This is clearly demonstrated in the articles included in the special issue *Technology and Culture* (1991), focusing on the historical formation of Western patent systems. This argument is more formally developed by Paul David (1992).

[2] As we will see, it is this role of coordination which renders patent systems superior to the system of trade secrecy from the welfare point of view.

[3] On the notion of diversity and the valorisation of diversities in Europe, see Cohendet, Llerena and Sorge (1992).

4   Moreover, one can hypothesise that great progress has been made today with respect to the technologies of codification of tacit knowledge (e.g. expert-systems software). The respective roles of tacit and codifiable knowledge would then be reversed in the research process. According to David (1992) : *"It would seem that the first-order effects of improvements across the whole range of information technologies would be to increase the extent of codification, as well as expanding potential international access to the stock of codified scientific and technological information"*.

5   For an analysis of the choice between these alternatives, see Wright (1983) who uses a model focusing on the differences in the informational roles of each alternative.

6   Even if the establishment of a patent only requires disclosure of a part of the information necessary for the implementation of the invention, it none the less provides a primary indication with respect to the possible success or "practicability" of a research orientation.

7   By model of innovation, we mean the process of seeking novelty, that appears as the "standard" in a given society. Thus, Aoki shows that this standard differs in Japan as compared to the US, that firms of each country, respectively, are not innovative in the same way, that what is considered innovative in one country can be considered entirely differently in another : *"the chain-link model by Kline and Rosenberg provides a good framework for characterizing the Japanese R&D process. According to the traditional linear model of innovation, the J-firm (the Japanese in general) may be characterized as uninventive and uninnovative"* (Aoki, 1984).

8   These legal and administrative arrangements include, on the one hand, public policy in favour of applicants, supporting them in the industrial exploitation of patents (for example, the "privilèges" in France, cf. MacLeod, 1991), and on the other hand, laws and jurisprudence regarding licences, which are more or less in favour of the inventors (Bouju, 1978).

9   For an overview on the works in these different organisations, see Reidenberg, 1988.

10 Trade, competition and technology policy

Peter Holmes *

I Introduction

Globalisation of business brings together the parallel issues of the regulation of national competition and that of international competition. With footloose investment, we can no longer clearly distinguish domestic and foreign producers. More sales by US firms come from overseas production than from exports, (Julius, 1990). Traditional instruments of trade policy do not work as they once did. Protecting one market will give most support to the strongest producers - who may be foreign owned - operating there. Anti-dumping duties and VERs (voluntary export restraints), intended to reduce the intensity of competition within the EC, may induce inward DFI (direct foreign investment) and so intensify internal competition. Competition policy can no longer be based on the premise that internal competition (good) is a different animal from foreign competition (dubious). At the same time globalisation does raise new possibilities for "unfair competition", via cross subsidy. We see an increase in "multi-market oligopoly" and an increasing importance of know-how generated at high fixed cost in one market but transferable at a lower cost to others.

Competition policy has always been ambivalent (see Hawk, 1988) about whether it is primarily protecting competition *per se*, i.e. consumers, or the rights of competitors to a level playing field, (Hawk, 1988). And what if more competition risks undermine European industry's competitiveness ? Conflicts between objectives were somewhat neglected in the 1980s. The conventional wisdom has been that promoting more competition within the

* This paper is based on a research project at the University of Sussex funded by the UK Economic and Social Research Council's European Initiative.

EC can benefit consumers and simultaneously enhance the dynamism and innovation of EC firms, (see Cecchini, 1988). There is much truth in this insight. Competition promotes diversity of sources of supply, pluralism of centres of decision-making and economic and political power, and promotes multiple avenues of innovation at the same time.

The logic of the benefits from a free competitive process, whether one takes a neo-classical or Austrian perspective, depends on there being a negative feedback loop in the reactions of one actor to the strength of another. The success of one firm, and any rents it earns, must make it either grow unfit or lazy, or act as a stimulus to others. This has been the great historic strength of market capitalism. If there are no sunk costs and no important learning effects, markets may approximate conditions of "contestability" so that even the threat of entry, or re-entry will ensure that the benefits of technical progress are passed on to consumers. In a neo-classical perspective the comparative advantages that emerge from such processes are exogenous. There is little firms or governments can do except exploit their natural advantages.

But to realise this balanced outcome, there must not be excessively great economies of scale nor, above all, irreversible dynamic effects. From a Schumpeterian perspective they are endogenous to the competitive process. The new literature on strategic behaviour and strategic trade policy show that there may be important market failures if there are cumulative dynamic learning effects, intra-firm and involving national or regional spillovers. Comparative advantage is thus endogenous and susceptible to collective action if the foregoing factors are responsive to public policy. (Krugman (ed.), 1986). In these circumstances there are possible legitimate policy concerns about where investments take place and the concentration of economic know-how and rents. We may still not care about the location of ownership, but we do have concern about where the "brain" of the firm is based.

The existence of sunk costs, including R&D, and even static economies of scale may give first movers' rents **by influencing rivals' expectations** via strategic pre-commitment; if so, such profits can be shifted from other regions if entry barriers are sustained (Smith, 1987).

In recent models of "endogenous growth", e.g. Young (1991) international competition may display "knife-edge" sensitivity to initial conditions, and in **extreme cases** lead to irreversible economic gains for one region not linked to initial comparative advantage. Economic policy may have effects out of proportion to its direct magnitude, but the impact will vary according to circumstances. Where durable rents were available, national income could have been more positively affected by ensuring that investment took place in industries that guaranteed a share of such rents rather than by ensuring that industries with the most favourable natural comparative advantage were chosen. There is thus a potential case for intervention, to correct spillover effects, to promote the capture of rents and to seek to prevent others from doing this at our expense. Stiglitz (1987, p. 143) has observed : "in the presence of learning by doing, one cannot rely on the standard welfare theorems to argue that market equilibria will be efficient".

Unfortunately the scope for strategic behaviour by firms and governments encompasses both positive- and negative-sum aspects from the point of view of the world as a whole. Dynamic learning effects may create informational market failures that can be improved on by such policies as generalised R&D subsidies etc. But with dynamic irreversibilities there is also potential profit from exclusionary tactics that have been traditionally dismissed by economists operating with a "contestability" model at the back of their minds. If there are major economies of scale it pays firms to invest heavily ahead of demand for two separate reasons : to capture potential forward-looking economies of scale and to pre-commit one's capacity to threaten credibly to make any new entry unprofitable.

Successful intervention depends on detailed knowledge and evaluation of scale economies and spillovers, the expectations and behaviour of firms, and the retaliation of rival firms and governments. Some institutional frameworks (notably Japan's) seem better able to allow firms to exploit strategic gains than others. The ability of firms to compete becomes a matter of both the cleverness of firm strategies and the degree to which the institutional environment allows them to engage in sound strategies.

International competition policy now acquires an unwelcome new dimension. It is not only concerned about levelling the playing field, but also with the asymmetries of outcomes as well as the asymmetries of initial conditions, which might be small or arbitrary, and perhaps long outdated.

Where such problems exist public authorities are faced with two risks. The first is that there will be "too much" competition. Suppose in an industry there are high fixed costs, and low marginal costs ; suppose also that there is scope for market segmentation across space due to international trade barriers. The strategic "predation" can be a profitable activity to enlarge market share, **even if there is no intention to raise prices for consumers to monopolistic levels.** Benefits from "market share predation" come not from higher prices extracted from consumers but from learning and other economies so obtained and denied to other producers.

Another danger is the very knowledge that such behaviour can be profitable for some but very costly for a large part of the industry. This may make firms seek cartellistic behaviour on a global scale. Globalisation of firms combined with residual barriers to trade, known as "multi-market contact" can make it profitable to enforce collusion in some markets by retaliation in other separable ones. This problem is exacerbated by the existence of networks of alliances. As Jacquemin (1987, chap. 5) notes, new organisational forms can be motivated either by pure efficiency considerations, or strategic considerations of the effects on rivals' choices, or both. With the same firms being sometimes rivals, allies, suppliers and customers in different markets, the significance of horizontal and vertical alliances becomes far more complex.

Industries characterised by the features noted above of high fixed costs and segmented "multi-market competition" thus offer strong incentives to firms to engage in collusive practices in many cases. And if this does not occur, such conditions provide opportunity for exclusionary behaviour, cross-subsidising one market from another, as Japanese firms are sometimes, rightly or wrongly, accused of doing. Competition rules need to guard against both these possibilities but experience in the EC and the USA has shown how hard it is to do this effectively. But it is very hard to distinguish dynamic competition from exclusionary behaviour, the latter being most easily defined as tactics that would be unprofitable in themselves if they did not lead to the withdrawal or non-entry of other firms. This leads to the view that it may be better, if difficult, to tackle the problem via an industrial policy intended to promote pluralism of supply, rather than by **ex-post** competition law.

In October 1990 the EC published a policy paper on industrial policy explicitly recognising the interactions of policy domains we have discussed here. In April 1991 it sought to apply these to electronics. In April 1992, the car sector was approached, but too late for this chapter to be able to comment.

Both the November 1990 and April 1991 documents enunciate principles but leave final solutions to be settled later.

II   The electronics and information technology (IT) sector

Electronics and IT seem to display the characteristics invoked by supporters of strategic trade theory, (see Krugman, 1987). This sector is rife with market failures, externalities, cumulative learning effects, etc. But, as Krugman is at pains to stress, the existence of market failures does not mean that the state can be sure of intervening wisely.

The European Community is committed to a two-handed approach to intervene, on the one hand, to combat "unfair trade", on the other, to promote EC technological collaboration, both inside and outside the EC framework (ESPRIT vs. Eureka) ; at the same time it seeks to promote competitive markets.

The EC's commitment to competition and to the extensive use of anti-dumping duties in electronics can only be sensibly reconciled by some idea of strategic behaviour. One is in favour of free trade, so long as the other side is playing fair, but in the case of consumer electronics and semiconductors, the presumption of many in the EC Commission is that the Japanese are not. This is based on both industry gut feeling and modern strategic trade theory which says we cannot rule out this possibility. Even though many theorists deny the industrialists' and officials' allegations, this is on empirical rather than **a priori** grounds (see for example Dick, 1991). Baldwin and Krugman (1988b) use a calibrated model to argue that the Japanese were only able to secure entry into the 16K DRAM market by some form of market exclusion, though they claim that benefits to Japanese producers were outweighed by costs to Japanese consumers. Their analysis does however omit intergenerational dynamic learning effects, and on this account it may underestimate the gains to Japanese firms. It also highlights the fact that the interests of producers and consumers need to be weighed up in a way that is different from traditional competition policy when profit-shifting is possible.

The US Supreme Court was heard on predation allegations in the Matsushita vs. Zenith case under US anti-trust laws. The Court rejected by a 5:4 majority the arguments of Zenith *et al.* that the Japanese were actually engaging in "collusive predatory dumping" of colour TVs (CTVs). Their conclusion has been widely disputed (e.g. by Scherer and Ross, 1990, p. 479).

The Court reasoned that if the Japanese firms had been unable to achieve a monopoly in the US CTV market after 20 years, there was no chance of them ever raising prices to monopoly levels. But the court did not address the issue of profit-shifting by "exclusionary" pricing at levels above Japanese long run marginal cost (LRMC) but below their own average cost (AC) and entry costs of US firms.   Blair *et al.* (1991) interpret Japanese behaviour as sales at or even below marginal cost in order to enhance the sales and reputation of Japanese firms, allegedly facilitated by cartel practices at home. There is evidence for these allegations (see Yamamura, 1986), notably via Keiretsu distribution structures and the absence of domestic entry in what has been a profitable industry within Japan. Blair *et al.* conclude that under US law the judges were right to decide as they did, but that on the apparent facts, the Japanese firms did appear to be exploiting a cross-subsidy possibility that seemed to be "unfair".

It is striking that this case was brought under US domestic anti-trust law. The Supreme Court in fact dismissed the US firms' case on "summary judgment" ; they took a brief look at the mountain of factual submissions and concluded that in the light of "economic theory", (read "Chicago economic theory") the allegations did not deserve a full hearing. The Court has in recent years sought to put the onus of proof overwhelmingly on the alleged victim in such cases. If a case is inconsistent with the Court's model of rational firm behaviour it will be dismissed without examination of the evidence.

There is no doubt that, in such circumstances with a different burden of proof, EC anti-dumping authorities would certainly have judged against Japanese firms. However, strategic behaviour by direct foreign investors who have amortised R&D costs at home could produce the same effect as alleged dumping, but be immune to action under trade law.

In the recent AKZO judgment the European Court of Justice provided for the first time a definition of predatory pricing (AKZO Judgment, European Court of Justice, June 1991). This is far more restrictive than the criteria currently used in anti-dumping cases, and poses political problems for future integration of trade and competition rules. It is thus far from clear that anti-dumping duties are only targeting practices that would be covered by Article 86.

In this industry the issue of unilateral vs. bilateral vs. multilateral action against "unfair competition" poses itself clearly. Ferguson (1990) clearly insists that the Japanese have engaged in predatory dumping in the semiconductor industry. The EC reaction has been to share US anxieties but to denounce the US bilateral approach. At the same time it is seeking such a solution itself with Japan. But ironically these measures serve essentially to facilitate the collusion among Japanese firms that is feared (see Flamm, 1990).

Anti-dumping actions also reduce competition in the short run and appear to allow anti-competitive behaviour; but in the long run they tend to attract inward investment (see Hindley, 1989 ; Belderbos, 1991 ; and Sharp and Pavitt, 1992). GATT has condemned the EC's "screwdriver" anti-dumping regulation which is intended to reduce competition via such investments. Though the latest EC report on anti-dumping activities states that this regulation will be kept in the statute book, it is clear it cannot be used on new cases without provoking a political storm.

There are serious possibilities for "predatory" exclusionary behaviour in electronics. Where there are very big economies of scale it may pay firms to deter strategically new entry. Where the institutional and financial systems of some countries make it easier to do this than others, there are real possibilities of "unfairness". But anti-dumping laws are a very unsubtle response. It may well be impossible and economically unprofitable for "victim" countries to retaliate (see Gasiorek *et al.*, 1989). The profit-shifting phenomenon does not involve any attempt to raise prices to final consumers, and once a first mover advantage has been gained by one party it may be of little profit to try and re-enter. Or if the Japanese have invested heavily to become the second player it may not pay to enter as the third.

The difficulty of distinguishing true motives for ambiguously competitive behaviour and the fact that one cannot reverse history put the competition authorities in a difficult position. The case for the maintenance of competition in electronics is a strong one, but how can it be done ? One is forced to ask whether industrial and technology policies to preserve pluralism of supply might not be desirable. Such policies may make their users better off even if there is retaliation, but if everyone does this there cannot be net gains.

III   Cars

The trade/competition/technology interface also manifests itself in cars. Mastery of "lean production methods" is at stake (see Womack *et al.*, 1990). Most commentators seem to feel that Japanese automobile production methods involve important learning-by-doing effects, and hence there is a possible risk of cumulative dominant positions. Public statements by leading car firm executives, notably from France, indicate that the firms believe they can only emulate Japanese methods at unacceptable social cost, and are demanding continued protection in a form that threatens the integrity of the Single Market and the Common Commercial Policy. But even industry leaders acknowledge that learning may be transferable by observation and that EC firms could learn by example, as is indicated by favourable interpretations of the US experience.

Although the Japanese have made huge inroads into the world car industry, it is hard to make a case for serious predatory behaviour. Instead Japanese firms have been remarkably willing to engage in "self-restraint" that saves them the expense of aggressive competition, while allowing their rivals to survive.

In the car sector, the Rome Treaty has been rather crudely distorted. National voluntary export restraints (VERs) and quota regulations (QRs) have been widespread and of doubtful legality, both under GATT and the Rome Treaty. The Commission has tried to bring trade policy into line with EC trade rules by negotiating a VER on cars with the Japanese government to run from 1 January 1993.

Until the signing of an EC-Japan car VER in the summer of 1991, the Commission has had no choice but to tolerate national "derogations" from the idea of a common commercial policy.   France has had semi-official administrative controls, and Italy a formal bilateral quota governing car imports from Japan. The UK has had a bilateral industry-to-industry VER restricting Japanese imports to 11 % of the market. Consumer groups have argued that such an agreement is illegal under the Rome Treaty : it represents a market sharing agreement by suppliers in a major part of the EC which keeps prices higher in one part of the Common Market than in the rest (BEUC, 1991). The jurisprudence on this kind of case is extensive since first EC Commission decisions and ECJ rulings (see Bourgeois, 1989 ; Marquez Mendes, 1991). And yet for obvious reasons the competition authorities have chosen to turn a blind eye.

A recent UK Monopolies Commission report recently criticised the arrangement without formally declaring it to be illegal.

European consumer groups submitted in September 1991 a complaint to DG-IV against the UK-Japan VER. The Commission's reply actually reveals the political problems of applying competition policy dispassionately in an international context, stating that since an EC-wide VER was to apply in

1993, there was no "community interest" in acting on the UK VER at this stage. But there is no "public interest" clause in Article 85 under which the complaint had been brought. To exempt the agreement from prosecution the authorities would have to show benefits to consumers or that it was the result of legal compulsion by a foreign government. But it is clear from GATT reports and extensive press reporting that the UK agreement was not covered by the "foreign compulsion" defence.

The EC Commission is clearly more independent than the UK Monopolies Commission and more powerful than the German Bundeskartellamt, and yet it is forced to acknowledge political pressures about technology and employment. But, as Japanese inward investment develops, EC firms will be putting on pressure to restrict sales from plants within the EC and the competition authorities will be forced to decide if they can swallow market sharing agreements inside the EC. It may be observed that the rules on vehicle distribution have in the past done just this, but the EC Commission is now committed to doing away with these forms of market segmentation.

The Commission is also searching for ways to improve the competitiveness of this sector without resorting to protection or subsidies, but has had little success even in devising instruments beyond retraining.

IV Conclusions

Traditional free traders would say that the Commission must be wrong to have allowed domestic car and electronics producers to demand higher prices and lower sales by their foreign competitors. But if there is anything at all in the new models of strategic behaviour and predation, this conclusion needs careful re-examination. The chances are that we will still conclude that more competition is the best way to improve performance in the car industry, even in employment practices and emission controls, etc. On the other hand, there is more scope for doubt about the unregulated market in chips.

Meanwhile, the approach to international alliances and collaborations in electronics is necessarily bedevilled by the fact that they have no simple and measurable effect on market shares that can be used to assess the obvious impact on competition.

Existing procedures for evaluating these issues have not caught up with technical change. We risk developing our industrial policy through selective exemptions from competition policy justified on grounds of technological and international trade. This has applied in the US and the EC towards research collaboration. But we have not had the overt policy debates and formalisation of criteria. Moreover, without international agreements there is risk of mercantilism over inward investment, and over the distribution of suspected "rents." It is surely better that we agree upon rules that ensure the dissipation and diffusion of rents than engage in zero- or negative-sum games to transfer them. The EC Commission has recognised the importance of confronting these issues, but at the same time the political sensitivity of the debate means that the problems are far from solved.

"Unfair competition" is more often than not just an excuse for demanding protectionism. Dore [1] has even argued that we might as well abandon the idea of defining unfair competition and design rules for tariffs designed to attract DFI! The EC Commission and the OECD have argued for tighter international competition rules (see also Ostry, 1990 ; and Soete, 1991). We need to find a way to curb both genuinely unfair competition and uncontrolled retaliation against others' alleged unfairness. At the same time states must be free to retain their national systems, and be free to emulate the examples of others (see also Holmes *et al.*, 1992). The EC, as Flamm (this volume) notes, is inching its way towards a two-pronged solution to this problem. On the one hand, it is a model for a set of rules under which states voluntarily, but bindingly, agree not to engage in zero-sum actions, e.g. destructively competitive subsidies etc., while preserving national diversity. At the same time, with limited success so far, it is trying to evolve industrial policies that maintain pluralism of supply.

Notes

[1]   "Preaching Pragmatism to Free Trade Church", *The Financial Times*, 8 July 1992.

11 Regional blocs, corporate strategies and government policies : the end of free trade ?

John Zysman

I   Introduction

The regional structure of a global economy is altering the management of technology, forcing governments and corporations to develop new strategies and policies. This chapter proceeds in three stages. The first sketches the regional character of the global economy ; the second considers how this regional structure affects the strategy options open to firms ; the third considers the consequences for national government policy. Those policy choices depend on judgements about the character of the linkage among economic activities and the way technology flows.

II   Regional trade groups in a global economy

The international economy contains three regional trade groups.   Not everyone agrees.   Evidence of global markets dominated by transnational corporations is often set against evidence of regional trade groups in which firms depend on their home base. The task is not to choose between two models or ideal types. Weighing the evidence to select between a proposition of globalization and a hypothesis of distinct and separable regions, or trying to measure how far we have come along the road to a global economy, would only miss the point. Rather, the task is to interpret the complex pattern of the global, the regional, the national and the local. We must understand how international markets are interwoven into regional economies. For example, international financial markets of enormous scale and significance have emerged over the past twenty years ; yet global wholesale banking rests firmly on national foundations because retail financial banking and financial markets remain national, or even local. There are transnational corporations, but their strategies and strengths are for the most part rooted in the character of their home base. Even as firms compete in international markets, their strategies and tactics are formed within particular regional contexts, often specific national and local institutional arrangements as well as supply bases that at once constrain and direct their choices.

There are three co-equal and distinct interconnected regional economies, three regional poles, each with its own technological base. These are natural groups [1]. First, global production is geographically concentrated in three places [2]. The United States/Canada and Western Europe each represent about 25 % of global GDP while Japan and the Asian NICs represent another 20 % (depending on the year, which countries are named, and exchange rates). Second, foreign trade for each region, if defined as exports and imports outside the area, is a very limited part of the GDP. Third, foreign direct investment is not blurring these regional boundaries, although it is rapidly expanding and often visible as well as controversial. FDI grew roughly three times as fast as world trade in the period 1983-89. But if we look closely, the regional pattern is there. There was a clustering pattern in which each region was dominated by investment from a single Triad member : Latin America by the US ; Asia by Japan and Eastern Europe ; as well as selected African countries by the EC [3]. Fourth, despite the continued dominance of the dollar in the international financial system, the yen in Asia and the German mark in Europe are given increasing regional importance. The natural trade groups could give rise to politically organized competing trade blocs [4], but that is a separate problem.

The three global economic regions have distinct trajectories of economic and technological development that rest on distinct institutional, industrial, and community organization as well as on separate supply bases. The notion that each economy is defined by distinct institutional and production systems that could be modeled, underpins the notion that we are experiencing the competition amongst different forms of capitalism. Each region is also characterized by a distinct "supply base" that both differentiates the regional production profile and has consequences for technological development [5]. The supply base has been defined by Borrus as "the parts, components, subsystems, materials and equipment technologies available for new products and process development, as well as the structure of relations among the firms that supply and use these elements. The supply base shapes the possibilities confronting users by enabling or deterring access to appropriate technologies in a timely fashion at a reasonable price."[6] The structure of markets and communities through which these elements reach producers is defined here as the "architecture" of supply. A market consisting of many "flexibly specialized" small firms all in shifting horizontal relations, each supplying components and know-how to the other, has a very different architecture from the vertically arranged keiretsu. The difference in architecture matters when it influences the access, timeliness and cost of technology.

Replaced in a more conventional language for technology debates, the supply base supports and is the result of a particular technology trajectory. There is nothing surprising here. However, for the notion of technology trajectory to have meaning, the variables that separate trajectories must be defined. Trajectory arguments hinge on the notions that the composition of production is significant, that activities are linked and grouped into development blocs, and that technologies spill over from one sector or activity into another. If, as is argued, the path of technology depends on learning, then that trajectory is by definition a function of the materials available to learn from and work with, defined here as the supply base. Similarly, generating that path of development leaves its traces in the form of components, subsystems and the like. Seen from this vantage of a supply base that underpins final production, Paolo Guerrieri's finding that trade in production equipment is linked to final output is not surprising [7]. Success in final goods and the production equipment that supports them are intertwined. Production equipment is an element of the supply base that is created by and makes possible competitive advantage in the final goods.

The character of each region's supply base differs, making a distinct trajectory of development likely in each place. For example, the Japanese domination of consumer electronics products produced an Asian regional supply base dominating in mechatronics and volume electronics. It is also significant that German export of capital equipment and Japanese export of volume consumer durables reflect the character of each nation's robots and machine tools - equipment that embeds production know-how. The actual character of the robots and machine tools in each case in turn reflect the two nation's characteristic production strategies.

Let us now link the fact of regions and regional supply bases to technology choices. For convenience, let us take as a stylized fact the existence of three regional supply bases. The first proposition is that it matters to a firm which supply base is its home, that the options open to the firm differ with its roots. This certainly assumes that firm strategies and organizational norms are a principal function of the national environment in which they are centrally rooted [8]. The second proposition is that the flow of technological and industrial know-how is denser within one region than across many regions, that there is not a single global market for technology, but rather three distinct supply bases.

How are these supply bases linked together ? How does technology flow among these regions ? If these three regions were simply geographic facts with no market significance, they would not be of importance to governments or firms. We must, of course, distinguish between **scientific knowledge**, formal and more specific, and **technological knowledge**, more implicit and less easily specified, noting that flows of scientific knowledge are much more open and much more international. To begin, let us specify three mechanisms of technology flow. First, industry technology flows through communities of company engineers. Such technological communities are inherently more local and national than international. Second, technology can flow through markets, but industrial structure and ordinary facts of distance and language can create a local bias. Moreover, national markets are often protected, and the flows of technology are distorted by trade protection. Not all buyers have equal access ; local buyers are likely to have some initial advantage. This is particularly important when production and design supply bases are in the same region as launch markets for innovative products, as is now the case in Asia for electronics. The result is that despite international markets for goods, technology still pools in local places. Third, multinational corporations may act as bees sampling pollen in each of the three regions. But they are still likely to make honey in their home base, have a root in the expertise and markets at home.

III   Corporate management of technological vulnerability in a world of regions and rapidly evolving technology

It is evident that in an era of rapid technological change, firms must continuously renew their core technological capacities in the form of worker skills, accumulated know-how, proprietary solutions and the like. Corporate management becomes more than resource allocation, but also - or more importantly - knowledge management. It is not just the speed of technical development that presses on firms. Developments, such as electronics, that recast competitive markets often come from outside an industry's traditional technology domain. The further the "technological event horizon" is from a company's original technical base, the harder it will be for the firm to recognize the radical disruptive technologies or to make appropriate responses. The faster the pace of technical change and the broader the horizon along which a radical change may emerge, greater will be the difficulty to maintain position and greater the risk.

The task is amplified because the sources of the technological advances and innovations often develop in different global regions than the home base of the company. The first question, clearly, is "how does a firm monitor the horizon in three regions for rapidly emerging opportunities ?" It does not suffice to say that firms require a presence in several regions, even a design and marketing presence, to answer the question. Certainly many large firms do not understand what they see ; and many small firms do not have the resources, depending for necessary information on trade associations, public institutions, clients, suppliers and the market. How, in any case, should firms respond to what they see ?

Often companies may have assured access to technology simply by buying it on world markets in the form of components or tools that embody technical know-how. That is often possible. Danish hearing aids and German machine tools embody and apply technology effectively. The core competence in the firm is the applications know-how. However, the difficulty comes when key technical knowledge required for application is not built into the equipment or machines but rather is intertwined with local know-how that is not transferred.

We might group possible corporate responses into three obvious sets : develop technology in-house (hierarchies) ; buy on the open market (markets) ; and team up with others (joint ventures and networks). The circumstances in which each has advantages have been widely discussed. In-house projects are needed for proprietary technologies critical to a particular company. But accumulating knowledge exclusively through internal investment is neither desirable, because of the inefficiencies of hierarchy, nor feasible, because of the limitation on resources. Markets are attractive for commodity products. Alliances may be attractive for projects that are too expensive or require technologies not under a firm's control.

When should a firm act and how ? The issue is not simply efficiency. Rather the choices are often central strategic issues. The strategic choices must depend on an assessment of the knowledge portfolio and technology needs of the firm and the position of its competitors. Clearly it must ask questions such as : (i) does the firm become dependent on outside sources for critical technologies and thus unable to sustain product or production advantage, that is, does it undermine its own critical capacities ; (ii) does the firm effectively transfer technology to competitors ; (iii) can the firm learn critical new technologies from a partner.

Does regionalization influence choice ? I think so. The risks involved in cross-regional sourcing of components, subsystems or production services in the form of contract manufacturing are greater or at least different and usually harder to manage. The networks concentrated in a region other than the firms home base may better serve the firm's competitors in the delicate problems of technology development, technology protection and technology transfer. We must certainly distinguish vertical arrangements in which a large customer - Toyota, for example - may dominate a pyramid of suppliers creating "virtual", albeit more efficient, vertical integration from horizontal networks of more equal partners. But in each case outsiders are at a disadvantage.

Strategic cooperation across regions is made more complex precisely because the several regions have distinct technological expertise. Consider electronics. For much of high volume digital electronics as well as the mechatronics and mechanical components that support final product, the core supply base is in Asia and is dominated by Japanese firms. Companies in Europe and the US often find that these networks in the supply base are closely linked to their competitors. Japanese network arrangements based on long-standing and deep linkages that include equity holdings make collaboration outside the group different from within. Contracting for components, technologies or services for that matter, often simply transfers technology to competitors. There are a few rather dramatic cases of this.

Certainly there are great risks when simply pursuing short-term efficiency with spot market purchases that hint strategies to competitors or what is worse, transfer technology knowledge. Yet collaboration is necessary. There are also risks in joint development. Those risks may be judged acceptable and manageable. But the risks are there, and become greater or at least different when the arrangements cross regions.

IV   Government technology policy in a world of regions : the end of free trade ?

Technology policy choices for governments are becoming increasingly difficult. Technological change is extraordinarily rapid and developments in one domain spread across to other sectors in often unexpected ways. Some technologies - such as semiconductors - appear as transformative, emerging and then altering the sectors they touch. But the transformative sectors themselves are the servants of the client sectors, semiconductors underpin computers, but computers underpin auto production and the product itself.

There are two polar views of how technology develops and flows, each implying different government choices and corporate strategies. We might define them best by looking at how they each interpret the European position in advanced electronics technology. Europe's computer and semiconductor producers have an extremely weak position in global markets. The first view would contend that Europeans should not be worried, that the capacity to apply and use advanced electronics technology is critical [9]. While there are some applications that may depend on having intimate access to the newest technologies in advanced electronics, for the most part the effective use of technology depends on a mastery of the application area. Consequently, European governments should desire only that there are multiple sources of advanced technology, that there are several firms (ideally firms of separate nationality) providing critical technology. Another policy focus suggested by this first view is to support public programs for diffusion and application expertise.

The competing view contends that only intimate knowledge of emerging semiconductor products can provide a foundation for volume electronics production in consumer goods from televisions to cars. Moreover, without the intimate knowledge that local development and production provide, application producers from a region weak in electronics may stumble. Firms from a region strong in electronics will find new solutions that will render obsolete established products. More broadly in this vision, governments should recognize that local producers of advanced technology do matter to the continuing development of closely linked activities, such as advanced consumer electronics, automobile electronics and other products where the knowledge simply spills over.

Assume for a moment that this second view is correct. Does a government need to promote the entire chain of semiconductor production or only parts of the chain ? Does it need to support billion dollar fabrication facilities or fund research in design technologies ? And if it supports design technologies, should it support device automation or system-level design ? My own position is that, at a minimum, the government must attempt to maintain open access to the technologies critical to its national producers, help assure that the foreign suppliers are unable to extract monopoly rents, slow product development in the country, or use their technology expertise to establish dominant application position. Equally important, the government must support programs for diffusion and the use of these transformative technologies. Growing regionalism raises two important questions. First, what difference does it make if the domestic producers are foreign firms ? For example, is the presence of Toshiba in the US, or of Texas Instrument in Europe, threatening or reassuring ? A judgement on the value or threat of foreign firms certainly hinges on how well the firms serve the application needs in the host region, on the technology a company brings with it, and on the technological opportunities that firm creates for local suppliers. If a foreign firm supports the interconnected web of local activity required to sustain technological developments in the particular country, a government may welcome it. Second, what if all the producers of an important input are concentrated in one country ? Assume, for example, that there are five producers - each with equivalent market share - of advanced nano-technologies, but that all are from **one region** - Europe, for example. Clearly, greater diversity of supply is attractive, but why regional diversity ? Should the producers in the other regions, America and Japan, be concerned ? Should the fact that the five producers are from one region matter ? There is no absolute answer to either question. The concern here is that the five firms are subject to home government choices and are particularly responsive to home country clients, meaning that they may not serve the interests of hosts as well. This is less likely if there is regional diversity. The concern is greater when the home market of the five producers is itself relatively impermeable and if technology flows centrally within that country. Then perhaps the potential host government contemplating entry of a firm from that semi-permeable base as a supplier of important technology should consider means of maintaining alternate sources of technology for their companies. If, on the other hand, the home market of the producers is open and if technology and supply relations are open, allowing entrance might be an effective way of securing a domestic supply base. What concerns Americans as well as smaller Asian countries - not always shared in Europe - is that Japan as the sole or dominant source of advanced electronics technology could make continued technological development for others difficult.

Unfortunately, the notions we are discussing here (technological security, supply bases required as the foundation for applications, competition, technology trajectories and strategic trade theory) define technology competition as the centre of trade wars. Marrying technology and trade theory produces a view that nations are competing for their economic future, that there are winners and losers. In some cases the language is "economics as war by other means". This supports a view that regional trade groups are rival blocs [10]. Indeed, a cult of the economic offensive in which early action is critical can result. States that wager successfully for technology early on may seize critical first mover advantages and capture whole downstream sectors of advanced economies within their borders. Others will be left behind. There are really three possible trade and security futures : managed multilateralism, regional autonomy and regional mercantilism. Those futures will not result from economic forces, but from political choices shaped by our ideas about how domestic development and international markets function. Consequently, those who determine domestic technology policy must consider the kind of international economic and security order that will result from their choices. An international framework, regime even, for the management of science and technology, and competition in technology will be needed. That regime must include : (i) access to launch markets ; (ii) access to emerging technologies and science ; and (iii) intellectual property rules.

V   Conclusion

The analytic argument here is very simple. The global economy is built around three somewhat separable economic regions. A truly global economy may someday arrive, but it isn't here yet. The substantive issue, avoided in these brief pages, is that Japan at the core of the Asian region has created a market and technology community that are asymmetrically permeable. It is accessible but in ways that alter the terms of access to launch markets, affect the profits of established markets, the character of partnerships and the problem of technology management. Because Asia has a dominant position in the emerging domain of high volume digital electronics this asymmetry poses difficult strategic problems for corporations. For governments it blurs the boundaries between trade and technology policy, making domestic promotion a controversial international issue. The problem is complicated because their choices will tip the balance between managed mercantilism of a global economy and competitive neo-mercantilism.

Notes

1 See Paul Krugman, "The Move to Free Trade Zones". Preliminary draft of a paper prepared for the Policy Implications of Trade and Currency Zones Symposium, Jackson Hole, Wyoming, 22-24 August 1991.

2 This argument is taken largely from Michael Borrus and John Zysman in BRIE (1992).

3 These materials are taken from "Foreign Direct Investment in East Asia" prepared by Sylvia Ostry for a joint research project designed by Sylvia Ostry, Center for International Studies, University of Toronto and the Berkeley Roundtable on the International Economy, 1992.

4 See chapter 6 Steve Weber and John Zysman "The Risk that Mercantilism will Define the Next Security System", in BRIE (1992).

5 See Borrus (1990).

6 See Borrus (1990) and Borrus and Zysman (1992), chapter 1, in BRIE (1992).

7 See Paolo Guerrieri, "Technology and International Trade Performance of the Most Advanced Countries", BRIE, Working Paper #49, 1991.

8 This has recently been argued by Y.S. Hu in *California Management Review*, "Global or Stateless Corporations Are National Firms with International Operations", as well as by van Tulder and Ruigrok in this volume.

9 This position is well argued by Gerd June "Competitiveness and the Impact of Change : Applications of 'High Technology'", in Peter Katzenstein, *Industry and Politics in West Germany*, Cornell University Press, 1989.

10 See note 4.

12 Seeking balanced trade and competition conditions in the context of globalisation : the case of electronics

Tora C. Lie and Gérald Santucci

I Introduction

This chapter deals with the notion of "unfair" competition in globalised markets and industries and discusses some fundamental issues including market access, predatory pricing and industrial targeting. It supports the view that the world community should seek a fair global competitive environment, where an open multilateral international trade system and the emergence of transnational companies are viewed as important elements.

Our approach to globalisation and the need of a level playing field could be used to study any industry but we selected electronics because of its alleged "strategic" importance for modern economies : as electronics pervade the modern economy, innovation increasingly depends on the access to, and availability of, core technologies combined to create new products and processes. Furthermore, the development of information and communication technologies has been a key factor in support of the globalisation process.

II   Three challenges facing the world economy

Globalisation versus regionalism

The world economy is today influenced by two basic trends, namely the globalisation of markets and industries, on the one hand, the constitution of integrated regional trading blocs, on the other.

The movement of the world economy towards globalisation started in the late 1980s. Globalisation is fundamentally a process of world economic fusion ; this process is made up of both the vertical relationships between states which belong to the same economic entity (e.g. Europe, North America, Asia) structured around the Triad (respectively the European Community, the United States and Japan) and the horizontal, mutually interpenetrating international relationships among the Triad. Another evolution of the world economy is the constitution of regional trading blocs such as the European Economic Area (EEA), the countries of Asia and the Pacific Rim, and the North American Free Trade Agreement (NAFTA). In this respect, the breaking up of the Comecon in 1990 and the fall of the Soviet regime appear to be exceptions.

Isn't the emergence of such regional blocs contradictory to the globalisation of markets and industries ? Does the intensification of regional economic blocs and the possible subsequent growth of protectionism constitute a threat to globalisation ? The internal European market has, for some time, been a cause of concern to EC trading partners due to what they have termed as the possible creation of a "Fortress Europe". Negotiations are under way to conclude NAFTA linking the United States, Canada and Mexico into the world's largest free trade zone, and an initiative to establish a free trade area for both North and South America is being considered. If such moves lead to regional blocs, market access for extraregional countries might be interrupted, and their export-led growth severely affected.

The danger of economic blocs, however, tends to be exaggerated. Regionalism and multilateralism are compatible with each other to the extent that the existing blocs are free trade areas which remain open to the outside world, welcome new members and respect the GATT disciplines. Regional blocs were not created with a view to achieving regional self-sufficiency, but rather to exploit fully the benefits of international trade. With modern economies being export-driven and increasingly dependent upon direct foreign investment, there is now considerable interaction among economic regions. In order for the EEA, the NAFTA and other arrangements to carve the world into a set of warring, protectionist trade blocs, they would have to break away substantially from the present international trade system. This is indeed a very unlikely event. Instead, by bringing evidence that increased local trade leads to economic growth, regional liberalisation has the potential of becoming a step on the road to global liberalisation.

If globalisation and regionalism as they develop today are not fundamentally incompatible, specific frictions are not however excluded. Such frictions have been revealed by the ongoing Uruguay Round negotiations; but what is involved there is not so much the regional blocs than the rise of protectionist forces exacerbated by a depressed world economy conjuncture.

Competition versus cooperation

By its very nature industrial cooperation is a threatening concept: why should a company choose to reallocate resources and share proprietary information with a real or potential competitor ? High-technology companies, particularly electronics companies, compete in an increasingly fast paced, expensive and demanding global business environment. State-of-the-art products have short lives due to the high speed of innovation and the continuous flow of new or improved products. The cost of research, development, engineering and manufacturing of these products is increasing rapidly : semiconductor manufacturers, for example, are expected to allocate nearly 35 % of total revenues toward R&D and capital expenditures in order to survive in global competition. Also, the level of expertise required is too broad to be handled exclusively by any individual company, and this explains why a swirl of alliances is taking shape.

Of all the changes in the world economy, the need for cooperation therefore has increasingly become the most vital. In the light of rising fixed costs and barriers to entry in new technological markets, it is no longer enough to think nationally and competitively ; one must also think globally and cooperatively. Here, governments play a key role. Where governments once created legal barriers to protect their industries and/or companies, it is now time to eliminate those barriers and provide companies with the necessary flexibility to form international joint R&D and manufacturing ventures in order to spread risks, pool resources, share technologies and combine production to lower costs.

Cooperation between companies is also an essential tool for those who must remain competitive while offering better service to customers. What should be avoided are cartel-like groupings of firms that are able to dominate the market, by controlling output and prices. This is a real danger because of the oligopolistic tendencies we are already seeing in the field of electronics, which again is closely connected to the globalisation of economies. It is therefore essential that firms which participate in alliances continue their own activities and remain real competitors in order to keep their dynamism. Competition and collaboration could take place this way side by side between companies, and still be beneficial to the prosperity of all parties without distorting the functioning of the market.

Free trade versus managed trade

The 1986 US-Japan agreement on semiconductor trade is the prime example of managed trade, it rejects traditional free trade notions in favour of negotiating specific trade results. Since it is clear that the three major trading areas each consider semiconductors as being so important, that they are determined to retain domestic production capacity, the temptation to "manage" semiconductor trade is increasing in relation to the globalisation of markets and production.

The attempts by the United States to get import quotas on the Japanese semiconductor market are clearly against the current tendency of free trade. Managed trade could affect business confidence in the free play of market forces. The appearance of regional trading blocs in the world context, while it can have a trade generating effect and contribute to the welfare of the partners, can easily be turned into an attitude of regional self-sufficiency and increase the danger of worldwide protectionism.

Advocates of free trade claim that any economic activity not driven by market forces soon loses momentum. On the contrary, those who support managed trade base their arguments on the logic that free trade is not realistic and that countries are likely to operate their economies in different ways due to cultural and structural differences. Consequently, the national and global interests would be better served by a regime that acknowledges the reality of managed trade, yet promotes competition, innovation and freer trade. Trade agreements should be used as a compromise to free trade where they are expected to function better than market forces. One serious problem is that this creates an environment where competition rules are different according to actors in the market, exactly the opposite of what GATT is working for. Furthermore there is a danger that the powerful countries will dictate the conditions and that these agreements will become permanent. Used correctly, managed trade could be a step on the way to freer trade, but if it is the ultimate goal it can severely disrupt trade.

III   Unfair global competition

Surveys on "unfair" trade practices have been conducted by various governments and organisations, e.g. "Trade Policy Review" (GATT), "National Trade Estimate Report" (the United States Trade Representative), "Report on Unfair Trade Practices by Major Trading Partners" (MITI's Industrial Structure Council in Japan) and "Report on United States Trade

Barriers and Unfair Practices" (the Commission of the European Communities). One is tempted to ask : "Who is the unfairest of them all ?" The concept of "unfair conduct" may refer to any practice or policy that is not consistent with GATT disciplines and other international conventions or to any course of conduct that differs significantly from those employed in their own country.

Indeed, factors such as government regulation, trade policies, government procurement and standards in various countries, influence the ability of producers to compete in global markets for electronic equipment, because of their impact on trade flows and on competition. However, it is worth noting that governments may be tempted to wave preposterous arguments of unfair trade and competition in the world economy with a view to justifying protectionist measures.

We will in the following paragraphs highlight some examples of "unfair trade practices" that exist in the electronics industry.

Market access

In principle, every economy wants its domestic firms to have access to markets, technology and investment opportunities in partner economies. Some countries, however, also want to control foreign behaviour in their domestic markets. That control may come by way of government restriction as in Korea, or, as in Japan, by sharp limits on the ability of foreign investors to buy into existing groups or exploit market opportunities.

This problem lies at the heart of contemporary disputes over trade and competition within the Triad. These disputes are about the impact and meaning of domestic industrial policies and business practices that are not transparent and that, above all, implicate a purposeful search for self-sufficiency at the national or regional level in contempt of international rules. While the degree of competition and openness to direct foreign investment is increasingly important in the context of globalisation, certain markets are still practically closed to the penetration of foreign investment and products.

In view of the difficulties the non-Japanese semiconductor and other electronic equipment manufacturers have in penetrating the Japanese market, it is not surprising that market access has become a fundamental issue with political implications. Various reasons can be found to explain the difficulties for foreign-affiliated companies to enter the Japanese electronics market, the most peculiar being the structural barrier that results from the Japanese Keiretsu system - massive industrial combines centred around a bank or integrated along a supplier chain dominated by a major manufacturer. This system excludes foreign companies from much of Japanese business by denying them acquisition of any Japanese company that could serve as a market entry point or by controlling the distribution system.

One of the consequences of these controlled distribution systems is that the Japanese producers are able to charge consumers with prices significantly above those which American and European consumers pay for the same products. With these superprofits the Japanese manufacturers are able to take risks and support new technologies that are not yet profitable, and still pursue their long-term goals.

After years of conflictual relations on trade issues, the United States have tried recently to compel Japan to open its market by negotiating bilateral agreements ensuring market access and competitive behaviour. Following the Structural Impediments Initiative (SII), the agreements under "Super 301" covering wood products, supercomputers and satellites, and bilateral agreements on computers, telecommunications, semiconductors, construction services and vehicles, *inter alia*, multilateral rules appear increasingly irrelevant to US-Japan trade relations.

Dumping

Dumping, which is commonly defined as the sale of a product overseas for less than the price on the home market or for less than the cost of production, is acknowledged to be a potentially damaging practice in international trade. However, anti-dumping rules and mechanisms are double-edged. They are needed to provide protection from a potential threat (dumping) but their presence may encourage the development of another threat, namely the seizure and use of these instruments by firms and industries which incorporate them into discriminatory strategies to compensate for the lack of corporate competitiveness. The recent spread of anti-dumping measures in the United States and the EC may be seen as a trend towards protectionism dissuading certain firms from competing effectively in an increasingly globalised environment.

Indeed, two different types of explanation can be put forward to analyse situations in which dumping is suspected in the electronics industry. The first stresses the role of **predatory pricing** behaviours by aggressive exporters seeking to increase their global market share through dumped prices. The second refers to the **divergence between long-term and short-term business strategies**. Average costs are used by some producers, in particular in the semiconductor industry, as a basis for pricing, in the perspective of a long-term strategy anticipating a progressive decline in marginal costs due to economies of scale and the learning curve. Such behaviour highlights the difference which is commonly acknowledged between the business behaviour of Japanese firms, on the one hand, and of US firms, on the other. The latter require quick profitability through prices related to actual average costs, while the former pursue rather more long-term planning in their business strategies.

In the semiconductor industry, the anti-dumping provisions under the 1991 trade agreement between the United States and Japan constitute an improvement in comparison with the previous system where government involvement had been more important. This is due to claims by the US computer industry that the "Fair Market Value" floor prices set by the United States only benefited Japan by provoking higher prices that disadvantaged US computer firms against their foreign competitors. They also claimed that the MITI under the aegis of the agreement orchestrated a sharp decline of the DRAM production that resulted in severe shortages in the US market.

One of the new elements in the 1991 US-Japan semiconductor agreement is the so-called "fast track" anti-dumping system that allows for a rapid determination of whether or not Japanese companies have been dumping, and would allow the US government to act quickly to stop dumping if it occurred.

Industrial targeting

Industrial targeting refers to a course of conduct involving elements of government/industry cooperation the purpose of which is to assist an industry to become dominant in one or more export markets.

Such a course of conduct may involve a broad range of measures including "strategic" industrial policy measures (protection of domestic industries from outside competition), macroeconomic policies tending to provide industries with substantial competitive advantages over foreign competition and tolerance of anti-competitive behaviour by domestic industries in their home and export markets.

Every individual activity included in the strategy is not necessarily unfair in itself, it is the cumulative impact of the improper course of conduct that defines targeting and makes it such a potentially destructive practice. Some industry leaders in the United States and the European Community have been arguing, for some time, that Japanese companies habitually dump products and use direct investment to seize control of key technologies to lock their foreign competitors out of promising new industries. In a report to the US Senate, the US General Accounting Office (GAO) developed information on whether US firms in the semiconductor, semiconductor equipment and materials, and computer industries were being denied advanced parts, equipment or technologies from Japanese suppliers. The semiconductor industry was particularly concerned in this matter. Withholding or deliberately delaying delivery of advanced technology is only one of several unfair trade practices that can be identified but it is also one which is particularly harmful to companies dependent upon critical technologies.

V   Towards a level playing field

For global competition to take place on a level playing field, it should be expected that legal and structural barriers which still exist in certain countries and regions will rapidly be lifted. Two major forces may contribute to achieve such a level playing field in a mid- to long-term perspective : the willingness of the world community to maintain an open, multilateral international trade system, and the emergence of genuine transnational corporations.

An open, multilateral international trade system

The issue of equitable conditions of competition and market access for both products and technologies at the world level is of great concern to all industrial economies. Multilateral concertation should be strengthened with a view to enforce strict reciprocal access to regional markets, investment opportunities and state-of-the-art technologies ; and to define international rules for "fair" industrial practices and policies. These two principles should delimit **a global level playing field**, i.e. an open and competitive environment characterised by fair international trading conditions. First, reciprocity of access to markets, investment opportunities and underlying technologies permit as much openness as each regional economy can tolerate and forces agreement upon mutual concessions in domestic practices that may be viewed as unfair. Second, some degree of agreement on appropriate international codes of behaviour is necessary. Although past experience shows that such codes of behaviour are extremely difficult to negotiate and then to execute and enforce, they are preferable to the proliferation of bilateral agreements which may lead to cartelisation of certain industries and to the exacerbation of conflicts between regional trading blocs.

This quest of free and fair competition on non-discriminatory terms in a liberalised global market could be pursued within both multilateral (GATT, OECD) and bilateral discussions. Priority objectives should include notably a successful conclusion of the Uruguay Round trade negotiations and/or any bilateral negotiations ; effective open, transparent and non-discriminatory procurement procedures and practices ; a stronger drive towards international standards.

In a resolution dated 18 November 1991, the EC Industry Council invited the European Community Commission to establish a so-called "Centralised Point of Information", in the field of information technology. Its mandate is to monitor marketing, market access and distribution practices throughout the main industrial areas in the world, focusing on those practices which restrain competition of extra-Communitary dimensions. The long-term task could be to make suggestions about modification of both internal and external legal environments.

The concept of global competition and the emergence of transnational corporations

A problem which is often a matter of concern to the policy-maker is the increasingly blurred boundaries of the "firm". The firm can no longer be considered as a well-defined entity with a single objective function, and this is particularly true in fast growing high-tech industries. For example, dramatic changes in the semiconductor industry over the past decade include the emergence of large, well-financed, vertically integrated manufacturers, the cost-of-capital advantage of some international competitors and aggressive pricing and market share strategies, that have imposed new ways of competing. These include financing activities to reduce cost of capital, reallocation of international activities, partnership with key customers and increasing the return on intellectual property.

It is development on a world scale of the activities of multinational corporations (MNCs) which has been the driving force for globalisation. Globalisation, especially by means of transnational mergers, acquisitions and alliances and of foreign direct investment, leads to a new concept of domestic interest. As Reich or Ohmae have suggested, governments should attract investment which can generate growth and employment independently of the nationality of ownership. Reich (1990, 1991) claimed that "today, the competitiveness of American-owned corporations is no longer the same as American competitiveness" and foreign companies which undertake research, design, development and manufacturing in the United States may be more "American" than American companies with international operations. This implies a dramatic revision of the role of governments and the objectives of industrial policy in a globalising economy. An example of the increasing divergence between domestic/regional interests and global interests is provided by the recent developments within Sematech, a government-sponsored consortium of US chip makers established in 1987 to restore America's leadership in semiconductor manufacturing technology. Since 1989, at least three of the 14 members of Sematech (Texas Instruments, IBM, AT&T) have entered agreements with non-US competitors involving the joint development of advanced 0.35-micron process technology - a goal simultaneously being sought after by the consortium itself. These R&D collaborations between Sematech members and off-shore suppliers may undermine the consortium's efforts to boost US manufacturing competitiveness but in return comply with the trend towards globalisation. In a globalising environment, it is likely to be increasingly difficult to forge international alliances and at the same time remain committed to a purely inward collaborative approach. The same argument applies to the European JESSI programme since Siemens entered a strategic alliance with IBM in 1990 to develop the next generation of DRAM products.

Interestingly, some analysts argue that the concept of a "multinational corporation" is either meaningless, misleading, or both. Multinational corporations, they argue, are merely national entities with foreign operations, or in some cases "binationals". Their argument brings to light two main points : the primary source of a company's international competitive advantage lies in its home nation ; the bulk of a company's research and development takes place in the home nation, where strategic and integrated decisions can be taken rapidly.

We may argue that the globalisation trend does not contradict the evidence about the strongly home basis of the competitive advantage of such emerging firms. It is indeed in the first instance the national virtues which create the opportunity to cross borders. However, this emphasis does underscore the new, emerging trend of globalisation and networking between such firms, becoming more and more global in their marketing, distribution and technology sourcing, as reflected for instance in the number of strategic alliances.

VI   Conclusion

There are several tendencies in the world economy today that may be contradictory to the globalisation of markets and industries, namely the establishment of regional blocs, the development of managed trade and the frequency of alliances and forms of integration between private companies. But instead of simplifying the situation and calling for global thinking, effective competition and free trade, we should accept the divergence of tendencies at hand. In trying to move towards *freer* international trade, we should recognise that this is a process where regional blocs will be playing a role and cooperative relationships between firms will develop. Global competition cannot be fair at the outset because the competitors and actors build on different cultures and social structures, but we should seek for mutually balanced conditions in world trade. Clearly, this will require time, a sense of vision and high commitment.

A number of analysts believe that globalisation is a natural trend, which is best served by competition and free trade. Regionalism would generate warring blocs; cooperation would generate large combines unable to foster innovation and to manage in a flexible manner in order to focus on evolving users' needs ; managed trade would reduce the benefits of international trade and lead to cartelisation of several industries. In fact all these tendencies exist in all modern economies, and when misconstrued, each can become a grotesque caricature. Interestingly, these tendencies need a form of Utopia to justify themselves. Utopia is not dead, nor are its ideological corollaries. But history has given us a chance to be realistic by acknowledging the complexity of modern societies and organisations.

Part III

Implications for countries

13 Foreign multinationals and economic competitiveness : the UK experience

Kirsty S. Hughes

I Introduction

This chapter analyses the role of foreign multinationals (MNEs) in UK manufacturing industry in the 1980s. It considers their structural and performance characteristics to assess whether foreign MNEs exhibit distinctive characteristics and strategies relative to UK firms.

The 1980s was a period both of major de-industrialisation in the UK and of high productivity growth (see for example Muellbauer, 1986 ; Andrews and Hughes, 1992). At the same time profitability improved but trade performance deteriorated - as the UK net trade balance in manufactures became negative for the first time in 1983 (and remained so). In this chapter we ask what light the descriptive statistics can throw on the role foreign MNEs played in these changes in the UK manufacturing industry.

II Foreign MNEs in the UK manufacturing industry

Using two main data sources we consider the characteristics of foreign MNEs in the period 1979-89. First, we use 2-digit data, which is published in the annual censuses of production, to present some descriptive statistics, 1979-89. Secondly, we use 3-digit data on foreign MNEs to analyse industry characteristics in more detail. This is also census of production data but it is not published - the data was purchased for 1983, 1985 and 1987 (the costs of data prior to 1983 being prohibitive). Data on UK industry characteristics is obtained from a major database on UK manufacturing industry 1979-88 (Andrews *et al.*, 1990). We start by considering the 2-digit data to consider overall MNE presence and trends and to consider sectorial distribution. We then use the 3-digit data to look in more detail at specialisation and performance. Our analysis will rest on a set of tables we have built from these data.

Table 13.1 shows the importance of foreign MNEs in UK manufacturing in terms of various indicators for the period 1979-89. Over the period as a whole the employment share stays roughly constant at around 14 % while share of sales, net output and investment increases - and is always higher than the employment share. The cyclical behaviour of the MNEs through the 1980/81 recession appears to be different from that of UK firms, thus in 1981 the employment share rises at the same time as the net output share falls. Subsequently in 1985 and 1987 the employment share falls, suggesting a delayed shakeout by the MNEs. The period 1983-87 was one of exceptionally high productivity growth. These figures suggest that part of this could be due to the MNEs delayed labour shake-out. Subsequently to 1989 the MNEs' employment share rises again, so that they are responsible for half the employment increase in manufacturing 1987-89 - the first time since 1979 that employment in UK manufacturing has stopped falling. Over the period 1981 to 1989 total manufacturing employment fell by 29.6 % while that of foreign MNEs fell by 25.7 %. Thus, MNEs did participate strongly in the major de-industrialisation of the 1980s but cannot be said to have led it.

Table 13.1   Proportion of foreign multinationals in terms of employment, sales, net output and investment in total manufacturing

Year	Employment	Sales	Net output	I
1979	14.07 %	21.70 %	20.25 %	21.46 %
1981	14.85 %	19.41 %	18.55 %	25.55 %
1983	14.49 %	20.37 %	18.97 %	23.05 %
1985	13.98 %	20.33 %	18.84 %	21.89 %
1987	13.37 %	21.00 %	19.05 %	21.32 %
1989	14.86 %	21.06 %	21.48 %	27.55 %

Source : Table 18, BM PA 1002, various years

Table 13.2 sets out the main source countries for foreign MNEs in the UK. The US remains the largest but its share falls over the 1980s while the EC's increases. The largest increase is that of Japan, which, while still relatively low, is increasing at a very high rate.

Table 13.2   Proportion of foreign enterprises from EC, Japan, US
and rest of the world

	EC *	Japan	US	ROW
1981	22.34 %	1.12 %	54.34 %	22.21 %
1989	25.59 %	6.34 %	46.68 %	21.39 %

* Not directly comparable ; Spain and Portugal entered after 1986

Source : Table 18, BM PA 1002, 1991 and 1989

Table 13.3 sets out the distribution of total foreign MNEs' sales across
2-digit manufacturing sectors to show where the largest absolute amount of
sales is. In 1991 almost 80 % of MNE sales were in six 2-digit sectors,
chemicals being the highest. Over the 1980s, the proportion in mechanical
engineering fell the most, followed by chemicals and food, drink and
tobacco. Motor vehicles showed a sharp increase, probably reflecting the
increased Japanese investment in this sector.

Table 13.3   Percentage distribution of foreign MNEs sales
- the largest sectors

2-digit Sector		1981	1989
Name	SIC	%	%
Chemicals	25	18.3	16.8
Food, drink and tobacco	41	15.1	13.7
Mechanical engineering	32	14.9	10.3
Motor vehicles and parts	35	14.7	17.9
Electrical and electronic engineering	34	9.6	9.0
Papers, printing and publishing	47	6.0	7.5
All other sectors		21.4	24.8
TOTAL		100	100

Table 13.4 shows foreign MNE presence by sector relative to the total
size of the sector in 1981 and 1989. In 1981, the sector with the highest MNE
presence is motor vehicles followed by office machinery but this ranking is
reversed by 1981, with both sectors showing substantial increases in foreign
MNE presence - to 64 % in office machinery. There is a large decline in
MNE presence in instrument engineering and man-made fibres, while the
previously noted absolute decline in mechanical engineering can be seen here
to have simply matched the decline by UK firms. MNE presence overall has
increased, in sales terms, from 19.4 to 24 %.

Table 13.4   Foreign MNEs participation in UK industry - highest
participation rates

2-Digit sector		Foreign MNE sales/ UK sales (%)	
Name	SIC	1981	1989
Motor vehicles and parts	35	46.3	55.7
Office machinery and data-processing equipment	33	42.9	64.3
Instrument engineering	37	38.1	27.5
Chemicals	25	33.5	36.9
Mechanical engineering	32	25.7	24.0
Rubber and plastics	48	24.8	23.5
Electrical and electronic engineering	34	23.3	25.1
Man-made fibres	26	19.3	13.9
TOTAL MANUFACTURING		19.41	24.06

Table 13.5 also shows foreign MNE participation by sector, but now by 3-digit sector in 1987. Only three sectors have a foreign MNE presence greater than 50 %. Out of a total of 65 sectors for which we have information (of 104 3-digit sectors in total) 17 have a greater than average foreign MNE presence and thirteen have a participation ratio greater than a third. The distribution can be seen to be quite highly skewed with only a small number of sectors where there is a very high presence. If we include UK MNEs, over a half of output on average comes from MNEs. Figures for 1979 show that on average UK MNEs accounted for 42 % of industry output (Hughes and Oughton, 1992).

Table 13.6 measures foreign participation (foreign/total sales) and correlates it with various measures of industry structure and performance in 1987 and with some changes (denoted by 'D') from 1983 to 1987. The measures are as follows :

> Prody = net output per head
> Exps = export-sales ratio
> Imps = import-penetration ratio
> XM = net trade ratio
> R&D = research and development/net output
> Scale = minimum efficient scale measured by median plant size
> CR5 = five firm concentration ratio
> SMFMS = proportion of small firms by number
> EMP200 = proportion of employment in small firms (less than 200 employees)
> TUs = proportion of work force covered by major collective agreements

Table 13.5 Foreign MNEs participation in UK industry - rankings by
3-digit industry 1987 (above average)

3-digit sector		Foreign MNEs /UK Sales
Name	Code	%
Specialised chem. prod. - ind. use	259	76.6
Agricultural machinery	321	67.2
Motor vehicles	351	60.1
Office machinery and data-processing eq.	330	48.7
Soap and toilet preps.	258	47.9
Non-ferrous metal	224	44.4
Miscell. electronic eq.	345	43.8
Optical precision instruments and photographic equipment	373	41.9
Starch and misc. foods	423	41.0
Pharmaceuticals	257	40.8
Specialised chem. prod. - home and office use	256	38.3
Rubber products	482	38.3
Domestic elec. appliances	346	34.5
Clocks, watches, etc.	374	31.9
Mining machinery, constr. and mech. handling equipment	325	29.0
Food, chem. and rel. machinery	324	26.5
Miscell. machinery	328	24.7

Table 13.6   Correlation of foreign MNE participation (foreign
sales/total) with industry characteristics 1987

Industry variable	Correlation coefficient
Prody	0.40
DPrody	0.15
Exps	0.52
Dexps	0.04
Imps	0.44
Dimps	- 0.09
XM	- 0.01
DXM	0.15
R&D	0.26
Scale	0.38
CR5	0.27
SMFMS	- 0.12
EMP200	- 0.32
TUs	- 0.36

The correlations are mostly as would be predicted. Foreign MNE presence correlates positively with the level and growth rate of productivity, with the level of exports and imports and with R&D, scale and concentration. It correlates negatively with small firms presence and with trade union presence, measured by coverage. Thus, we have a fairly typical account of foreign MNEs being present in oligopolistic industries that are very open in trade terms and that are R&D-intensive.

Table 13.7 sets out a variety of performance measures, calculated for each sector and then averaged in terms of sectors and years - 1983, 1985 and 1987. The performance measures are presented for foreign MNEs, for UK-only firms, and, where possible, for large UK-only firms, that is UK-only firms minus firms with less than two hundred employees (assuming all small firms to be UK-only). This latter adjustment allows us to observe whether or to what extent better foreign MNE performance simply means in fact better performance of larger firms. Table 13.7 shows that foreign MNEs have higher productivity - even relative to large UK firms there is a gap of 12 percentage points. They also have a larger investment to output ratio. Over time, 1983 to 1987, the foreign MNEs have a much better productivity growth rate, but this is due to lower net output growth and higher employment cuts than UK firms. This reinforces the suggestion made above that some part of the so-called 'productivity miracle' could be due to a delayed employment shake-out by foreign MNEs. Part (c) of Table 13.7 compares price-cost margins and average wages (thousands of pounds per head). Foreign MNEs have slightly higher price-cost margins but these grow at a much higher rate than UK firms. They have substantially higher wages but these grow at a lower rate, possibly reflecting the employment shake-out.

Table 13.8 also compares performance measures here by taking foreign relative to UK performance in each industry and then taking the average over industries and years. It also gives the number of sectors where the foreign level was higher, or, in the case of rates of change, the number where the difference between the foreign and UK rate of growth was positive. In terms of levels foreign MNE performance is superior for all the variables considered - productivity, profits, wages and investment. However, in terms of number of sectors only slightly over half have higher investment while almost all pay higher wages and three-quarters have higher productivity. The superior performance of foreign MNEs does not, therefore, appear to be dependent on their specific sectoral distribution nor on size alone. The rates of change demonstrate the pattern already discussed - productivity growth is greater but employment and net output changes are less than the UK firms.

Table 13.7   Foreign MNEs, UK firms and large UK firms - some measures
of relative performance

3-digit means, 1983, 85, 87, pooled

(a)	log productivity	Investment/output
Foreign	2.75	0.092
UK	2.58	0.075
Big UK	2.63	

(b) % change in net output, employment and productivity 1983-87			
	DNO	DEMP	DPrody
Foreign	8.3	- 12.8	24.5
UK	17.7	- 1.0	16.9
Big UK	16.8	- 2.2	19.7

(c) Price-cost margins, wages and % changes 1983-87				
	PCM	DPCM	Av. wage	D Av. wage
Foreign	0.56	5.8	6.37	14.6
UK	0.54	3.3	4.72	16.2

Table 13.8   Foreign MNEs/UK for various performance measures

(a) Foreign/UK 3-digit industry averages 1983, 85, 87 pooled		
		Prody no. of indus. with ration > 1
Prody	1.21	157
B Prody	1.15	149
PCM	1.04	128
Av. Wage	1.41	184
Investment/output	1.31	101
		n = 195
(b) Foreign rate of change - UK rate of change 1983-87, 3-digit means		
		No. of indus. > 0
DPrody	0.08	36
DB Prody	0.04	31
Demp	- 0.12	14
DNO	- 0.06	20
DInvestment	0.08	28
		n = 65

Conclusion

This paper has considered the role of foreign MNEs in UK manufacturing industry. Foreign MNEs exhibit many different characteristics from UK firms, in general appearing to be more efficient and more profitable than UK firms while at the same time paying higher wages. However, while their performance appears to be generally better, this does not imply foreign MNEs have a fully beneficial effect on UK industry. Since MNEs are located in oligopolistic industries, it may be questioned whether their higher profits are due to efficiency or market power (see for example Hughes and Oughton, 1991 and 1992). Similarly, we may ask whether foreign MNEs do make a substantial contribution to productivity growth or whether the data here represents temporary adjustments and equally what effect they have on trade performance overall. Earlier studies have suggested they may have a detrimental effect on UK trade performance (Panic and Joyce, 1980 and Hughes, 1986).

14 Risks and opportunities from Japanese direct investments : the French case

Françoise Guelle

I Introduction

The progression of Japanese direct investments in the French manufacturing industry is the result of a conjuncture of favourable tendencies : the growing internationalisation of the Japanese industry due to the appreciation of the yen, restrictions on Japanese exportations with anti-dumping taxation, and the European desire to develop alliances with Japan so as to counterbalance Japanese ties with the USA.

There are many good reasons for Japanese multinational companies to establish themselves in France in order to penetrate the European economic market, the largest in the world. France has the fourth GNP in the world, ranking also in fourth position for exportations after the United States, Japan and Germany. France's localisation in Europe, its endowment with an important domestic market, its high quality of labour and political leadership in European unification, these are the principal factors that attract Japanese firms. French policy towards foreign direct investment (FDI) became more favourable in the 1980s. This was at a period when Japanese multinational companies, looking for footholds in Europe, established subsidiaries in France as part of a global development strategy.

II The evolution of French policy towards FDI

Before the Japanese challenge, about 25 years ago, France was confronted with an "American Challenge" which encountered the resistance of French development policy seeking to establish national economic independence. At the beginning of the worldwide delocalisation of Japanese industry, France refused to follow British liberal policy in regard to FDI, then French policy became more open towards Japanese investments.

One important reason for this previous attitude resides in historically restrictive policies towards imports and foreign investments. However, in several steps and particularly since the beginning of the 1980s, legislation has drastically changed. Barriers to entry and penetration have vanished for greenfield investments which are no longer reviewed, but must be reported a posteriori. Only direct acquisitions of French firms valued over 10 million French francs by non-EC investors are still reviewed by the French administration.

III   The role of rivalry among regions of France

The context of the European Community obliges member countries to harmonise their attitude towards Japanese investments. Japanese MNCs strategy takes into consideration the whole European market, not specific national markets. If Japanese investments are preponderantly placed in other countries of the European Community, with the anticipated free circulation of products, there may be negative repercussions for French industries in terms of employment, without any counter reply for job creation, the balance of payments or the transfer of technology. Governments of European Community States are less and less able to regulate Japanese investment through administrative control and tariff barriers. However, the automobile, electronics and machine-tools industries will be the only ones protected until 1993. The countries of implantation, and regions within these countries, are openly competing to attract potential Japanese investments. Each sector of production, in different European countries where national production is deficient (automobiles in Great Britain, office automation in France, for example) gladly welcomes Japanese direct investments for these particular sectors. This results in a rise of local, regional, national and European subsidies and incentives to attract mobile international projects.

In the context of this rivalry, the French regional authority DATAR [1] has a mandate to attract FDI, in order to ensure maximum net benefits for France. In Japan, DATAR seeks to influence and orient prospective firms anticipating entry into the European market towards France. DATAR's incentives towards direct foreign investment comprise infrastructure support tax incentives, subsidies and capital grants. This strong regional development policy aimed at attracting investment towards peripheral regions does not generally distinguish between domestic and foreign investors. Until ten years ago, DATAR's policy focused implantation towards regions affected by unemployment. The reluctance of many firms to submit to imposed localisation led to a gradual change in DATAR's policy to allow potential investors to choose the most adapted sites for their needs. The tendency in France today is a move towards basic framework or business climate policies in order to create more employment in the regions and to increase R&D and headquarters functions in France.

IV Levels and trends of Japanese direct investments in France

Japanese FDI towards France remained extremely modest in the 1970s. The attraction of FDI increased by globalisation strategies pursued by Japanese MNCs after the appreciation of the value of the yen in 1985. In 1990, France became the third largest country to host Japanese FDI in Europe. According to DATAR, Japanese companies had established 155 manufacturing plants in France by the end of June 1991 comprising greenfield plants, joint ventures and acquisitions. These plants employed a total of 25,683 workers as of June 1991, with a distribution of 8 % of plants over 500 workers and 46 % between 100 and 500 workers. In terms of employment, the most important region is Picardie with more than 4000 employees in Japanese plants.

Japanese direct investment into France still remains, however, very limited, even if its level has multiplied by more than 10 since 1982. Average Japanese penetration from 1981 to 1989 represented approximately 4 % of total foreign investments ; 1 % of total Japanese investments abroad ; 3 % of direct foreign investments in the French manufacturing industry (Table 14.1). Three-quarters of these Japanese investments are oriented towards the tertiary sector and real estate in France. A remaining 25 % consecrated to industrial investments represented only 1 billion French francs in 1989. This rate of 25 % is however very high compared to overall Japanese investment in Europe, which represents an average of 18 % for the manufacturing industry.

However, it should be noted that in 1990, a year marked by a slight reduction of total Japanese investments abroad, investment in France progressed to 6 billion francs. This corresponded to 6.8 % of total foreign investment in France and 2 % of total Japanese foreign investment abroad. Since 1990, Japan has become the sixth important foreign investor in France, advancing from ninth position in 1989. This evolution results particularly from the behaviour of long established Japanese firms in France. Four of the most important investment operations (of a value superior to 100 millions FF) were implemented by Japanese industrial firms which had been installed in France for more than eight years. French Ministry of Industry statistics show that the weighting of industrial enterprises controlled by Japanese capital has remained weak in comparison to German and American investment (Table 14.2).

Table 14.1 Japanese direct investments in France 1981-1989 (FF Million, %)

	1981	1982	1983	1984	1985	1986	1987	1988	1989	1981-1989
FDI Total	13222	10343	12509	19299	19947	19162	27860	42798	60945	226085
Japanese inv.(a)	270	352	608	579	607	907	998	1705	3911	9937
Japanese %	*2.04*	*3.4*	*4.8*	*3*	*3*	*4.7*	*3.6*	*3.98*	*6*	*4*
FDI in industry	6267	3205	4565	6951	5564	5177	12089	19160	7620	70598
Japanese inv.(b)	18	57	109	338	205	376	161	263	1041	2468
Japanese %	*0.28*	*1.78*	*2.38*	*3.42*	*3.68*	*6.75*	*1.33*	*1.37*	*14*	*3*
(b) / (a)	6.6	16.2	17.9	41.1	33.7	41.5	16.1	15.4	27	25

Source : Banque de France

Table 14.2 Distribution of principal foreign investors in France (1.1.1989) (%)

	Japan	Germany	EEC	USA
Number of firms	1.4	19.4	50.2	20.0
Employment	1.8	16.1	43.2	30.6
Sales	1.5	15.2	41.8	34.6
Investments	1.9	15.0	42.0	35.5

Source : French Ministry of Industry, SESSI, "L'implantation étrangère dans l'industrie au 1er janvier 1989", February 1991

As to the sectorial classification of Japanese investments, they are distributed in fifteen sectors. The leading sector is the rubber industry, followed by the machine-tool industry, and well penetrated sectors are those quite well penetrated by foreign capital. The rate of Japanese penetration in the French manufacturing industry remains, however, very low when compared to the global penetration of foreign direct investments in France (Table 14.3). Recent investment tends to be in the "De Luxe" industry (fashion and leather goods) and the distribution system (acquisition of tyre distribution systems).

Table 14.3 Weight of Japanese investments and FDI by major industry in French manufacturing industry (number of employees, FF Million ,%) as of 1.1.1989

Major industries penetrated by Japanese investment	Japan		FDI Total	
	Employment (%)	Sales (%)	Employment (%)	Sales (%)
Metal fab.	287 (0.46)	255 (0.24)	11235 (22.54)	27492 (30.9)
Parachemical ind.	831 (0.29)	841 (0.28)	54106 (47.35)	67826 (54.3)
Fabricated metal	367 (0.14)	232 (0.18)	33801 (11.94)	19572 (13.5)
Machine-tools	990 (2.74)	670 (3.4)	12249 (32.42)	6939 (33.5)
Electronical prod.	785 (0.34)	910 (0.54)	61341 (26.75)	51617 (32.1)
Transport equip.	1655 (0.44)	960 (0.24)	68076 (17.62)	66511 (16.35)
Clothing industry	169 (0.12)	84 (0.15)	10787 (7.7)	5426 (9.4)
Rubber industry	5232 (6.4)	3644 (8.7)	20758 (24.9)	13156 (30.9)

Source : See Table 14.2

V   Conclusion : Risks and opportunities

The main recent growth of Japanese investment in France, but which still stays at a low level in terms of total FDI, doesn't permit us to draw definitive conclusions in regard to their full economic impact. However we are able to analyse the opportunities and the risks of Japanese investments in regard to their potential effects on French industrial and economic development.

Local economic development : regions of implantation benefit from Japanese investments in terms of employment, industrial competitivity and their international image. While Japanese firms are obliged to search for a significant level of integration, local industries benefit from subcontracting. This is often seen as an opportunity for these local industries to familiarise themselves with Japanese skills in terms of management and organisation.

However, it is still possible for Japanese subcontractors to settle into these areas and therefore to become tough competitors for local firms.

Employment : this is positively affected in the short term and especially when Japanese investment does not compete with the local French industrial production system. However this may backfire if the investment concerns products for which national or European production exists and that progressively get through existing commercial barriers (for example the Japanese automotive transplants in Great Britain).

Trade balance : Japanese industries mainly produce for the European market. If they contribute at present towards French exportations to other European countries, they rarely export outside of Europe. Japanese investments can also replace the flow of imported finished products by a flow of spare parts, more or less important in regard to the rate of their local content and the technological level of locally produced parts.

Flow of technology : except in a few cases of balanced partnerships, Japanese investment doesn't result in a real transfer of Japanese technology towards France. Conversely, there are some examples of Japanese buying local enterprises and transferring their techniques to Japan.

If we can anticipate those possible negative effects in regard to the observations which we have described above, the relatively low level of Japanese investment in France may very well be explained by the fact that it is often concentrated in certain sectors which can be vulnerable because of possible negative consequences on technology (electronics) or employment (automobile). Local integration (see Guelle, 1990) seems to be one of the essential factors so that Japanese investment may induce positive consequences for regional development, employment and commercial balance. This is another concern which is also shared by other countries of the European Community, in order to compete with the dynamism induced by the growing industrial cooperation with Japan.

Notes

1   Delégation à l'Aménagement du Territoire et à l'Action Régionale.

15 Globalisation and performance of small firms within the smaller European economies

Dermot P. O'Doherty

I Introduction

This chapter is based on a number of key premises regarding the impacts of the current globalisation process on the current and future performance of small firms, particularly within the smaller economies : (i) the major share of industrial activity and employment continues to be in small and medium-sized enterprises in all the OECD countries, as well as in the European Community. The majority of these firms are affected, to varying degrees, by increasingly influential international economic forces and pressures whether they themselves are playing an active or a passive role in the overall internationalisation-globalisation process. The nature and level of their participation in inter-firm cooperation can be taken as an important indication of their response ; (ii) some of the economic actors perhaps most affected by the movement towards a global economy are small firms in small economies. These firms must learn to cooperate with other firms within an integrated strategic management approach if they are to survive, not to mention prosper ; (iii) the "public authorities" must directly participate both with "industry" in the wide sense and with specific firms in designing and implementing such strategies - to compensate for the lack of strategic planning and other resource capabilities in the individual firms and to create the critical mass and necessary level of coordination between firms to allow them to succeed in international markets - ; (iv) the "public authorities" must now include not only local/regional governments or even "the State" but for the small, less developed European countries at least there must be a more direct approach from the European Commission/Community. This is because nation-states in general and the smaller countries in particular are no longer in a position to mediate and influence all of the economic forces at play within their boundaries.

II   European small firms

There were approximately 1.9m manufacturing firms in the European Community in 1986 [1]. Of these only 7,400 or 0.39 % were classified as large (employing 500+) with nearly 1.6m or 82.7 % employing 1-10 people. The remaining 321,000 or 16.9 % employed from 10-500 with most of these in the less than 200 category (Figure 15.1).

● Size of firm

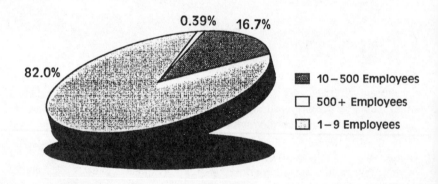

Figure 15.1   European firms

Small and very small firms obviously dominate the European industrial scene, although the pattern of employment in European manufacturing is somewhat different from the structure of firms with 72 % of employment in small and medium-sized enterprises (SMEs) with up to 500 people.

While we have relatively little knowledge of the extent of formal small firm to small firm cooperation (not to mention informal networks both national and international) and only a partial view of small firm-large firm links across the European Community (Hagedoorn *et al.*, 1991), there is evidence that quite a complex set of relationships is emerging. We do know that small firms appear to have a preference for linking up with firms of a similar size (Rotwell, 1989), and that where small firms have participated in European Research Programmes, informal relationships with existing or former "formal" partners have ensued (Fitzpatrick Ass., 1990). We also know that small firms are often rooted in their own localities or "milieu" and that this involves a whole range of cooperative relationships with customers, suppliers and competitors (Camagni, 1991) as well as local universities, research institutes and other parts of the development infrastructure - complementing those which have developed explicitly within the internationalisation-globalisation process.

Evidence of the cooperative involvements of a group of such firms comes from a study carried out in Britain in the mid-1980s [2] on the relationships established with other companies by 100 small and medium-sized innovative firms. This showed that : (i) 39 % contracted-out research and development, 85.7 % of subcontracting R&D relationships were with firms employing less than 200, 50 % of the subcontractors were located within 49 miles, 47 % of the subcontractors were supplier firms and 18.5 % were customers ; (ii) 26 % of firms engaged in some form of collaborative R&D venture, 56 % of the collaborations were with firms employing less than 200, 46.6 % of the collaborations were with suppliers and 34.6 % were with customers ; (iii) 68 % of the firms subcontracted a proportion of their manufacturing, 66 % of the subcontractors were within 40 miles of the contracting firm.

The authors concluded that "these data suggest the importance of strong technical links between small firms ; a strong pattern of quasi-verticality in technical relationships and the importance of proximity to their R&D and manufacturing partners."

III   Small countries and economies

Alongside increased inter-firm cooperation and interaction, there are other aspects of globalisation which are important for small firms. Small countries and economies offer a useful context in which some of these wider impacts can be assessed. In the Irish context for example, globalisation operates at three significant levels : (i) economy-wide, where it is reflected in : the increasing openness of the economy in general (see Table 15.1) ; the flows of inward and outward foreign direct investment (FDI) with the associated high levels of repatriated profits (see Table 15.2) ; (ii) at the industry/firm level, where it is reflected for example in the ownership structure of Irish-based firms. Some 1000 overseas firms employ 90,000 people or 40 % of the industrial work force and generate 50 % of manufactured output and 75 % of industrial exports ; (iii) at the technological level, reflected in the high share (65 %) of Irish Business Enterprise R&D (BERD) performed by foreign subsidiaries (Figure 15.2).

Table 15.1   Openness of Irish economy

	Export of Goods & Service % of GDP (1988)	Imports of Goods & Services % of GDP (1988)
Ireland	65	55
Netherlands	54	51
Belgium	69	66
Denmark	29	29
Greece	23	31
Portugal	35	42
EUR 12	27	27

Source : Annual Economic Report 1988-89, European Commission

Table 15.2   Profit repatriation (% GNP)

	1985	1986	1987	1988	1989
Profit repatriation (% GNP)	- 8.4	- 7.9	- 7.2	- 10.1	- 11.2

Source : Central Bank of Ireland

Many multinationals, in particular US firms in the high-tech sectors, have tended to operate in a "global" manner right from the early 1960s, in setting up and operating subsidiaries expressly directed to external markets on mainland Europe and elsewhere and receiving the bulk of their technology from their parents. Essentially they short-circuited the "international-multinational-global" paradigm.

By contrast, many of the 6,500 Irish indigenous manufacturing companies, (all of which are small by international standards), are in the very small category and operate in the vulnerable, low-tech, traditional sectors. Until recently at least, they have been narrowly focused on the domestic market. In general, Irish SMEs have tended to react passively to the globalisation phenomenon, so that the continued survival of many of them in the face of international competition is now in question. However, a minority of around 600 have adopted international strategies, rapidly increased their output and export performance and are now looking to product and process innovation and cooperation for their further growth and development.

● Level of R&D performed 1990

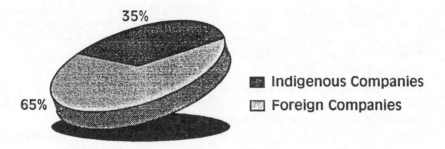

Figure 15.2   Irish-based firms

Ireland, Greece and Portugal differ in their relative scientific and technological capabilities and their wider industrial and economic situations, but are experiencing many similar effects from the process of globalisation. They share many of these experiences with the small more advanced EC member states which in general also have small firm-based industrial structures. The effects on these countries have recently been analysed in the Globalisation project of the EC MONITOR/FAST Programme (1991). These studies [3] (to be published by Blackwell) stress that firms themselves, their national authorities and the EC must all take action to ensure their best position and prospects within the internationalisation and globalisation process.

The structural characteristics of the small economies have an impact on the nature of the cooperation activities in which their firms tend to become involved. Because of the restricted and highly competitive nature of the domestic market, formal horizontal relationships will generally be formed with foreign-based partners to have access to distant markets or vice versa. There is more scope for vertical cooperation, i.e. with suppliers and customers, particularly in the areas where the small economy has tended to specialise. An "external" orientation can obviously assist in encouraging the cooperation process. Involvement in foreign markets and in various European Community programmes for example can be of disproportionate importance for small firms in small economies.

IV   Innovative small firms in Ireland - cooperation and competition strategies

For innovation and cooperation to be successfully integrated into the strategies of small firms, in small economy environments in particular, they must be trading internationally or planning to do so in the near future. The difficulty of promoting innovations from Ireland can be seen in the fact that "technology offers" tend to exceed explicit requests for licences and other forms of disembodied technology from indigenous industry.   This is evidenced by the imbalance of ca. 150 offers to ca. 120 requests that came forward for the EC SPRINT Programme-sponsored National Technology Transfer Days, (4 to 5 May 1992) as well as by the direct experience of professional brokers and intermediaries who are members of the Licensing Executives Society (LES).   This is somewhat surprising given that Gross Expenditure on R&D (GERD) varies between 0.7 and 0.9 % of the GDP and that most indigenous firms spend little or nothing on formal R&D. However a subset of the group of small innovative firms already referred to (308 out of 2,000+ surveyed) are estimated to have spent an average of 7.1 % of turnover in 1990.

The number of Irish-based firms, both indigenous and foreign, involved in the "R&D Consortia" in 1990 compared to 1988 was :

Table 15.3   R&D Consortia 1990 (1988)

	Irish firms involved		Overseas firms involved		Total	
Located in Ireland	50	(32)	20	(9)	70	(41)
Located outside Ireland	93	(44)	98	(75)	191	(119)

Source : EOLAS Surveys of Technology in Irish Industry 1988 and 1990

Up to the end of the 1980s, 16 foreign subsidiaries had been involved in EC ESPRIT Information Technology projects compared to 13 Irish-owned firms.

The figures for EUREKA, a programme which covers a much wider range of industries and technologies, were only 5 subsidiaries and 4 Irish firms. Participation in EUREKA is self-funded, which largely accounts for the low level of involvement. University participation is also low compared with their involvement in a relatively large number of funded projects in ESPRIT and other parts of the overall EC FRAMEWORK Programme.

The number of Irish firms transferring-in technology through licences and joint ventures is estimated at not more than 150 in 1990. The surprisingly low level of formal licensing and joint venture agreements in both Ireland and Portugal has already been noted [4]. One of the ways in which this appears to have been compensated for in the Irish case is through technology transferred in subcontracting arrangements with foreign companies located both in and outside Ireland. Here, however, there has been a worrying fall in the number of firms indicating their participation in sub-supply arrangements involving technology transfer between 1988 and 1990. The relevant data are given in Table 15.4.

Table 15.4   Subcontract manufacturing for overseas companies
1990 (1988)

	Irish firms involved	Foreign firms involved	Total
Located in Ireland	122 (179)	61 (54)	183 (132)
Located outside Ireland	89 (166)	57 (135)	146 (301)
Total	211 (345)	118 (189)	329 (433)

Source : EOLAS Survey of Technology in Industry 1988 and 1990

This trend could be very worrying if it were part of the process of reducing the number of supplier firms and developing increasingly closer links with the remainder, this has been observed elsewhere as being an important aspect of globalisation.

Reverting for a moment to the issue of the licensing-in of technology in the Irish case, the evidence cited earlier indicated a low level of involvement by Irish firms in terms of the number of formal agreements. However, where agreements have been concluded many have tended to operate with a high level of interaction between the partner firms and with informal spin-off effects similar to those already referred to for participation in EC projects (Fitzpatrick Ass., 1990). The success and failure characteristics of these partnerships should be observed in the near future as well as the more difficult question of why so few contacts between Irish- and foreign-based firms lead to formal agreements.

One of the factors here may be the need for a higher and better level of "mediation" between firms. Because of the information deficiencies of the technology market, more professional intermediaries and brokers need to be trained and promoted by the public authorities and, most importantly, used by small firms.

There is a tendency for small firm managements (and governments) to assume wrongly that everything is all right with the ordinary production, quality and human resource aspects of the business. Up to 200 "matched pair" company comparisons between a number of Irish and British regions (O'Farrel *et al.*, 1989), and subsequent comparisons with firms in the former FRG & DDR (West and East Germany) have indicated product quality, production costs and skills-related deficiencies in the British and particularly the Irish firms despite the ready availability of capital grants for new plant and equipment.

The quality-related deficiencies are now being tackled through the installation of quality management systems, certified under the International Standards Organisation's "ISO 9000", in a rapidly increasing number of firms (Table 15.5).

Table 15. 5   ISO 9000 quality management systems (end 1991)

Ireland	420 firms
Denmark	60 firms
Australia	45 firms

Source : National Standards Authority of Ireland

Production costs are being reduced through national wage and salary agreements and a growing number of technology/manufacturing audits at individual company level. The skills deficiencies are more intractable and can only be addressed on a long-term basis at both the firm and national levels, with the German model of apprenticeships and other related manpower policies being seen as the ideal.

The importance of an integrated strategically planned and managed approach at firm level has been affirmed in a recent survey of 75+ Irish Chief Executives (CEOs) [5] which indicated that "Customer Service" in the new Single European Market and "Strategic Planning" are the two major management issues for the '90s. Strategic Planning was rated as being of major importance across all industry sectors with subsumed issues such as strategic alliances, mergers, etc., as well as the quality and production issues referred to above.

V   National roles

Ireland and Denmark have both tried to stimulate inter-firm cooperation as an integral part of national industrial policy. In Ireland the issues currently exercising policy-makers include : (i) how to turn a commitment to reorienting overall industrial policy towards investment in "intangibles" such as technological and marketing cooperation in an industrial structure which continues to be highly fragmented ; (ii) how to revamp both a long established R&D Grants Scheme which has focused on individual firms and a relatively new Technology Acquisition Grant Scheme (which has so far assisted less than 15 firms) to ensure more co-operative R&D on the one hand and a higher level of licensing-in agreements on the other : both schemes can be used to subsidise consultants but there is no training or "panel" system involved ; (iii) how to organise and deliver industrial and technological policy on an integrated institutional basis.

On the other hand, in Denmark : (i) new industrial and technological policies are being implemented - leading to major structural changes in Danish industry in terms of mergers and alliances which may leave the country with 20 strong groups by 1995 [6] ; (ii) a "Network Programme" aimed at encouraging export and technical cooperation is in its final year, with ca. 150 networks in place and a significant focus on training and employing a panel of professional brokers and intermediaries ; (iii) a new institutional framework is in place in the form of an integrated "National Agency for Industry & Trade" with an explicit "Internationalisation and Market Development Division."

Major efforts are now being made in Ireland to ensure that an integrated technological and industrial policy and a new agency infrastructure will be set up by the third quarter of 1992. The electrical and mechanical engineering areas, and particularly their automotive and aeronautics segments, have been chosen as the basis for Irish "Porter-like" clusters of interacting firms (Porter, 1990).

VI   European Commission and Community role

From the point of view of the less developed member states in particular [3] the mutually reinforcing processes of globalisation and European integration have led to a situation where not only are national governments no longer free to promote policies or take decisions at their own discretion but also there has been a shift of power and influence from the public authorities generally to the large private firms of the larger countries. In these circumstances it is necessary for the Commission/Community to "fill the gap" in terms of promoting and enhancing the innovation and cooperation opportunities and capabilities of small firms in small countries.

It is now assumed that the 4th EC FRAMEWORK Programme will generally move "nearer to the market". This should certainly suit SMEs, as illustrated in a comparison of small firm involvement in the ESPRIT and EUREKA programmes [7] which showed a 44.2 % participation level of SMEs in EUREKA compared to 27.4 % in ESPRIT. Given that only 1 or 2 % of small firms have been involved in any European programme resolving this SME issue, however, may lead to the institution of a European version of the American Small Business Innovation Research Programme (SBIR) in which a proportion of the budgets of all US Federal Agencies involved in funding research is reserved for small firms.

Even if a European SBIR-type programme were to be set up, the bulk of European SMEs, even innovating small firms, would still be excluded. That is why an extension of SPRINT - the EC programme explicitly aimed at encouraging innovation and technology transfer, largely under the guidance of professional intermediaries - would be so important. With a budget of 120 million ECU - a fraction of that of such research programmes as ESPRIT and RACE within DGXIII which along with the programmes of DGXII have a budget of almost 6,000m ECU in the 3rd FRAMEWORK Programme (1990-1994) - SPRINT can only act as a catalyst. It is also restricted to encouraging and funding formal intra-European agreements. In the context of operating in a global economy SPRINT must be permitted to encourage the exchange of technology on a worldwide basis and to include informal as well as formal relations between firms.

The Commission has already made some moves to improve the position of subcontractors within the Community. However, it does not appear to have any kind of "model approach" to which it is aspiring. In Japan large assembly firms and their component suppliers are organised in what are known as production keiretsu. The keiretsu "lying in-between the in-house system and the autonomy market" (Yoshitomi, 1992), is based on a framework for determining quantity, costs, prices, profits and rewards for improvements. "U.S. and European manufacturers provide component suppliers with detailed drawings of parts and simply ask for price bids. In production keiretsu, by contrast, quantity adjustments take place monthly, while price adjustments occur every six months. Suppliers develop 'relation-specific skills' to meet the demands of the parent companies, through their own drawing capability." The Commission might fruitfully investigate the positive aspects of this approach to managing subcontract relationships in Europe.

VII   European Community principles

If the Commission/Community is to effectively assist small firms it must look again at **principles such as subsidiarity and the concept of "precompetitive"** activities. These restrict the role of the Community to areas where there is no private sector or national competence. But small firms and small countries do not have the same competences as their larger counterparts. A more pragmatic approach is now required if the Commission is to assist small firms and the smaller economies in both adjusting to and influencing the growing impacts of the globalisation process.

Notes

1   *Enterprises in the European Community,* EC Commission, DGXXIII, Brussels : 1990.

2   Rothwell and Beesley quoted in Rothwell (1989).

3   *Globalisation and the Small Less-Advanced E.C. Countries* : Greece (T. Giannitsis), Ireland (D. O'Doherty and J. McDevitt), Portugal (Vitor Corado Simões), Synthesis Report (D. O'Doherty); *Globalisation of Science & Technology & the Small Advanced Countries,* Jacobs, D., A. Braendgaard & P. Boekholt.

4   V. Corado Simões, "Licensing Agreements in Portugese Manufacturing Industry", and T.J. Allen, D.J. Cogan, D. O'Doherty and B. O'Sullivan, "Direct Acquisition of Technology by Irish Industry", in O'Doherty, D. (ed.), *The Cooperation Phenomenon - Prospects for Small Firms and the Small Economies,* London : Graham & Trotman, 1990.

5   *The Challenge for Management in the 1980s,* Dublin : Ernst and Young, 1991.

6   "Back to Basics - but with a Difference", *Danish Review,* no. 3, 1990.

7   Roscam Abbing M. & J. Shakenraad, "Intended and Unintended Effects of Participation in ESPRIT and EUREKA for Small Countries Industrial Policies", in Hilpert, U (ed.), *State Policies and Unintended Effects,* Routledge, Chapman & Hall, 1991.

16 Going global or going European ? The case of Portugal

Vitor Corado Simões

I   Globalisation and European integration : the issues

The last decade witnessed the development of the globalisation phenomenon, largely dominated by a Triadic race of the main world economic powers - USA, Japan and Europe - and their respective firms. This drive includes at least five interrelated currents :

(i)   globalisation of markets, since an increasing share of products, services and brands is addressed to world markets, while national boundaries are losing relevance as criteria for market segmentation ;

(ii) globalisation of production, namely through the setting up and strengthening of worldwide integration strategies, characterised by the specialisation of plants across borders into integrated multinational manufacturing networks ;

(iii) globalisation of technological innovation: firms are increasingly eager to tap new developments worldwide, to strengthen and/or to defend their competitive positions. While in the fifties and sixties there was a leading technology pole - the United States -, today technological power is multipolar, with three areas struggling for leadership. Therefore, firms establish "antennas" in the most promising innovation areas, in order to keep aware of new developments, and cooperate among themselves, through different forms, ranging from cooperative R&D and cross-licensing to joint-production. Technological cooperation is thus envisaged not only as a cost-sharing device, but mainly as a mechanism for achieving global leadership and for strengthening their capacity to internalise knowledge on a worldwide scale ;

(iv) globalisation of information networks, linking the whole world, such as the banking network SWIFT, the airlines network IATA or financial information systems. These networks are a consequence of the globalisation process, but at the same time largely contribute to shape and to strengthen it, so that they may be envisaged as globalisation enabling devices ;

(v) globalisation of banking and financial activities, translated in a wave of mergers and acquisitions and in an increasing interdependence among the main financial centres.

Simultaneously with the developments in globalisation, the second half of the Eighties and the beginning of the Nineties were characterised by a new momentum in the process of European integration that culminated with the Maastricht agreements. Although there were strong European specific factors behind it, such a process is not without links to the globalisation drive. On the contrary, there is a significant interaction between them. European integration corresponded to a large extent to a struggle of the main European countries to play an increased role on the world economic scene. As a matter of fact, none of the European nations had the power needed to challenge the United States and Japan. The Single Market programme emerged therefore as the European response to the globalisation challenge, by providing European firms with a "domestic" basis large enough to enable them to compete against their American and Japanese counterparts. More recent developments, such as the launching of the Economic and Monetary Union process, with the aim of setting up a single European currency by 1999, and the building up of the European Economic Space (creating a common market between EC and EFTA countries) may also be seen, to a large extent, as steps to meet the globalisation challenge.

The globalisation drive has largely been shaped by strategies of the world-embracing multinational corporations. But it was also reflected by the behaviour of the governments that are increasingly acting as purveyors of resources and based infrastructures to enable their home-based multinationals to win in the global competition arena. There is therefore, a "mutuality of interest between Governments and firms" (Dunning, 1990, p. 33) or a "new alliance", largely based on the rationale that the "success of the national enterprises on the world scene is a prerequisite for the achievement and preservation of a country's technological and economic autonomy" (Petrella, 1990, p. 102).

The globalisation process does not affect, however, all European countries in the same way. The challenges met by small countries are different, and probably more formidable than those faced by larger nations. On the other hand, globalisation is perceived from a different perspective by countries with their own multinationals and by those that lack enterprises strong enough to compete in the global arena.

Portugal is a small country without multinational firms. The purpose of this chapter is to assess how the globalisation drive has impinged upon the

Portuguese economy and upon the behaviour of economic agents with activities in Portugal, both national and foreign-owned. It is shown that the process of European integration has been the driving force behind Portugal's internationalisation pattern since the mid-eighties, so that the impact of globalisation has not been felt directly, but rather indirectly via the challenges raised through the increased relations with other EC partners.

II   Recent developments in the internationalisation of the Portuguese economy

General perspective

The last half of the eighties and the early nineties were marked by a strong internationalisation of the Portuguese economy. Links with foreign countries and organisations developed swiftly, though not in a uniform way. This internationalisation process might be characterised, in general terms, as a Europeanisation of the Portuguese economy. Let us start with a broad analysis of its main dimensions, to focus later on a geographic approach.

Before entering the Community, Portugal was already a relatively open economy, member of the EFTA and with a trade agreement with the EC. However, EC entry, in 1986, laid down new conditions for Portugal's involvement in international trade, despite the existence of a transition period. The ratio of foreign trade (exports plus imports) to GDP reached around 70 % in 1990, as against only 57 % in the early eighties. Portugal's specialisation pattern did not undergo significant changes. In fact, despite a growing share of machinery, equipment and transportation material in overall exports, these remained largely dominated by traditional and resource-based industries ; some developments might be anticipated in the years to come, due to recent export-oriented foreign investments in transportation equipment and chemicals. A relevant, and troubling, feature was the boom in subcontracting relationships with foreign firms, especially in consumer goods industries, that led to a "divorce" of many Portuguese firms from international markets, despite increased exports.

Concerning international investment, FDI inflow experienced a remarkable boom, increasing more than 11-fold between 1986 and 1990[1] ; expressed as a percentage of GDP, foreign investments reached 3 % for 1990, as against 0.5 % for 1980-82. Foreign investments were directed towards three main areas of activity : manufacturing, financial services and tourism, and real estate. Investments in manufacturing were concentrated in the automotive sector, where a handful of significant projects, mostly by large multinationals, took place. The ranking is led by a joint-venture created in 1991 between Ford and Volkswagen, to manufacture a new multi-purpose vehicle ; it is the largest foreign investment ever made in Portugal, involving an overall investment in fixed assets of almost 450 billion escudos. Worth mentioning also are the investments undertaken by General Motors (electronic devices and ignition systems), Ford (auto-radios), Valmet (tractors) and the Brazilian firm Cofap (automotive components). All these projects benefited from significant cash-grants under EC sponsored incentive systems.

The boom in inward investment was not paralleled by a similar expansion of Portuguese investments abroad, the ratio of inward to outward investment declining from 11 % in the early eighties to less than 9 % in 1990. There was nevertheless an increase in Portugal's investment penetration abroad, since 1988, which translated into an annual average growth rate of 50 % for 1988-90. Investments were mostly concentrated on the financial sector.

Turning now to the pattern of internationalisation of R&D activities, available data suggests that the main thrust in that direction came from participation in European-based R&D projects, such as EUREKA and especially the EC sponsored cooperation under the R&D Framework Programme (ESPRIT, RACE and BRITE/EURAM). This led to significant changes in the sources financing the Portuguese R&D system and enabled a sharp growth of the Private non Profit R&D sector, where some organisations achieved significant international involvement.

In contrast, the participation of business enterprises in R&D activities in general and in technology-based cooperation in particular has been very small. It may be said that Portuguese firms have remained absent from the wave of technology-driven agreements that took place in the last decade. Sound empirical data on inter-firm linkages involving Portuguese firms are very scarce and based on press surveys [2]. Existing studies are however unanimous in suggesting that the majority of inter-firm agreements is inward-oriented, referring to activities to be undertaken in Portugal and not so much to the extension of Portuguese firms abroad ; according to Maria Teresa Miranda, only 23 % of the agreements identified were related to the internationalisation of Portuguese firms. Furthermore, marketing-oriented agreements largely exceeded technology-based ones ; these have only a small stake in the overall number of agreements entered into by Portuguese firms.

Therefore, the involvement of Portuguese firms in technology trans-border cooperation has been feeble and has mostly concerned what Hagedoorn and Schakenraad (1990b, p. 4) label "one-directional technology flows". Those firms lack, in general, the technological assets needed in order to be envisaged as interesting partners for joint R&D or for technology sharing agreements. They are mostly technology purchasers and not technology suppliers or developers.

Despite this fact, disembodied technology imports by Portuguese firms are low and have not increased significantly in recent years. Technology inflows at the firm level have taken place mostly through the purchase of machinery and equipment and through direct foreign investments. Payments stemming from licensing-in agreements, according to the Bank of Portugal, accounted for almost 11 billion escudos in 1990, corresponding to an annual growth rate of 5.2 % only, since 1985.

In short, the strengthening of the internationalisation of the Portuguese economy has mainly been driven through inward investment and international trade flows. The broad picture just presented needs, however, to be analysed more in depth to really grasp the driving forces behind this internationalisation process.

Trading and investment partners

Tables 16.1 and 16.2 depict Portugal's main trading and investment partners throughout the eighties and early nineties. They both tell the same story : a strong concentration of flows intra-EC. This means that following Portugal's accession to the EC there was a Europeanisation - or, to be more precise, a Communitarisation - of Portugal's trade and investment flows.

Table 16.1   Main trading partners (%)

	Exports				Imports			
	1980	1985	1989	1990	1980	1985	1989	1990
EEC (1)	58.2	62.5	71.5	73.7	45.2	45.8	67.4	69.2
Germany (2)	13.5	13.8	15.7	16.7	11.7	11.4	14.3	14.4
France	10.6	12.7	15.1	15.5	7.3	8.0	11.5	11.5
U. Kingdom	14.8	14.6	12.3	12.1	8.6	7.5	8.1	7.6
Italy	5.7	4.0	4.2	4.0	5.2	5.1	9.0	10.0
Spain	3.6	4.1	12.5	13.3	5.5	7.4	14.4	14.4
Netherlands	4.7	6.9	5.7	5.7	2.9	3.2	5.4	5.8
EFTA	13.9	10.8	10.2	10.2	7.6	6.1	6.2	6.2
United States	5.7	9.2	6.0	4.8	11.0	9.7	4.4	3.9
Former colonies	5.9	3.9	3.3	3.4	0.6	1.2	0.4	0.4
Oil-export countries	2.1	2.5	0.7	0.6	19.7	17.6	6.1	6.8
Others	14.2	11.1	8.3	7.3	15.9	19.6	15.5	13.5
TOTAL	100	100	100	100	100	100	100	100

(1) Includes Spain for all years   (2) Includes the former GDR for 1990

Source : Instituto Nacional de Estatistica and Direccao General do Comercio Externo

Table 16.2   Main origin and destination of FDI flows (%)

	Inward		Outward		
	1980-85	1986-91	1980	1985	1988-89
E.C.	54.7	71.2	55.2	8.0	86.7
Belgium + Lux.	1.4	6.8	0.2	0.1	2.9
Germany	4.8	10.5	4.5	1.5	0.3
France	13.7	10.5	9.1	1.2	30.3
Netherlands	3.9	3.2	..	..	0.8
Spain	5.1	10.3	2.9	2.8	23.8
UK	20.8	25.4	38.5	1.8	26.1
EFTA	11.0	8.1	..	..	0.9
Japan	1.5	1.2	..	..	..
USA	19.8	6.3	7.0	29.3	1.1
Brazil	-	3.5	27.0	0.9	0.1
Former colonies	-	-	2.9	27.2	4.0
Macao	-	-	0.2	32.1	5.6

Notes :   .. Below 0.1 %   - Not separately identified in data available

Source : See note 3

With regard to trade, EC shares for exports and imports respectively expanded from 58 to 74 % and from 45 to 69 % between 1980 and 1990. EC membership simultaneously entailed a strengthening of trade relations with the majority of the other EC countries and a decline in trade links with the United States. Therefore the significant increase in Portugal's foreign trade reported above was almost exclusively due to the intra-EC flows. It should be stressed that the entry of Spain in the Common Market played an important role in this move, trade with Spain being responsible for almost one-fourth of the increase in trade with the EC. In fact, common EC membership provided a basis for intra-Iberian trade, due to the progressive removal of tariff and non-tariff barriers. From a low rank in the early eighties, Spain became in 1990 Portugal's second trade partner. A significant share of Portuguese-Spanish trade takes place intra-firm, between affiliates of multinational corporations, translating an overlapping of regional and corporate integration.

However, Spain was not the only trade partner to show remarkable growth : Germany and France (on both imports and exports) and Italy (mostly on the import side) strongly increased their shares. The only EC country to experience a decline was the United Kingdom, Portugal's traditional partner in trade.

Inward investment from the EC amounted to more than 70 % of the total for 1986-91, as against 55 % for the first half of the eighties. A similar picture is shown for outward investment, despite its lower figures and the modest degree of internationalisation of Portuguese companies : EC share raised from 55 % in 1980 to 86 % in 1986-89 [3].

These data concern the immediate sources of investment and not the location of foreign investors' headquarters and decision-making. This means, for instance, that an investment undertaken by an American multinational whose funds are transferred from its French affiliate appears in the statistics as coming from France. This introduces a bias in the statistics, but it also informs about the "hierarchisation" patterns of multinational firms' networks.

The United Kingdom was the main origin of foreign investment throughout the eighties, accounting for 25 % of total in 1986-91. British investments were mainly oriented towards services (financial activities, tourism and real estate). Other relevant sources of investment in the post-accession period were France, Spain (including several projects by Spanish affiliates of multinational firms) and Germany (where Volkswagen had a significant share, of about 45 %).

In contrast, investments from non-European countries have been relatively small, especially when compared with their weight in worldwide investment flows. The only exception was Brazil, a country without a tradition of investing abroad, that accounted for almost 4 % of FDI in Portugal in 1986-91. Brazilian capital was attracted due to three main factors : the psychic proximity between the two countries, the advantages offered by Portugal as a gateway to the EC and the instability of the Brazilian economy. Investments from the United States reached 6 % only, although it should be remarked that this share barely translates the importance of the projects undertaken by US multinationals, whose funds to a large extent came from European affiliates, particularly those based in the United Kingdom or in Spain ; if such indirect investments were considered, US share would be as high as 12 %. However, this pattern of investments by US firms clearly suggests the integration of Portugal in European production and distribution networks. The case of Japan is different : in spite of a few projects carried out by European affiliates, Japanese investment in Portugal was, on the whole, very small. Portugal has not been considered by Japanese companies as a privileged location in the EC, a feature that might be associated with the relative immaturity of Japanese manufacturing investment in Europe.

III   Globalisation or Europeanisation ?

The brief perspective of Portugal's internationalisation pattern presented above enables, in our opinion, the identification of the main actors and the driving forces behind the process.

First, **the actors**. An assessment of the roles played by domestic and foreign firms suggests that the latter have become the prevailing authority. Portuguese firms have been relatively passive, adopting in general a reactive stance rather than a proactive one. They have remained largely specialised in traditional industries, employing competitive strategies based on cost and not on product differentiation. Marketing has been given low priority and links with final customers have tended to be weak, most firms lacking their own distribution channels abroad. Furthermore, cooperative agreements have been, as remarked, largely inward-oriented : only a few cases have involved cooperative approaches to enter European markets. Foreign investment data points to a similar direction, since the projects undertaken abroad by non-banking firms have been scarce and unsuccessful. Several firms have considered Africa as a countervailing factor to the fierce competition faced in Europe and to conceal technological weaknesses. These have also been at the root of very low involvement in EC-financed R&D programmes. All in all, and with the exception of a few success stories, Portuguese firms have been largely passive in exploiting the new opportunities generated by European integration.

Conversely, foreign firms have been very active. Their share in Portugal's exports have experienced a significant increase, through either direct exports by affiliates or subcontracting relationships established with Portuguese manufacturers. Foreign investment has boomed, profiting from the advantages provided by Portugal as a manufacturing location and as a market : low wages, relatively skilled and adaptable labour, good working relationships, development of physical infrastructures, increasing domestic demand and generous financial incentives. Both greenfield investments and acquisitions have increased sharply, strengthening the level of foreign penetration in the Portuguese economy.

It may be argued therefore that Portuguese firms have "suffered" international economic changes without taking a significant role in the process. From this perspective it may be argued that the swift internationalisation of Portugal in recent years has been to a large extent a "passive internationalisation".

Second, **the driving forces**. The recent internationalisation of the Portuguese economy has been the result of three interrelated factors : EC accession, the progressive liberalisation of the domestic economic system and the globalisation drive. The first has been, in our opinion, the leading one. In fact, the liberalisation of the Portuguese economy has been to some extent the consequence of engagements taken under the Treaty of Accession to the European Communities, as well as of the movement towards the building up of the Single Market. Furthermore, EC membership has had a powerful effect on the launching and the development of an extensive programme of infrastructure modernisation and the granting of significant incentives to private investments. The internationalisation pattern presented above can be characterised by a growing engulfment of Portugal into Europe or, more precisely, into the European Community. This means a sharpening of intra-EC trade, an increasing importance of EC funds to finance the Portuguese

R&D system and an expansion of intra-EC investment flows. There has been a simultaneous loosening and strengthening of the links between Portugal and the world economy. Strengthening, in so far as Portugal is more open to international economic relationships and worldwide networks, is increasingly pervasive. Loosening, to the extent that European integration has acted as a "mediator" between Portugal and the world economy and that the development of intra-European links has conditioned the preservation or the building up of relationships with non-European areas. This process should not be interpreted as a stiff opposition between European integration and globalisation, but rather as an interaction and a mediation. European integration has largely shaped and "filtered" the impact of globalisation on the Portuguese economy.

Globalisation has not been perceived as a significant challenge by most Portuguese economic agents. The main, and the immediate, challenge has been European integration. Portuguese firms are primarily concerned with an increasingly fierce competition within the EC and with the attack on the domestic market by foreign competitors. A few have responded to the challenge by setting up marketing channels abroad, especially in Spain. Others have tried to squeeze costs to remain competitive or have accepted to work as subcontractees for large European distribution chains. Still others have looked towards Africa to withstand the European challenge. But, for most of them, globalisation has been envisaged as something distant - what has been perceived as really important is the process of European integration.

Foreign firms, and especially large multinationals that have invested in Portugal in the last few years, are clearly more concerned with globalisation. Several of them are relevant actors in the globalisation process. The joint-venture between Ford and Volkswagen to launch a new multi-purpose vehicle follows other cooperative moves between the two firms in other areas (such as Brazil, for instance), and may be envisaged as a strategic decision to challenge some of their global competitors, like Renault or Toyota. However, the choice of Portugal as an investment location was taken because Portugal is a member of the European Community. Portugal is mainly perceived as "a place in Europe" and not as an independent location. A great deal of foreign investments in Portugal were not mainly and immediately driven by globalisation pressure, but were rather undertaken to take advantage of Portugal's position in the EC setting. This happened with several projects in the automotive industry where Portuguese plants are strongly integrated in European manufacturing networks, with investments in domestic electrical goods to supply the Iberian market or with the acquisition of former Portuguese contractual partners to strengthen the integration of Portugal into European distribution networks. Therefore, even for foreign firms the impact of globalisation pressures on the decision to invest in Portugal was to a large extent "mediated" by the very process of European integration. It may be argued that the wave of foreign investments in Portugal was mainly due to new opportunities opened up in relation to overlapping between corporate and regional integration.

To sum up, we think that, from the Portuguese standpoint, the effects of globalisation have been mainly felt through an increased inter-twining with the other EC member countries. However, when looking ahead it is necessary to bear in mind that Portugal's international economic relationships should not be confined to the European Community as they stand now. Being anchored in Europe and firmly committed to the process of building up the Economic and Monetary Union, Portugal also needs to strengthen links with the other continents, through a pro-active approach. Its long history of forging international relationships should be ranked as an asset in a shrinking world.

Notes

1   Global data on inward and outward investment are based on information supplied by the Bank of Portugal.

2   As far as we know there are only two studies in this field. One was undertaken by Maria Teresa Miranda, from the Universidade Nova de Lisboa, the main conclusions being published in *Expresso*, 25 April 1992. The other was led by the present author, with the cooperation of Artur Ferreira, and its main findings were reported in Simões (1991).

3   The geographical breakdown of inward investment is based on data published by the former Foreign Investment Institute and the Institute for Foreign Trade (ICEP). Destinations of outward investment were taken from data supplied by the Bank of Portugal.

17 Globalisation, technology factors and industrial structuring in southern Europe : the Greek experience

Tassos Giannitsis

I   Introduction

For many national economic systems in Europe the transition from the 1970s to the 1980s was associated with strong tendencies of integration into the world market. During this period, the second EEC enlargement, the various agreements between the EEC and third countries, the disintegration of the centrally-planned economies of Eastern Europe, the move towards the Single Market and the Economic and Monetary Union has had as an effect the reduction of national market barriers and the enhancement of the unification of economic conditions in broader economic spaces.

The aim of this chapter is to analyse some of the implications of globalisation in the case of Greece, as an intermediate economy. It should be stressed that although analysis focuses on globalisation, this factor cannot be isolated with regard to its implications for industrial structures. It is the interplay of external factors and internal capabilities, structures, weaknesses or strengths and policies that determines the form and the importance of the direct and the indirect implications of the phenomenon of globalisation.

In many studies globalisation is conceived as a general trend towards worldwide expansion of firm activities, as it emerged during the 1980s. However, in this approach globalisation is seen "as a wide set of processes and relationships as a result of which firms, industries and nations derive competitive advantages by integrating activities on a worldwide basis" [1]. From a single country's point of view, what is important is that competitive advantages of the global players derive less from where they perform activities and more from the way they organise and perform on a worldwide basis [2]. This means that there are emerging new forms of competitive advantages that no longer depend on geographical location. They are not specific to the location but to the activity of the firm as an entity [3].

However, our understanding of the complexities created by the new realities would remain incomplete if considerations were centred on micro-economic actors and strategies alone. Globalisation is only partially a micro-phenomenon. Foremost it is associated with serious changes in the macro-economic context and in the determinants of firm activities, as a result of which the latter shape their strategic actions. Complementary therefore to its micro-economic foundation, globalisation has to be seen in the context of broader changes encompassing three major areas.

Firstly, globalisation is closely linked with the dynamic process of the reallocation of functions between the State and the Market in the regulation and shaping of industrial structures. As a result, this substitution leads to the dissipation not only of state, but also of national economic decision-making power, which is transferred to or at least benefits a worldwide population of private actors [4].

Secondly, globalisation is also linked with a redistribution of policy-making power from individual states to a central authority (e.g. the EC Commission).

Thirdly, one major implication of the increasing role of technology as a factor determining competitive advantages in global markets is that such advantages are becoming more and more internal to firms and external to markets. The consequence for technologically weaker countries is that they have to form their policies in an environment which on the one hand leads to the dissolution of state power in order to promote industrial transformation, while on the other the shift of emphasis towards technological issues implies the linkage of decisive industrial policy instruments with the capabilities and strategies of firms.

In fact, although competitive relations appear to function under increasingly open market conditions, new forms of barriers to entry are appearing in the form of technological relations. Economic policies of all industrial economies tend to multiply technological schemes in favour of national-global players. In the EEC too, technological support is not considered to distort the competitive positions in the market. This shift of emphasis combined with deregulation deprives technologically weak actors from important development instruments for the simple reason that their specialisation patterns and industrial structures are posing severe limits to technologically oriented policies. A new reality is visible, where feasible industrial strategies lead increasingly to innovation and technological policies, thereby limiting the possibilities of technological weaker actors to follow within visible time limits.

II   The integration of industry into global economic structures and implications for key variables of the economy

The Greek economy, as well as the other Southern European countries of the second enlargement, experienced during a very short period the most radical exposure into world competitive forces of its history. World market integration had important consequences for two key variables : market shares and profitability.

The reallocation of market shares

World market integration homogenised the conditions of entry for broader segments of the industrial (and service) markets between national and international firms. For a range of industries this homogenisation implied the elimination of substantial entry barriers against international players. As a consequence, domestic firms experienced severe losses in market shares. Import penetration in industry increased from 25 % in 1980 to 43 % in 1989, while in specific branches (mostly in light industries) percentage increases of 100 % to 300 % could be noticed.

The transition from quasi-monopolistic profits to competitive markets

Globalisation affected economic processes through its impact on a central variable of the economy : profitability. In particular, profitability was squeezed because of the move from protection to competitive conditions both in the goods and in the capital market. In particular, the elimination of tariff and non-tariff barriers had not only market share effects but was also associated with a decline in industrial value added, mostly at the expense of profits, at least during the early 1980s. Equally, liberalisation of the capital market affected the costs of industrial production. As a consequence, profit margins, profitability perspectives and the whole hierarchy of profitability between the industrial and other sectorial activities in the economy were altered.

It has been estimated, that for many industries, nominal tariff protection alone represented about 100 % to 500 % of their profits before trade liberalisation [5]. This high dependence of profits on protection is indicative of the fundamental destabilising effects exerted on the industrial sector when it is removed.

A reversal of the downward trend in profits was achieved through persistent restrictive income policies during the second half of the 1980s. The weak technological capabilities of most industrial firms posed severe limits to their possibilities of escaping competitive pressure by improving productivity rather than depressing labour remuneration. As a result, the struggle for income shares became a central element of the Greek economic scene during the 1980s.

III   Changing relations to the world market and forms of industrial adjustment

Pressure on industrial profits and on market shares had important implications for the following key issues : (i) the stagnation of industrial production and a reallocation of resources from tradeable to non-tradeable areas of activity ; (ii) the internal organisation of industries ; and (iii) the in- and outward capital and technology flows (foreign direct investment and licensing).

De-industrialisation and the reinforcement of unofficial activities

De-industrialisation characterises the whole period after 1974 and in particular the 1980s. The expression of de-industrialisation consists in stagnant growth rates of manufacturing (0.8 % per year for 1981-89), in the absolute drop in employment in most industries as well as in the decline of the industrial index by about 14 % to 37 % for seven of the 20 two-digit industries and by 2-5 % for another three. As a result, the position of manufacturing in the national production system shrunk by about three percentage points between 1980 and 1990 (from 21.4 % to 18.5 %).

The destabilisation of large parts of the industry in combination with the pressure on industrial value added indicate that both capital and labour forces were adversely affected, the first because of the elimination of quasi-monopolistic profit margins and the latter because of the subsequent austerity programmes. It is not surprising that as a consequence, a reallocation of resources seemed to take place during the 1980s, moving away from activities exposed to world market pressure and towards the production of non-tradeable. It has been estimated [6] that unofficial activities increased from 11 % of the GDP in 1980 to over 35 % in the late 1980s. The reinforcement of tertiary and unofficial activities as opposed to industry seems to imply that national economic actors tried to adjust to international competitive pressure by moving towards activities, which are less exposed to competition, and ensure less risky combinations of viability, profitability and security.

Firm exits and size adjustments

Globalisation of competition had the following further effects on industrial organisation and on development prospects :

(i)   it forced a range of firms out of industry. In general, during the 1980s many important firms were faced with increasing difficulties, leading either to complete closure and exit from the market, or to the phenomenon of "ailing firms", to shrinkage of activity, to shifts from industrial production to import activities, to acquisition strategies of other firms, etc. ;

(ii)   with regard to the size classes of firms leaving the market, it has been found that liberalisation of trade during the 1980s rather than encouraging the formation of bigger firms favoured the small ones. Statistical evidence reveals that firms with over 20 employees shrunk by about 400 units or about 10 % of their total number, while smaller firms increased in number. Equally, the size class of over 100 employees experienced similar trends [7]. As a result, the organisation of many industries consists of fewer units and smaller average sizes. The substitution of smaller units in medium and large industries has had severe implications for the development perspectives of the industry in this period of market opening. Indeed, the shift to smaller sizes can be considered as an adjustment of firms to scales which from a micro-economic point of view can be more viable and resistant to competitive pressures. However, at the macro-economic level this affects negatively the development process. Small size implies insufficient resources for innovation activities, for the upgrading of the value added, for expanding into export activities, for bargaining the cost of inputs, and for participating in global networks in large consumer markets. The capability of such organisational forms to push forward the development process is faced with serious barriers, and micro-economic adjustment is associated with shrinking capacities for production and competition and increased imbalances at the macro-level ;

(iii) in contrast to the above trends, the exposure to higher competitive pressure led a number of firms to modernise and upgrade their competitive capacities. This ongoing adjustment process had uncertain results as regards the position of industry as a whole. This contrasted development at the micro-level reflected the existence of a two-tier system, whereby, under the influence of competition, the performance of about two-thirds of firms revealed some form of positive adjustment (including M&A, see below), while for the rest, structural weakness seemed to result in persistent negative profits, followed by closures and other forms of failure ;

(iv) the opening of markets in the case of East European countries exerted also a positive effect on a range of Greek firms. For the first time (with some exceptions) Greek firms are expanding through outward direct investments (subsidiaries or joint ventures) into these countries. An unquantified number of such firms has been created during the last few years, by both medium and large firms. However, these initiatives are aiming more at distribution, commercial and other service activities and less at industrial ones ;

(v) an additional trend that deserves reference is a slight increase in research and development activities. Fierce competition appears to generate a tendency among industries for increased attention on research and innovation. Since however, the share of R&D in total production is under 2 %, its impact until now has been concentrated in some more technology aware players and cannot be seen as a decisive factor in shaping industrial competitiveness above the firm level.

The changing importance of foreign direct investment and licensing

Trade liberalisation, apart from its impact on industrial profits, exerted significant effects on the relative profitability of exporting in comparison to foreign direct investment (FDI) or to licensing as alternative vehicles of penetration into the Greek market. The liberalisation of trade broadened significantly the opportunities of multinational firms to export to the Greek market from EEC and non-EEC zones of production. In particular, the most important factors determining the impact of globalisation on FDI in the country were the following :

(i) the elimination of protection of final products squeezed significantly the profit margins of industrial firms and consequently of the subsidiaries of MNCs established in Greece. On the other hand, this factor opened up the market for foreign products, since it created the possibility to expand sales as a result of changes of the relative prices between previously protected goods and the rest of goods and services ;

(ii) the effect on profit margins reduced on the one hand the oligopolistic rent from the use of licensing, and on the other the profitability of the potential licenser firms since they could no longer share part of this rent with their buying partners ;

(iii) the development of generalised and more transparent incentives for industrial firms in the place of a previously highly individualised and variable system of concessions which varied according to the activity and the bargaining power of the foreign firm and its state of origin.

The precise impact of these changes is difficult to assess. The empirical evidence of the 1980s reveals a large penetration of the Greek market through trade and to a much lesser extent through direct investment. However, as regards FDI, a more differentiated pattern of behaviour is visible. In some industries foreign investment has increased, while in others it has declined, so that in fact, the specific foreign firms established in the market are changing. The apparent stability of FDI as a whole is therefore associated with significant diversification as to the specific actors and their sectorial interests. Under the influence of the above factors, patterns of foreign direct investment in Greek industry reveal two major trends [8]. In the period from 1972/73 to the early 1980s a sharp decline of FDI took place, both in absolute and relative terms. Its main manifestation was the absence of significant new projects, the relatively slow growth of established foreign firms, the retirement of some large firms out of the market, and the transformation of some industrial firms to commercial ones, as well as the bankruptcy of some others. Indeed, after about two decades of activity, many of the foreign firms established in Greece in the 1960s, reached a point where they had exhausted most of the benefits of the old protectionist regime, were faced with the opening of the market and with significantly different conditions of functioning, and had to decide on a new strategy, i.e. whether to modernise obsolete production capacities, to expand, or to withdraw from local production. As a result, a sharp decline of their share in manufacturing occurred during the 1970s. Furthermore, most of the intermediate and capital goods industries, the expansion and diversification of which was driven in the past by the activities of MNCs dropped to relatively slow growth rates. What differentiates the 1980s from the earlier period is the reversal of the downward trend of FDI inflow, the establishment of new small and medium-sized firms and the coming into the market through the acquisition of medium and large domestic firms. The share of foreign firms in industry stabilised at around 23 % in 1988 as against a similar figure in 1978 and at about 33 % in the early 1970s. However, in contrast to the 1960s, new FDI did not help to expand the industrial specialisation of the country. It led rather to a differentiation of existing products, while their acquisitions (see below) were not contributing to the growth of productive capacity of the industry either.

Acquisitions, mergers and the emergence of new networks

The broader liberalisation of the markets and the expected increase in competitive pressure seems to have been a decisive factor behind the wave of acquisitions of industrial firms during the second half of the 1980s, similarly to many other countries. M&A represent a serious restructuring effort from both domestic and multinational firms with regard to competitive positions, economies of scope, control of sources of competitive advantages and/or opportunities to take over advantages owned by firms failing to face market pressure.

M&A took on an important dimension in industry albeit on a highly selective basis. They mainly concentrated on the food and beverage industry as well as those of paper products, chemicals, non-metallic minerals and electrical appliances. More than 90 % of the value acquisitions were concentrated on these six industries between 1985 and 1989. Multinational firms played a dominant role since they obtained over 75 % of the firms acquired in terms of various criteria (e.g. total assets, gross income). At the sectorial level these ownership changes represented from 4 % (chemicals) to 20 % (beverages) of the turnover or other variables of the respective branches, indicating important reallocations of responsibility among domestic or new foreign actors.

Globalisation seems to affect this restructuring process in multiple ways, and in particular :

(i)   the significant losses in market shares of domestic firms over a very short period, and their exposure to tougher competitive pressure, with uncertain implications as to the future flow of profits, the viability and their position exerted a downward pressure on their asset value. As a consequence, their acquisition constituted for stronger competitors a relatively cheap and quick way to enter the market or to upgrade competitive positions. This was reinforced by the important debt settlements which accompanied the privatisation of many firms after their inclusion in the specific government support schemes of the 1980s ;

(ii) the opening of the market induced the acquisition of firms with important distribution networks with the aim to benefit from the more liberal conditions in trade flows. This case concerns mostly acquisitions by foreign firms which were more interested in exploiting this asset in order to enhance their overall competitive position in the Greek market rather than to build up the productive capabilities of the acquired firm ;

(iii) firms of non-EEC countries (USA, Switzerland, Sweden) revealed a particular interest for strengthening their position in view of the Single Market. The prospect of the unified European space in the case of EFTA firms, or the goal to counterbalance trade advantages of EEC competitors by local presence in the case of US firms are factors which have to be taken into account before attempting any interpretation ;

(iv) the situation created by the complex interrelation between trade liberalisation, failing firms, free capital movement, fiscal deficits and deregulation permitted MNC's to enter, for the first time, in otherwise physically protected markets (e.g. in beverages, construction materials, etc.) by buying leading firms which were faced with significant difficulties of adjustment.

Acquisitions can contribute substantially to the creation of more competitive units and to the exploitation of advantages at the national level. However, the final realisation of this effect will depend on the role attributed to the acquired firms in the framework of the global activities of their new owners. In particular, the integration of parts of the country's productive system into global enterprise spaces can contribute to the improvement of its competitive position, as far as the restructuring and the reinforcement of the productive capacities of these firms is pursued. If instead, the role of these firms is reduced to that of an agent for products of their international group through their distribution networks, there is a danger that the productive capacities and the external macro-economic imbalances will further deteriorate. In this case, forces towards de-industrialisation and a more general destabilisation of the economy will persist and will continue to hamper transformation towards more dynamic structures of organisation.

IV   Global markets, global strategies and small countries

An important result of this analysis is that the globalisation of technologically weaker countries can be associated with four particular characteristics :

(i)   it takes a "passive" form, in the sense that domestic firms do not possess the necessary capabilities to follow global strategies [9]. They are rather the "target" of similar strategies of MNCs and not main actors ;

(ii)   it takes the form of market unification through trade liberalisation and integration rather than through the creation of local productive structures which would be integrated into global firm activities ;

(iii)   it generates significant changes with regard to established competitive advantages of firms and industries. Capital and labour are no longer considered the basis for success. Old competitive advantages based on non-diversified labour inputs have been seriously eroded. At the same time new technologies imply spectacular changes in labour cost structures. To the extent that markets have become global, technological capabilities in the broadest sense of the term have become the key factor in diversification and in the creation of competitive advantages ;

(iv)   globalisation and the key role of technology in shaping competitive advantages seem to support the conclusion, that small countries and, accordingly, small markets, can be disadvantaged to the extent that the life cycle of new technologies and products is shortened [10]. This factor limits seriously the possibilities of domestic firms to participate in such processes if they are not highly specialised and outward-oriented. It can also affect their comparative advantages for the attraction of FDI as compared to third economies with large internal markets.

Given this   reality, Greek industry is hampered by   two serious constraints :

(i)   increasing difficulties have appeared in the absorption and exploitation of production technology. Several factors in technology transfer reveal a declining trend ;

(ii)   the technology base of the Greek economy seems to have become weaker. Light consumer goods industries, which are technologically less intensive, service and unofficial activities are gaining in importance while industrial FDI is not associated (at least at this stage) with additional investment, but with the acquisition of existing firms and assets.

Countries in such a position will obviously have difficulties benefiting from globalisation if they fail to realise substantial and structural shifts in their productive and technological base. Otherwise, the danger exists that they will gradually "delink" from the world market to the extent that parts of their productive activities will move towards the more protected non-tradeable goods and/or unofficial activities, with adverse implications for their overall internal balance and position in the European system. Broadly speaking, it seems that a new pattern of relations has been created, between technologically powerful and weaker actors, in which the possibilities to achieve economic and social convergence has become more difficult than in the past. The difference with previous paradigms does not lie in a more unequal distribution of knowledge and power. The new qualitative element consists in the deprivation of significant degrees of freedom in shaping industrial and development strategies as a result of the complex interrelation between globalisation, deregulation and technology. In fact, in the past, development has only benefited those countries which succeeded in implementing a particular balance between discretionary intervention and competitive pressures. Under the new conditions, such strategies become less feasible, affecting   thus the broader macro-economic and development performance. In fact, as traditional forms of development policies are eroded, new concepts of action at the national or supra-national level are lacking. In particular, with regard to the EEC, the shift to global structures (not only at the level of concrete economic and technological relations, but also at that of policies and institutional framework) with the gradual elimination of traditional forms of national state intervention, raises new and   critical questions as to the instruments for coping with micro-restructuring in the small intermediate member countries. In a system where room for differentiated policies is substantially restricted and significant decision-making is gradually transferred to Community institutions, the question is which policies are appropriate but also feasible for preserving at least the relative position of these countries in a balanced European hierarchy ?

Notes

1   See M. Porter (1986b), p. 13 ; OECD, TEP, Draft Background Report, General Introduction, p. 7 (Paris, 1990) ; D. Ernst, D. O'Connor, 1989, p. 25 ; R. Petrella, "Europe", in A.W. Betts, E.L. Gavlick (eds), Proceedings of the Forty-Second Annual National Conference on the Advancement of Research (Lancaster, Basel, 1988), p. 112.

2   M. Porter, (1986b), p. 26.

3   Ibid., p. 25.

4   St. Thomadakis, "European economic integration, the Greek state, and the challenges of the 1990s" (mimeo, 1991), p. 3ff., and J.M. Cypher (1979), for a review of the major changes in the State functions.

5   T. Giannitsis, "Integration to the world market and implications for industrial and technological structures" (mimeo, Athens, 1992, in Greek).

6   M. Delivani, *The economics of unoffical economy in Greece*, Athens : Papazisis, 1991 (in Greek), p. 94.

7   See Ghemawat, P., Nalebuff, B. (1990), for a review of the explanations of the closure of large plants in declining industries.

8   For more details on FDI, licensing agreements, and the merger and acquisition activities see T. Giannitsis (1991), pp. 24-49.

9   Compare the analysis of V. Corado Simões (1991), p. 50.

10   See also *Small countries, science and technology and EC cohesion. Issues and opportunities*, CEC, FAST, Exploratory Dossier no. 14 (1988) ; Ernst and O'Connor (1989) ; O'Doherty and McDevitt (1991).

Part IV

Challenges for firms

---

18 Firm strategies, globalisation and new technological paradigms : the case of biotechnology

Vivien Walsh and Ilaria Galimberti *

I   Introduction

This chapter examines the strategies of large multinational firms, mainly in the chemical, pharmaceutical and agri-food industries, faced with three trends : a decline in their core businesses and traditional paradigms ; the emergence of biotechnology, a new paradigm largely outside their accumulated competences ; and increasing globalisation. It also examines to a lesser extent the strategies of the independent start-up firms which first commercialised the new technology. The strategies of small biotechnology firms have been examined in more detail elsewhere, by one of us together with other colleagues (Oakey *et al.*, 1990).

With increasing maturity, the chemical, pharmaceutical and agri-food sectors experienced something of a crisis : a levelling off or decline in the markets of their core businesses ; declining returns to effort from R&D and the exploitation of their traditional technological paradigms ; and increasingly complex regulations concerning unwanted consequences of innovation. Freeman (1990) [1], for example, notes a decline in chemical process innovations from the 1970s, and an even more dramatic fall in chemical product innovations. In the case of pharmaceuticals, Sharp (1989) shows an escalation in R&D costs with a levelling off and decline in numbers of new chemical entities marketed during the 1970s and 80s.

* *We are grateful to the colleagues listed in notes 4 & 11, plus François Chesnais, Rod Coombs, Ken Green, Keith Pavitt, Paolo Saviotti and Margaret Sharp for discussions, comments, ideas and pre-publication copies of papers over many years.*

Biotechnology [2] is a new technological paradigm in Dosi's (1982) sense, in that it has changed the way in which old problems are approached and opened up new possibilities for development. For example, it has provided the means to search for drugs, pesticides, food additives and other chemicals designed for a specific end use ("designer chemicals"), potentially replacing the old system of "molecular roulette". (That is, the systematic preparation and screening of as many chemical entities as possible, in the hope of finding something that offers the desired properties, but not the unwanted ones.) Similarly it offers the design of food crops resistant to pests or climatic change as a potential replacement for the slow and uncertain process of conventional plant breeding, or the design of micro-organisms to render specific toxic wastes harmless. Biotechnology thus offers, or has already provided, a paradigm change in the technological bases of a range of industrial sectors. In doing so it has already rendered obsolete some of the skills and competences accumulated by existing firms in those sectors, and has the potential to carry this process further, even though it is now recognised that, in time-scale, early predictions of commercial benefits were wildly optimistic.

Globalisation is a general trend affecting sectors besides those discussed in this paper, as other chapters in this volume indicate. The OECD (1992b) defines it as a dynamic process which develops at the interface of three continuously evolving phenomena : trade, the multinational structure of business firms, and the nature of financial markets. As Chesnais (this volume) shows, foreign direct investment has grown much more quickly than trade, and the movement of capital is closely related to a process of international mergers and acquisitions. Globalisation affects the competitive environment of the firms discussed here ; but, as others (see van Tulder and Ruigrok, this volume) argue, it is itself a **strategy adopted** by firms.

The chemical, pharmaceutical and agri-food sectors are highly globalised in all the OECD's senses of the term, but their responses to the emergence of biotechnology were (at least for a period) something of a departure from globalisation strategies. The aspect of globalisation in their competitive environment that particularly influenced them was the increase in international competition which, together with shortening product cycles, provided pressure to launch products more quickly, and enter more markets, both geographically and in terms of end-use applications. In addition, the increasingly science-based nature of innovation and its reliance on the convergence of several disciplines, has meant that scientific and technological competences in increasing breadth **and** depth are needed. This adds to the cost of innovation, and the need to recoup costs from as wide a series of markets as possible.

These trends have together stimulated the increase in cooperation between firms as a means of sharing costs and risks and gaining access to other skills and markets. Many such cooperative alliances cross national borders and so represent a (relatively new) aspect of globalisation [3]. It was the phenomenon of cooperative alliances which was particularly important in the initial strategies of the firms dealing with the emergence of biotechnology. Alliances were a major source of complementary knowledge and competence for both large and small firms, of vital importance to the commercialisation of the new technology.

II   Two apparent paradoxes

This paper explores two apparent paradoxes. The first one concerns firm size and innovation. The general consensus in innovation literature (e.g. Pavitt, 1984, 1991) is that small firms may make a contribution to innovation and economic growth disproportionate to their size ; but that this phenomenon is usually confined to certain sectors, such as mechanical or instrument engineering or electronic components, where entry barriers and static economies of scale are low. In contrast, innovation in the chemical, pharmaceutical and agri-food sectors is typically dominated by the large, well-established firms with multinational operations, and which are involved in global markets.

The first commercial **applications** of biotechnology were found in these latter sectors : but commercialisation was **first carried out** by new, small, specialist firms (known as Dedicated Biotechnology Firms or DBFs). They were established to exploit commercial opportunities following the scientific breakthroughs of the mid-1970s, typically in the United States, Canada and the UK. Furthermore, it might at first seem that biotechnology had proved to be an exception to recent trends in globalisation, since the small firms were not already involved in multinational operations, or active in concentrated, global markets.

The second paradox concerns new entrants and established firms. New technological paradigms, which can make obsolete the skills and competences of established firms, can appear from outside those firms. Such firms are often locked into old established procedures, research perspectives, dominant designs, industrial standards and so on. On the other hand, established firms have, over the past century, learned a great deal about survival and growth, starting with the organisational innovation of the in-house R&D laboratory. In particular, they have learned how to use their accumulated and firm-specific technological advantages and their market power to avoid being pushed out of the way by new entrants growing and forming the basis of a new industry.

The question is, how and why was it that the new paradigm of biotechnology was first commercialised by the new entrants ? Why was it not seized upon by established firms in the sectors where the applications were to be made, especially as the established firms concerned have generally been among the most research intensive and innovative in the economy. The chemical and pharmaceutical firms especially had a long-standing presence in industrial production, a strong tradition in R&D and a sustained rate of innovative success over many decades (Walsh, 1984), although neither the food processing nor the waste treatment firms have been very R&D intensive, even in conventional terms.

III   Small, independent firms' strategies for commercialising biotechnology

A large number of DBFs were established in the USA and the UK in the wave of commercial enthusiasm following the breakthroughs in genetic engineering in the mid-1970s. The largest number of new firms formed in any one year was 43 in the USA in 1981 (OTA, 1988) and 10 in the UK a year later (Oakey *et al.*, 1990). The DBFs were set up with the aim of manufacturing products for sale to final end users, though many of them failed to do so.

We have argued elsewhere (Walsh *et al.*, 1991) that the main problems facing the small firms were : shortage of finance, a longer time than anticipated for development work, a forecast level of demand that failed to materialise, and a lack of the complementary skills, assets and technologies (Teece, 1986) necessary for successful commercialisation of the technological knowledge they clearly had.

To commercialise biotechnology, firms needed networks of doctors, farmers, ecologists, agricultural experts, nutritionists and others prepared to carry out tests on the efficacy and/or safety of drugs, food additives, new crops, agrochemicals, waste treatment systems, diagnostic kits and enzymes, and later to recommend them to final end users. They needed well-established relationships with regulatory authorities and licensing bodies, in order to negotiate the tests required for new products to be approved, to steer the new product through the regulatory process and in some cases to agree on the prices to be charged and the conditions under which the product would be used.

The future economic impact of biotechnology depends not only on the expansion of demand but also on the existence of appropriate institutions within which demand can be articulated and met (Walsh, forthcoming). Consumers buy products, but their expectations are shaped and their choices limited - in some cases decisively determined - by intermediaries who exercise their professional judgement, and by the effects of a series of government regulations. For commercialisation to be successful, it was necessary to influence the professionals and lobby governments [4]. The complementary assets did not just enable the production and marketing of innovations, but shaped the selection environment in which they would be accepted or not.

These kinds of skills and experience, or networks of established relationships have to be built up over a period of time, while compliance with the public regulation and control of new products also requires heavy expenditure on screening and marketing. Small firms had two options. One was to sell services such as information, consultancy and contract R&D, or intermediate products such as reagents, enzymes or specialist equipment, to other manufacturing firms instead of final products to end users such as farmers or the health care system. A large majority of the UK firms whose main source of continued investment finance was their own profits, were firms selling mainly services rather than products. Forty % did contract research, while services accounted for more than 50 % of turnover for 35 % of firms [5]. Doing substantial contract research and thus acting essentially as the external research laboratory for an existing firm, represents a change in the boundaries within which innovations are produced and commercialised. Over most of this century the trend has been towards increased in-house R&D (Mowery, 1983 ; Teece, 1988). Subcontracting represents an increase in arms-length transactions in the market place, in technological know-how.

The other strategy open to them was to enter agreements with established firms in order to gain access to their funds and their complementary assets, sharing expertise in biotechnology in return. Collaborative agreements represent a shift in institutional boundaries in which R&D is located which is neither market nor hierarchy (Williamson, 1975, though Amin and Dietrich [6] describe the collaboration between large powerful firms and small vulnerable ones as a new form of hierarchy) and needs to be examined in its own right. Even the most successful of the independent firms - Genentech, Amgen, Cetus, Celltech and a few others - only succeeded in marketing final products as a result of various kinds of agreement with large established firms. There was, of course, a third option, which was to adopt both strategies. Several firms did so. Nevertheless, even with these strategies, the small firms faced substantial difficulties. By 1990 only six independent firms were making a profit in the USA [7]. Many of the independent firms in the UK have yet to produce a product or generate any profits. On the other hand, some of the small firms have done well, grown and established their own international operations (e.g. Dodgson, 1991).

IV   Large firms and their strategies

In Europe and Japan, it was large, established firms, rather than small start-ups, which were the prime movers in biotechnology, although they followed developments initiated by the US start-up firms and based their strategies on the establishment of collaborative links with them. This chapter concentrates on European firms' strategies and not the rather different ones adopted in Japan.

Globalisation and large firms

This section summarises the international operations and globalised nature of some of the sectors which adopted or have the potential to adopt biotechnology. The food processing market is highly concentrated (Yoxen and Green, 1990). A large growth in international merger and acquisition of food processing firms (Hamill and Crosbie, 1989) has strengthened brands in international markets and given access to the most innovative marketing skills. In seeds, ten firms have 30 % of an estimated $10 billion world market (Walsh *et al.*, 1991). In chemicals increased market concentration in the form of a variety of mergers and acquisitions took place in the late 1980s, notably between US and European companies. European firms dominate the world chemical market with eight of the largest ten firms.

In pharmaceuticals, 100 firms have 80 % of world sales ($145 billion in 1990) (Walsh *et al.*, 1991). Among the 30 largest drug companies, 12 are based in the US, 11 in Europe, 5 in Japan and 2 are US-European mergers. A variety of mergers in the pharmaceutical industry took place between 1985 and 1991 (in addition to acquisitions of biotechnology firms), many of them across national borders. Diagnostics has been an area with most potential for small firms but here, too, the large ones such as Abbott, Bayer and Ortho dominate the world market. Waste treatment is one of the smallest of the industries in which biotechnology has an actual or potential impact, and the least globalised. The largest firms are American and only beginning to expand into European markets. They have revenues of $11 billion [8] out of an estimated world market of $100 billion [9] .

Several of the industries using biotechnology provide an exception to Patel and Pavitt's (1991) observation that R&D is concentrated in the home country, even by firms otherwise highly globalised. The multinational location of drug company activities have shown the concentration and internationalisation of pharmaceutical R&D. This trend in drug R&D was noted back in 1967 [10] , but other sectors, such as seeds for instance are now following the same pattern. ICI seeds, for example, has plant-breeding research activities in 14 countries, production and marketing in 12 countries, and plant bioscience research (the most high-tech area) in 4. If the internationalisation of R&D in the chemical and pharmaceutical industry is exceptional, clearly the chemical companies have transferred their exceptional behaviour to other fields into which they have moved.

The established firms would appear to have been as well placed as any to move into a new technological area, building up their own R&D as they had always done, using their more-than-usually internationalised existing R&D

activities for widespread sourcing of new knowledge, and their traditional strategies of merger and acquisition to move significant investment into new areas of R&D, production and marketing (as ICI and Ciba-Geigy did with conventional plant breeding).

Initial strategies

However, in the sectors where applications for biotechnology have been developed, the large established firms continued to concentrate on the old paradigms they had established, well after the new entrants had been set up to commercialise an entirely new technology in the established firms' traditional markets. This was not necessarily short-sightedness, or poor forecasting on the part of the large firms, (though it may have represented a ponderousness and lack of flexibility in re-orienting a large institution). Many of them **carefully worked out** a strategy of caution.

At about the time that DBFs were beginning to appear, the large firms were entering a period of strategic re-orientation and organisational restructuring in general, as a result of the crisis mentioned earlier. This led to a move away from bulk chemicals towards high value added products, and a shift in R&D towards activities that would lead to higher value added production. It also led to the establishment of small groups, usually attached to corporate headquarters or a central strategic research department rather than any of the product divisions, to carry out exploratory basic research in a wide variety of new areas of potential interest necessary for the general move away from bulk chemicals, and to identify new commercial opportunities.

Bayer, Hoechst, Ciba-Geigy, ICI and Montedison, for instance, all underwent (major or minor) restructuring from the mid-1970s to early 1980s. In the case of Bayer, investment in life sciences was increased from 30 % to 57 % of R&D from 1970 to 1988. Re-orientation led ICI to increase the share of its turnover in fine chemicals from 40 % to 52 % between 1982 and 1986, with a corresponding decrease in bulk chemicals, plastics, fibres and petrochemicals. The Italian firms Enichem and Montedison did not so much initiate a re-orientation as a major upheaval in the early 1980s (and again in 1989). The Montedison group sold almost all its petrochemical and bulk chemical activities to the public company ENI while the remaining Nuovo Montedison has reinvested in high value added activities [11].

Among the exploratory activities mentioned, were investigations into biotechnology at quite an early stage. For example, Bayer had a small molecular biology group at Wuppertal in the 1970s. ICI created a Bioscience Group in its Corporate Research Laboratories in 1976. Ciba-Geigy in 1975 created molecular biology and human and plant cell biology groups at the FMI in Basel, an independent foundation almost entirely financed by the company in exchange for the first option on commercial exploitation of its results. Montedison had research groups at its Istituto Donegani and the CNR Genetic Engineering Research Centre in Pavia [9]. These small groups acted as pressure groups within the firms, making central R&D management aware of the commercial opportunities of biotechnology, and arguing for links with external sources of the new technology.

Despite these explorations in the 1970s, the established firms did not make their first serious investments in third generation biotechnology until the early 1980s, when the establishment of DBFs was already at its high point. Had they relied entirely on in-house R&D and building up the new capability from scratch, the established firms would have had to make the commitment of investing in new facilities and recruiting staff in a very wide range of disciplines in what was a quite distinct area from their traditional knowledge base, and this with no clear idea at that stage which ones (if any) they would wish to pursue further. Instead, they made alliances with external sources of the new technology (academic researchers and DBFs) which was not only a lower risk strategy than building up the necessary competences, but also a faster one.

In-house technological strengths of the chemical companies have always been supplemented by "many linkages to external sources of scientific and technological information and ideas as well as to markets, user experience and production" (Freeman 1990, see note 1). But, in establishing close R&D linkages with small firms as well as academics, the chemical and pharmaceutical firms were essentially **breaking with established practice**. Traditionally they funded projects at the "research" end of the R&D spectrum in the public sector and had relationships with other commercial organisations based on licensing and/or contracting out R&D at a later stage of product development, e.g. toxicity testing (Faulkner, 1989).

The established firms provided a significant slice of finance for the DBFs in the form of venture capital/equity investment and research funding. Equity investment of $119 million was made by established firms in 1982 (OTA, 1984), as part of the collaborative agreements through which technological knowledge was made available to them. In some cases European companies opened laboratories in the USA for closer interaction with the scientific infrastructure there. For example, Bayer bought 40 % of Molecular Diagnostics' equity in 1982 and in 1984 created Molecular Therapeutics which was wholly owned, both in New Haven Science Park. Ciba-Geigy created its Agrobiotech Research Centre in North Carolina and established cooperative research agreements with various DBFs [11].

Table 18.1   Commercial Biotechnology Investments in 1989

	From Europe	From USA	From Japan	From others
To Europe				
Start up	TM Innovation Immunology Ltd Biocon, Genset Duclos Fermentech Serono (Spain) Scottish Beef Dev. Bioresearch Ireland Knoll, MOC Tech		PGS British Biotechnology AGC	
Corporate	Inov Elf Biotech. Inv. Finbiotec, ICI	Johnson & Johnson Smith Kline G D Searle	Chugai Japan Tobacco	
To USA				
Start Up	Genentech Cultor/Kodak Bissendorf Peptide Incstar Separex DNA Plant Tech. Cytel Karo Bio	Integr. Gen. Genzyme, Ingene Viragen, Xoma La Jolla Pharma Cy. Oncogenetics CT Biosciences Metabolic Biosys. Epicor, Transgene Receptech Athena Neurosciences Affymax, Mimesys Cent. for Innov. Techn. Delphi Biovent. Biolistics, Genecor Bioscience, Epicor Agridiagnostics Infergene	Native Plants Inc. Mycogen	.../...

	From Europe	From USA	From Japan	From others
To USA				
.../... Corporate	Wacker-Chemie Hoffman-La- Roche BASF, Schering Bayer Organics Intern.	State Farm Fritzsche Dodge 3i. D. Blech Boston University Delco, Upjohn Paine Webber Equity Tr. IO Publishing D.M. Blair, Mercon Labs. Calgene, Gen- Probe Cartel Acquisitions	Kaken Chugai Kubota Sumitomo Chemicals Japan Tobacco	USSR Acad. of Sciences Institut Merieux (Can.)
To Japan				
Start Up			Daiichi Seed Plantech Sumitomo Metal Bionks MT Science Co. Ltd.	
Corporate			Toray, Mitsubishi Izaki Glico Sumitomo, Mitsui Sanyo Chemical Dowa Mining Nippon Roche .../...	

	From Europe	From USA	From Japan	From others
To others				
Start Up	Connaught (Canada) Unipharm (USSR) Biotech. Austr.	Un. Biot. Lab (China) Cibran (Brazil)		Gene Shears (Austr.) Pacific Biotech. (Austr.) Vepex (Hungary) Unicorn Biotech. (India) Hong Kong Inst. Biotech.
Corporate				Cortecs (Austr.) Wheat Pool (Canada) Apotex (Canada)

Source : SAGB (1990), Economic Benefits and European Competitiveness, Senior Advisory Group, Biotechnology, Conseil Européen des Fédérations de l'Industrie Chimique

A new phase in strategy

The interactive learning stage continued until the late 1980s [12], when a new phase emerged, in which longer term technology strategies were developed towards biotechnology. Established firms which had developed a competence in diagnostics, enzymes and reagents - products with commercial potential in the short term - consolidated their position as did firms which had developed pharmaceutical applications such as human insulin, interferon, interleukins and human growth hormone, while also using biotechnology as an important tool for basic research in pharmaceuticals. However, firms which had pursued agricultural opportunities (which turned out to be much longer term and more risky commercial propositions), like Bayer and Hoechst, reduced their biotechnology investments in this area to that of maintaining "windows on opportunity", and reinforced their positions in traditional agrochemicals. On the other hand, some (e.g. Ciba-Geigy, ICI) which had acquired positions in the seeds market and skills in (traditional) plant breeding as well as competences in relevant areas of biotechnology, invested strongly in R&D in this area. Priorities for investment (as opposed to monitoring) were distinguished by the established firms. They redefined their overall efforts in terms of skills and expertise to be deployed, and they selected areas of R&D to be internalised. Biotechnology moved away from centralised units in firms and became more integrated into the product divisions [11]. Investments in DBFs and corporate R&D are shown in Table 18.1, according to source and destination of finance (Europe, USA or Japan). Table 18.2 lists the biotechnology areas in which leading European firms had investments by 1990.

Table 18.2   Main area of investment in biotechnology by some
European firms, 1990

Firms	Therapeutics	Diagnost	Agrochem	Seed	Fine Chemical
Bayer	X		X	X	
Sandoz	X	X	X	X	X
ICI	X	X	X	X	X
Akzo	X	X			
Ciba-Geigy	X	X	X	X	
H. La Roche	X	X			X
BASF	X				
Rhone-P.	X	X		X	
ELF-Sanofi	X			X	X
Glaxo	X	X			
Giest B.	X				X
Novo-N.	X	X			X
Enimont	X	X		X	
N. Montedison	X	X			

Source : Annual Reports and interviews with firms

Once the established firms started making serious investments in in-house biotechnology R&D, they were able to devote far more resources to it than even the largest DBFs. As soon as they were able to see clearly which areas of biotechnology were going to be vital to their future business activities (and which were not), they began to build up this in-house capability. One important way of doing so quickly was to buy a biotechnology firm, possibly one with which they already had collaborative links and therefore knowledge of its competences. Table 18.3 lists acquisitions of American DBFs by established European firms in their end-user industries. Collaborative alliances depend on the needs of both partners. When large firms no longer needed access to a DBF's knowledge base, the reason for the collaboration vanished. Acquisitions and in-house R&D in areas with established commercial potential have become the order of the day, while collaborative agreements continue to be established in new areas of uncertainty. Hagedoorn and Schackenraad (1990) show an increase in biotechnology alliances to the mid-1980s, followed by a levelling off and a decline while our own data (Walsh *et al.*, 1991) also shows a relative decline in alliances and an increase in mergers, acquisition and equity purchase in the late 1980s.

Table 18.3 Acquisitions of North American companies by European firms

Year	Purchaser	Acquired firm	Area
1986	BP Nutrition (UK)	Edwards J Funk & Sons	Plant genetics
1987	Glaxo (UK)	Biogen	Therapeutics
1987	Montedison (IT)	Plant Cell Res Inst	Plant genetics
1987	Ferruzzi (IT)	CPC Int	Plant genetics
1987	Pharmacia (Swe)	Electro-Nucleonics	Diagnostics
1987	SDS Biotech (Swe)	Techamerica	Therapeutics
1988	Novo Industri (DK)	Zymogenetics	Therapeutics
1988	Biodor (Swi)	Calbiochem	Speciality chemicals
1988	Ciba-Geigy (Swi)	Cooper	Therapeutics
1988	H La Roche (Swi)	*Biogen	Research
1989	Bissendorf (Ger)	Biosciences	Diagnostics
1990	Porton Int (UK)	Hazelton Labs	Reagents
1990	Inst Merieux (Fr)	Connaught Biosci	Therapeutics
1990	Hoechst (Ger)	Gene Trak Systems	Diagnostics
1990	Cultor (Fin)/ Eastman Kodak (US)	Genencor	Therapeutics
1990	H La Roche (Swi)	Genentech	Therapeutics
1990	Schering AG (Ger)	Codon	Therapeutics
1990	Schering AG (Ger)	Triton	Therapeutics

* Division only

Source : compiled by authors from various sources

V Conclusions

All the chemical, pharmaceutical and agribusiness firms which adopted biotechnology were highly globalised in all the senses generally understood by the term (OECD, 1992b). They exported worldwide, had subsidiaries in a great many countries, manufacturing as well as marketing their products. They were able to act as centres of finance capital and cross subsidise activities in one market with profits from another. However, their approach to the new field of biotechnology was not typical of their global (or globalisation) strategies. The moves towards merger and acquisition on the one hand, and the building up of in-house R&D and production capability on the other, were late ones in this field. Their first move was to establish small central research groups whose role was exploratory basic research and identification of business opportunities. Their second move was a learning strategy based on collaborative alliances with specialist biotechnology firms. Although many of these alliances crossed national boundaries, this was a relatively new strategy rather than a continuation of the trend of increases in "conventional" globalisation. The third stage was undertaken once some of the uncertainty had been reduced, and when both commercial opportunities and less promising areas had been identified (and the latter abandoned) : increased in-house R&D, merger and acquisition, and more conventional alliances with academics (for which the learning phase had enabled them to be more specific and selective).

It might at first seem that the established firms' clinging on to their old paradigms when new entrants were introducing potentially competence destroying new paradigms would put them at a disadvantage. But it was transformed into an advantage [13]. They did not generate a new wave of innovation as a result of their accumulated in-house skills in the way described by Pavitt (1991). But they did use these accumulated competences to shape their selection environments, and to negotiate collaborative agreements which gave them access to the new knowledge. In their learning processes, the development of large firms' capacities for exploiting the new technology was based as much on their ability to appropriate exogenous knowledge as it was based on their own R&D. Indeed, in some senses it could be argued that the new entrants' skills and knowledge in the new technological paradigm were not, after all, really competence destroying. To be competence destroying in Schumpeter's sense ("gales of creative destruction"), they would have had to be combined with the necessary complementary skills, technologies and assets.

Innovation literature [14] suggests that firms' technological resources and performance can shape market structure as well as vice versa (Metcalfe & Boden, 1992). In this case, the new technological resources appeared outside existing market structures, but the established firms' technological competences and market power proved strong enough to absorb it.

The established firms therefore maintained their existing markets, innovated in a lower risk way, and moved into new markets. When they began to acquire DBFs, they contributed to the generation of more concentrated market structures. They acted as "nets" in both senses of the word, as described by Chesnais (1986): they established international networks of horizontal and vertical flows of finance and other inputs, intermediates, finished products and information ; and they acted as nets in which to catch, appropriate and exploit all kinds of productive resources, inputs and information. Large firms thus maintained their dominant role and in many cases prevented the autonomous development of the independent firms.

Notes

1   "Technical Innovation in the world Chemical Industry and Changes of Techno-Economic Paradigm", in Freeman and Soete (eds), 1990.

2   Strictly speaking, biotechnology is the commercial processing of materials by biological agents. It therefore includes some of the earliest, pre-capitalist activities such as brewing (1st generation biotechnology) ; and the development of large-scale industrial capabilities for microbial production of antibiotics in the 1940s (2nd generation biotechnology) ; as well as the applications of monoclonal antibody and recombinant DNA techniques (3rd generation biotechnology) made since the mid-1970s. For the purposes of this paper, however, biotechnology is taken to mean 3rd generation biotechnology.

3   There is now a substantial literature on inter-firm agreements. Major theoretical and empirical studies reported in the literature include Teece (1986, 1988), Chesnais (1988b), Mowery (1989), Mariti (1990), Katz and Ordover (1990), Pisano (1990), Hagedoorn & Schakenraad (1990a) and Mytelka (1991), and OECD (1992b, chap. 3).

4   For example, the Senior Advisory Group on Biotechnology is made up of senior executives seconded from the major European chemical and other firms affected by biotechnology, whose job is, among other things, to lobby the European Parliament and European Commission about regulations and policies likely to affect their interests.

5   A survey of 43 UK firms formed after 1974 and independent at formation was carried out by the author together with colleagues Ray Oakey, Wendy Faulkner and Sarah Cooper. This was almost the total population of such firms that we were able to identify. Full details of the study appear in Oakey *et al.* (1990). Thanks are due to the UK ESRC-SERC Joint Committee for financial support.

6   Amin and Dietrich (1991), "From Hierarchy to Hierarchy : the Dynamics of Contemporary Corporate Restructuring", in Amin, A., and Dietrich, M. (eds) (1991).

7   See *Chemical and Engineering News*, 1 April 1991.

8   See Zagor, K.,"Rubbish industry Smells New Profit", *The Financial Times*, London, 29th May 1991.

9   See Davies-Gleizes, F., "US Cleans Up Europe's Act", *The European*, 17 May 1991.

10   See Lord Sainsbury, Report of the Committee of Inquiry into the Relationship of the Pharmaceutical Industry with the National Health Service, Cmnd. 3410. London : Her Majesty's Stationery Office.

11 A second study carried out by the authors with Jas Gill, Albert Richards and Yogesh Sharma, and funded by the EC-FAST Programme as part of its report on Globalisation of Technology and Economies (Walsh *et al.*, 1991), consisted of : i) A survey of the large European firms involved in Biotechnology with in-depth interviews in 8 of them. This paper draws heavily on this information ; ii) Interviews with 5 major US independent biotechnology firms ; iii) Assembly and analysis of statistical material. Thanks are due to the EC-FAST Programme for funding.

12 There were differences in the strategies of firms depending on their market orientation. Multi-product firms ICI and Ciba-Geigy invested heavily in plant breeding and the seeds market. Multinationals with a stronger base in bulk chemicals took longer to enter biotechnology and investment has been less. Agri-food firms' involvement in biotechnology was relatively minor throughout the 1980s, involving a close monitoring of the technology with only small investments. Pharmaceutical specialists (e.g. Schering, Glaxo, Beecham and Boehringer Ingelheim), diversified fine chemicals groups with major pharmaceutical interests (e.g. Hoffmann La Roche & Sandoz) and firms with experience in second generation biotechnology, such as fermentation, single cell protein, insulin and enzymes (e.g. Novo and Nordisk in Denmark, now merged) have been relatively quick to move into biotechnology with large investments. These firms already had well-developed relevant complementary assets plus established collaborations with basic research institutions, and were able to build up their in-house capability in biotechnology more quickly than other chemical companies. The established firms were also influenced by country specific features ("National Systems of Innovation") such as the quality and organisational structure of public research systems, education systems and regulatory régimes.

13 Although they might have moved into biotechnology more slowly had it not been for the structural crisis of the industry which coincided with the emergence of the new paradigm.

14 See Teece *et al.* (1990), *Metcalfe and Boden 1992* and also Coombs, R., Saviotti, P., and Walsh, V., "Technology and the Firm : the Convergence of Economic and Sociological Approaches ?", in Coombs *et al.* (eds), op. cit.

19 Small and medium-sized firms in markets with substantial scale and scope economies

Paolo Mariti

1   Introduction

Some of the main current conditions shaping global markets are said to be : (i) homogenisation of consumer tastes for final goods implying price and quality advantages of large size and long production runs ; (ii) the existence of substantial economies of scope ; (iii) increased price sensitivity of buyers of raw materials and industrial goods under pressure to keep their costs as low as possible [1]. However a number of other trends are apparent as well : (i) rising standards of living that allow people to indulge in their tastes for variety, quality and novelty, for aesthetics, for social distinction ; (ii) a resurgence and strengthening of regional and local differences in tastes ; (iii) a request from industrial buyers for greater specialisation in the supply of intermediate goods, machinery and industrial services ; (iv) technological developments leading to smaller operational scales. Small firms cannot affect globalisation trends and indeed their main passive strategy should be to avoid any direct attempt to compete globally. Their main active strategy should instead be to evaluate carefully those other trends and squeeze the best out of them. This chapter is directed towards spotting some of the benefits and risks of a number of alternative courses of action that could be taken by small and medium-sized firms in such mixed contexts.

II   Reasons for coexistence of small and global businesses

Even though both static and dynamic economies of scale exist in relation to a given production, this market may not in reality be dominated by a global firm for several reasons : (i) economies of scale can often be fully exploited also at levels of output that represent only a small share of total market demand ; (ii) the competitive relevance of unit cost advantages is largely established by the cost reduction rate, which may be such as to grant competitiveness even operating at a scale significantly smaller than the most efficient one and/or with short production runs ; (iii) in some markets demand expands rapidly - as in the case of geographic areas under economic integration or previously separated by transportation costs, tariff and non-tariff barriers - and this makes new entries and survival profitable for small firms ; (iv) there is also a strong tendency in modern industrial systems towards the development of so-called "decentralising technologies" that make possible economic production with smaller capital outlays, thereby stimulating entry of new smaller firms and the restructuring of existing ones [2] ; (v) customers, and especially industrial buyers, may act to maintain alternative sources of supply to avoid the exploitation of monopsonistic power.

There is empirical evidence that small firms can compete successfully with only a few firms even in the presence of substantial economies of scale in their trades [3]. Of course they would not be able to tackle large firms in motor-cars, motor-cycles, aeroplanes, bulk chemicals, cosmetics, consumer electronics, breakfast cereals or the like or when large economies are related to ranges of products. A three-product firm can enjoy economies of scale for each individual product, yet not enjoy economies of scope. For example, the firm runs efficiently all three plants but does not take advantage of economies of scope because its products are so different that the joint use of inputs is not feasible or marketing programmes are separate. Economies of scope imply that it is more efficient to produce two or more distinct products together rather than separately. A common inference is that if they existed, the products would be made by larger firms making a range of products thereby minimizing average costs. Other firms would be forced out of business or acquired by larger multi-product firms. One should note in the first place that only *if* markets are perfectly competitive, (i.e. absence of niche markets) this outcome is correct. Besides, empirical evidence of economies of scope conveys the impression that they are somewhat limited in the field of production [4]. Rather they seem to operate mainly in the areas of selling and marketing, especially of low priced, standard, high quality, reliable products to different countries or many geographic markets (Pratten, 1991). The suggestion is that they may be related not so much to joint production in the narrow sense of the term, but more generally to the joint exploitation of some ability of a firm or the sharing of intangible assets : the ability to market commodities may be similar in such fields as ball-point pens, safety razors, shoes, carpets, cosmetics, cameras, safari trips, etc. that require instead very different production abilities.

The implication is that although economies of scope dictate that it is efficient to market two or more products together, they do not necessarily imply that these products should be produced by a single very large firm. In short, very many conditions exist which grant market segments and niches where small and medium-sized firms can enter, survive and prosper.

III   Advantages of small and medium-sized firms over global firms

Small firms have the advantage over global firms from several points of view : (i) they are "geographically" in a better position to monitor local markets and thus to cater to local or regional differences in tastes and spot changes in them ; (ii) in sectors where fashion and style are important (clothing, garments, ornaments, but even in house building, furniture, etc.) they can make recourse to distinctive styling. Small firms appear more suited to exploit negative network externalities in consumption as implied by a "snob effect" (i.e. the increase of price insensitivity of product demand when the number of customers is kept low by a careful use of market power). They appear less apt for exploitation of positive network externalities of the kind implied by a "bandwagon effect" (i.e. the shifting of market demand at higher level for any given price as the number of adopters increases) : inducing such an effect may require high advertising costs and/or costly forward integration into marketing and retailing ; (iii) they may have greater flexibility (Carlson, 1989). With marginal (and thus average costs) increasing less steeply in response to a change in output beyond a range around the level at which total unit costs are minimised, they are more willing to react and can react faster to erratic fluctuations in market demand, as is the case with custom designed products - including many industrial goods - and with sudden changes in tastes.

Some current developments in manufacturing flexibility granted by Computer Integrated Manufacturing (CIM) however, seem to provide a technological solution to flexibility problems. These techniques imply in general substantial investments, often of a rather specific type. Thanks to them, larger businesses can quickly change products on the assembly line and fill different market segments or niches at the same time and at lower costs than small specialized firms. Flexible manufacturing techniques could act to negate some of the advantages of small firm flexibility and reduce its scope. With reference to Japan, there is however some support for the idea that CIM may in fact be restricted to single applications, though important, to solve specific production problems (Pracentini, 1990).

IV   Risks of a niche strategy in global markets

A niche strategy, usually recommended for small firms, has two interrelated aims : product differentiation within the selected niche and/or cost leadership. It is not without risks however : (i) it is true that niche firms can often prosper because of regional or national loyalties, but differentiation advantages offered may be eroded by price disadvantages. More generally differentiation advantages offered may not be sufficient even in the medium term to overcome price disadvantages. There are always buyers on the margin progressively switching towards surrogates or alternative sources of supply ; (ii) present day shortening of product and technological life cycles may create an additional "R&D trap". Some small firms try to capitalise on their technological advantage with new products in reasonably high-technology sectors or with early products. They normally imply the production of low-volume high-value products requiring long-term and continued R&D efforts to keep up with developments. However focusing on too narrow a niche, given the rapidly changing scientific and technical environment, may require ever increasing resources to devote to R&D. Though in a framework of basically non-price competition, small firms may run into difficulties in funding them. Global firms may be interested in small firms' technology achievements and try to acquire them. The strategy is sounder however if the firm aims at establishing, or becoming itself, a specialized service company (Daly, 1985) ; (iii) attempts to achieve greater economies of scale to face price competition in established or late products may create a "distribution trap" owing to required costly forward integration ; the same trap may exist in the case of small firms with knowledge and competence dealing with high-technology products, but lacking skill and experience in marketing and commercialisation (Walsh, this volume) ; (iv) firms comparable in size may enter the niche market through sheer imitation or cheap substitutes ; (v) last but by no means least, the niche is not well protected (see section V below) and a global firm, seeing how successful the small one is, spans the niche demand.

V   Conditions for "safe" niche markets

Some of the necessary conditions for the existence of segments and niche markets were dealt with in section II above. What are the strong conditions that make a niche strategy truly safer ? In broad terms, niches should be large enough to make reaching significant economies of scale possible, but such that global firms will not want to fill the niche. Reasons why a leading global firm might not want to fill a niche are : (i) the niche is too small and to conquer it would not significantly increase the dominant firm's overall efficiency or its market share ; (ii) the niche is large enough but it is so well protected by local legislation, trade barriers, transportation costs, local tastes, habits or others, that it would be too costly to conquer it. More generally, the effects of lower prices and/or the extra marketing costs of squeezing out a number of small and medium-sized firms could prove prohibitive ; (iii) the specific products would detract from its market lines and/or from its overall reputation or image. A leader in disposable items may thus be uninterested in non-disposable ones, or a leader in a high priced line may not want to fill a low priced line (and vice versa).

VI How to manage some other limits of niche strategy

As to R&D, large firms with many different projects have scale advantages when externalities or spillovers are widespread. Small firms will not be at a disadvantage when technology is advanced and only if they deal with small-scale research projects directed at the particular problems of that industry. In other words, the rate of technological advance in the niche should not prevent smaller firms from keeping up. The best market for R&D purposes is one where the small firms can invest in enough R&D to prevent entry by imitators, but where the costs of R&D are not too much for small firms. An example of a good market : a given country language computer software ; a bad example : English language general purpose software for IBM PCs.

For sound product differentiation small firms should look carefully at after sales requirements. Many products such as consumer durables, machinery and the like require significant after sales servicing and other types of support. Furthermore, many service industries are typically characterised by the indivisibility involved in diagnosing a problem (you need one person physically present to do it) ; it would be inefficient - and costly for the customer - if that unit were unable to solve a wide range of problems. (A case in point is provided by a plumbing firm that should be able to handle a wide variety of plumbing services ranging from installation to repair of central heating systems as well as bathtubs, showers, sinks, etc.)

This leads to a more general point. Service industries are by their very nature less inclined to be acquainted with very large economies than manufacturing industries. However the global firm is at a disadvantage, since the labour required to produce the service will not be appreciably less. Customers are furthermore likely to prefer local firms providing the service directly (office and house cleaning,) and would prefer to come into contact with familiar people (personal services). Besides, if a global firm happens to develop a dominant strategy, or a better way of performing the service, it should be easy to imitate by local firms since this improvement can not be patented.

When supplying some part of the product line or input to a global firm, it is important not to allow such a firm to believe that it could after a time make the input or product cheaper itself. This can be done through step-by-step or continuous product advancements and the exploitation of learning.

VII   Other lines of action

Other main actions available to small firms to strengthen or exploit their niche strategy in global markets are : (i) exports ; (ii) direct investment ; and (iii) cooperative agreements.

Exports are traditionally made by using a wholesaler in the host country to reach retailers or consumers. The main advantages are : low cost ; low financial commitment ; few barriers to exit ; low organisational requirements and above all the possibility to export to many countries at one time. However, the firm has little control over price, product presentation to the consumer and after sales servicing. Foremost, contacts with customers are mediated through the wholesaler and these may impede early spotting of changes in tastes and shifting demands. This may turn out to be a poor alternative for a policy largely based on product differentiation.

Direct investment abroad, particularly when building a plant, has several advantages. The firm can preserve control over price, product presentation to the consumer and after sales servicing and it is able to monitor directly local market changes thanks to close contact with consumers. Production abroad is a frequently sought after advantage because it provides safe protection against changes in currency values for product costs, though of course not for repatriated profits. Other interesting advantages are : the exploitation of concessions offered by states or regions to attract jobs and also the possibility of escaping from protectionism since tariffs do not apply to inland production. Over and above capital requirements and management time constraints (Buckley, 1989), the main disadvantages of this strategy are barriers to exit, especially if the plant is characterised by sunk costs and/or local currency has become expensive.

Cooperative agreements include joint ventures, consortia, subcontracting, long-term marketing agreements, production rationalisation agreements, equity purchase, and technology licensing. Even though there are differences, let us consider them as a whole.

Second to the niche policy, the form of policy suggested most often for small firms in global contexts is that of diversifying into other product ranges and selling to different markets. The suggestion has much appeal, but it is complicated both in terms of finding new lines and choosing between them as well as getting organised for producing and selling. A new perspective is possible if we look at a firm in terms of activities carried out instead of describing it as usual in terms of its production function only. Firms' activities may be as diverse as those relating to search and assessment of consumer wants, research and development, product design, monitoring execution and coordination of processes of physical transformation, administration, marketing of goods, searching for resources and financial means or for suppliers, transportation and delivery of goods, after sales services and so on. **Firms could thus diversify, not away from their current markets, but into the realm of their activities** by : (i) dealing with a narrower range of products but increasing activity content (e.g. after sales servicing) ; (ii) performing fewer but higher quality operations on the same range of products.

If agreements are designed carefully (and transaction costs are not high), there are specific advantages to cooperation in both directions as compared to the two transactions just mentioned [5] : (i) the opportunity to achieve full-scale economies for their distinct product(s) while preserving the economies of scope in marketing that come from having a full product line (e.g. through reciprocal buying agreements). Multiplant specialisation through direct investment could be beyond the reach of a small firm ; (ii) greater flexibility in the sense that fewer fixed commitments are necessary in assets and activities which are alien or not essential to the core of their undertakings. This in turn implies lower investment costs than direct investment with much lower exit barriers ; (iii) the opportunity to obtain up-to-date technical expertise and advice, especially when working with a large concern ; (iv) greater closeness to final markets than granted by exports and greater attention to local market conditions thanks to partner's familiarity with the local market even in distant markets. This may be crucial : in distributing faster than others, since cooperative linkages can allow a greater speed of introduction to markets in the first instance relative to direct investment ; in finding or adjusting to new markets, since local firms may be able to provide information (on trends, quality, compatibility and safety standards, etc.) about such markets not otherwise obtainable by small firms located in distant areas ; in expanding the distribution network with low investments ; in reducing the cost of advertising .

There are some aspects that may lead to unsuccessful operations and limit the scope of cooperation for small firms : (i) the sharing of proprietary technology and R&D research entails the risk that partners may use it secretly or in ways not agreed upon. Risk of spillovers to other firms is also increased. Of course contract design is critical but small firms are ill-suited for writing contracts ; in addition, it is usually very difficult even for large businesses to get full protection or to foresee future developments of the relationship. This last point reminds us of the fact that a relationship is never static and develops over time : a partner may reveal himself to be as suitable as was initially expected or may fail altogether. There are no standard and easy ways out of these problems ; (ii) profits must be shared ; (iii) formal contracts may turn out to be a barrier to exit. This is more likely when firms share too many of their activities. Small firms are well advised not to form very demanding agreements requiring deep involvement especially in terms of financial and managerial resources ; (iv) there is also the danger of clashing in the same market once the agreement is over. This situation is more likely to occur when according to the agreement each firm must sell the other's products while introducing a series of technical adaptations and modifications which make them suitable for a market. This may provide part of the explanation why horizontal agreements are rare.

Notes

1   See, among others, Ballance (1987).

2   These new technologies are to be found principally in new forms of materials (plastics, "high performance" composites, new forms of concrete), new ways of creating power (batteries) and new ways of employing electronics. See Blair (1972).

3   See Pratten (1991), chapt. 6 ; and Nguyen *et al.* (1991).

4   See Bailey and Friedlaender (1982). As an instance, Friedlaender *et al.* (1982) have estimated a multi-product cost function for each of the four US auto makers on the hypothesis that costs depend on prices of various inputs and on the group of outputs such as small cars, large cars and trucks. One of their findings is that no economies of scope arise from producing trucks together with small and large cars.

5   For an expanded analysis, some bibliography and references to empirical evidence see my paper Mariti (1990).

20 Small firms facing globalisation in R&D activities. Lessons from case studies of Spanish small firms

Jaume Valls

I Introduction

Following Spain's EEC entry, the Spanish economy has gone through a series of far-reaching changes to become one of Europe's most dynamic economies. A policy of strong support from foreign investment together with the declining importance of traditional sectors has resulted in industry's growing dependence on decisions taken by multinational companies. The experience of small and medium-sized enterprises (SMEs) has varied widely depending on the industry involved. Those industries which are strongly internationalised (for example chemicals and pharmaceuticals) have experienced difficulties and the question facing many of the more competitive companies is often whether to sell out or to hold out. The expectations generated by a high growth economy and the multinationals' interest in obtaining distribution networks and strategic positions in Southern Europe has produced substantial changes in industry over the last few years.

These changes have had a strong impact on company behaviour as far as technology is concerned. However there is as yet little data and analysis available on the impact of these changes [1]. This chapter sets out the results of a group of case studies on R&D activity in SMEs in Catalonia. These cases are analysed in an attempt to reveal various general trends in company behaviour regarding R&D and, in particular, the means adopted to strengthen R&D and to give it an international dimension as a way to remain competitive. This chapter tries to provide an insight into the difficulties which SMEs face in internationalising/globalising their R&D activities ; to identify company strengths and weaknesses, and to determine the role played by government policies in this respect.

II   The context

In 1983 the ratio of R&D expenditure to GDP was just 0.47 %, putting Spain near the bottom of the OECD ranking in terms of technological effort. One of the government's objectives was to boost the level of Spanish technology. The government concentrated on putting an innovation policy into gear while devoting much greater resources to R&D. From the middle 1980s onwards a variety of factors began to make a big impact on the nation's industry and its level of technology. On the one hand, Spain began a period of higher economic growth and was beginning to emerge from its industrial crisis, on the other hand, Spain became a full member of the EEC in January 1986. The Science Law was also passed in the same year. This law gave rise to the subsequent National Research Plan which began in 1988. Another notable development was the University Reform Law. The impact of these changes on R&D in Spain was as follows :

(i)   Spanish EEC entry meant that companies could now consider participation in EEC research programmes. In addition, the votes and participation of new members (Spain and Portugal) were seen by existing EEC members as a means of lobbying for the approval of particular projects. In addition, companies now had access to a new source of R&D support, giving them a further incentive to internationalise their research.

(ii)   The National Research and Development Plan set new priorities, permitting publicly-owned research centres and universities to draw up and implement projects which were generally much larger than those hitherto in practice. Moreover, the plan provided incentives for collaboration between the private and public sectors (the latter comprising public research centres and universities), particularly in the fields of basic and applied research.

(iii) The University Reform Law made university links with the outside world easier and more flexible, removing the legal obstacles to such collaboration and permitting teaching staff to receive payment for their work on joint private-public projects. This, together with the subsequent creation of Technology Transfer Centres (CCTs) in the Universities, made company/university links in general and company/university R&D links in particular far more dynamic and market-oriented.

These changes have taken place over a very short period and in this respect (as has occurred in other countries) training, technical scientific know-how, and carrying out R&D have increasingly been recognised as important factors in achieving growth and competitiveness. The introduction of the National Research and Development Plan has meant an important infusion of funds (to the order of 57,000 million Pesetas for the 1988-1990 period). One should note the increase in the CDTI's (Centre For Industrial Technological Development) funding of low or zero interest loans for innovation purposes, and the Ministry of Industry's sectorial subsidies for modernisation. The Ministry of Industry provides financial support for the R&D stage through their Plans for Technological and Industrial Measures (PATI). The ministry also covers the gap between R&D and innovation by providing subsidies for plant and infrastructure in particular sectors. This policy of support for innovation has been complimented by regional governments' policies in supporting services and infrastructure. In so far as real services are concerned, the involvement of regional authorities has increased. Regional support for innovation (involving a wide range of measures) has been maintained and reinforced since the economy began to grow more rapidly and it became generally accepted that "innovative environments" have become a key factor in regional development. Figure 20.1 summarises this support for innovation and the R&D environment (which is only applicable to the most industrialised regions of Spain). The figure does not include public research bodies or the educational system.

Central government (R&D subsidies and funding)	Regional governments (infrastructure, services, information)
National R&D Plan CDTI loans Industrial Technology plans	Information services Infrastructure and technical services Support for industrial associations
Promotion and support for participation in European programmes	

Figure 20.1   The R&D support environment in Spain : main fields of regional and central government measures

III   The company sample and the methodology

An R&D study of 15 SMEs was carried out during 1991 [2]. The SMEs were independent companies (mainly from Catalonia), employing not more than 300 workers - 60 % of them employing 50 workers or less. These companies can be considered to be successful in their markets and to have expectations of international expansion or to continue existing expansion over the next few years. Six of them are international leaders. These companies have significant R&D [3] which they have begun to contract out over the last few years. This contracting out may take the form of collaboration with universities or participation in European programmes or commissioning specific, important R&D jobs to an outside company or laboratory. In some cases there is an international dimension to the R&D. However in all cases the companies concerned are interested in assessing the chances of giving their own R&D an international dimension (Escorsa and Valls, 1992). The companies' interest in technology is evidenced by the fact that : the majority have registered patents (11 out of 15) ; all of them have received public R&D support ; 14 out of 15 companies have carried out R&D with a Spanish public research centre.

Analysis of companies focuses on their technological level, their degree of openness, and their management capabilities. These parameters have been used (Figure 20.2) to evaluate the position of each company as far as internationalising its R&D is concerned [4]. Of the factors analysed, points which stand out are : company strategy ; use of public aid ; formalising the R&D team ; relationships with universities and public research centres ; the internationalisation of research ; participation in European R&D programmes.

Research potential	Openness	Management ability
Scientific level of the R&D team	Knowledge of company environment	Level of organisation (planning, quality, cost accounting...)
Capitalisation of know-how	Existing cooperation (industry, universities, services)	Initiative
Technological standards	Foreign languages	

Source : Euromanagement project (1991)

Figure 20.2   Analytical framework of R&D internationalisation capability

IV   SMEs and R&D. The path to internationalisation

Strategies

Companies which have consolidated their position and which have better prospects have invested in the quality of their products and have taken the greatest advantage of the flexibility which their size affords them. Extensive use is made of manufacturing subcontracting in all these companies. Likewise, in six cases the companies do not keep stock, instead they work on an order only basis, and have adopted modern production planning techniques. Three companies have adopted a technology cluster strategy, oddly enough without having explicitly formulated the concept beforehand.

In other words, they have entered new fields over the last few years thanks to technologies which they had already mastered. They have tended to take maximum advantage of different applications and products which have been made possible by their technological capabilities.

As far as markets are concerned, it is interesting to note that for the 4 biggest exporters in sales volume terms, the South American market is a very important one. This is because South America is one of the few cases where Spain has a clear-cut technological advantage. The fact that they have begun to tackle the European market is a measure of the level of expertise which these companies have acquired. In these 4 cases the companies have managed to penetrate successfully the German market. In the chemical and metallurgical/industrial plant sectors such penetration would appear to confer a certain cachet as far as excellence is concerned. Small and medium-sized enterprises clearly consider this market entry as a sign of the quality and technological level which they have reached.

Use of public R&D aid

In Spain the number of companies availing themselves of public aid has grown considerably over the last few years. The resources set aside by the government have increased along with the interest demonstrated by companies in modernising their operations and carrying out research. The data shows very significant increases in the volume of subsidised loans provided by CDTI [5]. Despite the frequent criticism of the red tape and bureaucratic processes involved in obtaining this aid, empirical evidence concerning innovating companies reveals that companies value this aid highly and are increasingly interested in availing themselves of it. In the case of the companies studied, all of them have received public assistance. One can say that companies with at least some real interest in R&D have benefited from one or other types of aid over the last few years. To some extent, over the last few years, R&D aid and innovation have become second nature to companies.

Case studies reveal that a particular sequence of events has become established when SMEs take up aid (Figure 20.3). SMEs often begin by making use of aid which relates to an isolated case and which does not involve complicated management. Examples of such assistance might be an energy audit or Ministry of Industry assistance for industrial equipment. The loans provided by the CDTI represent a second step in the process. In order to obtain such loans it is necessary to establish a work schedule and set objectives to be achieved as part of the R&D process. It is necessary to bring project expenditure to account (something which is relatively new and unfamiliar) and in general a certain degree of formalisation of these activities is imposed from outside the company. For SMEs which are not well versed in

R&D, reaching the goals set in their first CDTI project involves some sort of formal recognition of their R&D capability. Usually this encourages the R&D team to participate on further projects. A third level of public support is company participation in European R&D projects. The company needs a consolidated R&D team (whatever the company's size) with a tradition of research and openness wedded to proven management ability. R&D is jointly managed and hence requires international meetings and exchanges. The time-scale with respect to the market goes beyond the short term. Participation in the EUREKA programme has been taken as an example. Participation in the programme has been strongly supported by the Ministry of Industry and one can say that a EUREKA project could be considered as a CDTI project with a European dimension [6].

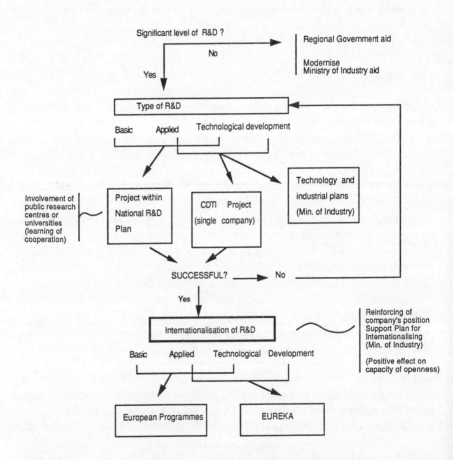

Figure 20.3   Public aid and internationalisation of R&D.
The Spanish case

More and more companies are following this sequence and to some extent also the progression which supports the internationalisation of R&D for the most dynamic SMEs. Of the 15 companies studied 12 companies have clearly followed this progression, even though not all of the companies currently find themselves in the same position. The sector is obviously an important conditioning factor. Thus in sectors such as industrial plants there is interest and conviction for internationalising R&D. However in sectors which are clearly high-technology fields such as biotechnology, companies do not merely show interest in internationalising R&D but perceive it as an indispensable strategic need over both short and medium terms. In two cases of high-technology companies, public assistance is considered vital as the companies are concerned with maintaining their technological position, which is based on continuous research.

The relationships between SMEs and universities/public research centres

The setting up of Technology Transfer Centres in Universities in 1987 was intended to re-launch the role of research in the universities, and forge links between university research on the one hand and industry and society at large on the other[7]. Against a background of growing collaboration between universities and companies, the participation of SMEs is still very low (Solé and Valls, 1991).

Those SMEs which have commissioned research from universities can be placed in one of two groups : first, those SMEs with a high level of excellence ; second, small companies (less than 50 employees) which have signed a collaboration agreement with a university, the project having either a low-technology content (tests, incremental development in well-established technologies) thus involving less risk and an easier learning curve or, if the overall project is high-tech, falling within the National Plan for Scientific and Technical Research. In the latter type of project, a condition for government financing is that the project is a joint venture between a public research centre and a university. In some cases it is obvious that the SME has gone into the research partnership because this implied receiving research funding.

In none of the cases studied here has any criticism been levelled at the university in connection with its level of technology[8] or because of obstacles encountered which rendered collaboration impossible. Company opinions/comments were more directed towards the problems involved in coordinating different paces of work. The results of collaboration with universities and public research centres were considered to be positive by 13 out of 14 companies.

Formalisation of the R&D team

Company relationships with university and public research centres have shown the importance of effective R&D teams and the difficulties involved in consolidating them. The greater the external contact involved, the greater the formalisation of the R&D department. Organisation is vital in order to effectively manage complex projects. The requisite management and external R&D skills have had a strong impact in this respect. In general, the inherent conflict between creativity and organisation was apparent in companies employing less than 25 employees. R&D teams comprise 3-4 people (not always employed full-time) and are used to responding quickly and producing research linked to short-term goals. Medium- and long-term research obliges them to formalise their way of working, which they do not always achieve in practice.

It is also significant that many companies have a technical department and not an R&D department. This is an old chestnut in the study of company R&D. This fact implies that such activities as quality control, time-and-motion studies, technical matters and R&D are lumped together. In this respect, especially in the smallest companies, carrying out R&D in collaboration with other countries makes it vital to formalise the R&D department combining it with the decision-making process while monitoring the R&D process itself. Formalised R&D teams occur frequently in companies with over 50 workers and this is even more pronounced in companies with over 100 employees. These companies carry out Technological Scanning, with someone responsible for systematically monitoring changes in the technological field. In this connection nearly all the companies place great importance on forging and maintaining informal relations with research centres and companies with leading technology.

Global strategies versus internationalising R&D

One of the EEC's concerns is to increase SME participation in European R&D programmes. In Spain in general and in Catalonia in particular this participation is low. However statistics show that participation in European programmes has increased in both quantitative and qualitative terms. In Catalonia the problem is that many SMEs are unreasonably concerned that such participation may mean losing their independence, sometimes compounded by an underestimation of their own capabilities. It is paradoxical that Catalonia is still considered to have a negative R&D balance in BRITE when this is the industrial technologies programme par excellence.

Experience to date of participation in European programmes makes one think that they have often provided companies with their first step in internationalising their R&D. This participation is also interesting (among other reasons) for its stimulating effect on medium- and long-term R&D ; the incorporation of companies into international research networks ; companies' assimilation of technology which involves project participation ; and learning to manage international R&D. This may well encourage a company to embark on similar projects later on and provide the company with decisive competitive advantages beyond the context of European programmes.

Up until comparatively recently SMEs seldom : contracted part of their manufacturing to other parts of the world ; had substantial R&D projects; were prepared to recruit the requisite experts wherever necessary on a worldwide scale ; were involved in international research ; exported to seventy or eighty countries. Four of the SMEs studied were, or were rapidly becoming, more substantial companies of the type just mentioned. These are SMEs which are becoming small multinationals (with between 100 and 200 employees, although less in some cases) and which have their own production facilities or sales facilities in various countries. Their market segment is very limited and the companies' aim is not to grow a great deal in size. In such cases the solid expertise gained through an aggressive marketing policy and international presence around the world appears to give them an incentive to decentralise research. The cases involved comprise companies in sectors such as metallurgy and industrial plants which have long been established in Catalonia. High-tech sectors are perhaps more difficult to identify. These are companies which, because of their size, cannot become world leaders but have managed to get among the 5-10 leading companies. They do not aim to have technology creation as their *raison d'être*. They are highly dependent on new components to incorporate into their products, and hence they need to monitor accurately technological trends. As soon as they find a new technology which they know to be reliable, they incorporate it in their products. Such companies have a strong regional base, and a higher technological level than other Spanish companies. These enterprises develop a markedly international view of markets and technologies, and thus become small multinationals [9]. There has been little study of the strategies adopted by such companies (sometimes very small) which are capable of structuring and organising themselves beyond the limits of conventional internationalisation. This is an area which needs to be studied in light of the effort being made to understand and analyse the globalisation that will take place over the next few years (amply evidenced by this book).

V   Some final remarks

Without attempting to draw general and definitive conclusions, these case studies appear to illustrate a set of phenomena concerning recent SME R&D in Spain. There is a very weak tradition of R&D in Spain. Some sectors are gradually latching on to the process of technology creation. In other cases

SMEs are modernising their technology but still lag behind in a number of areas.

SMEs with a significant R&D capability seem to share a number of features : (i) request of public assistance and attempt to take advantage of the various support measures introduced by different government bodies ; (ii) mastery of subcontracting and taking full advantage of the flexibility it provides the company. Knowing how to manage the complexity involved in having numerous suppliers of technology ; (iii) having more or less formalised technological scanning drawing on specialised services in this field ; (iv) having carried out research (with a greater or lesser technological content) in collaboration with universities or public research centres ; (v) having a significant export market (itself an indicator of competitiveness).

Every company has its own way of conducting R&D, however when public R&D is requested and used, it provides some sort of confirmation that the company concerned has reached a given technological level. The internationalisation of R&D requires a high R&D level, management capability and a certain degree of openness [10]. Receipt of public aid and carrying out research in collaboration with Spanish universities/public research centres appears to satisfy the first two points in the foregoing paragraph : level of R&D, and management capability. This is the case with the National R&D Plan or the CDTI projects. The need for openness is strongly linked to the international dimension or otherwise of the company's existing markets and the skills and training of scientific and technical staff. European programmes often are SMEs' first real experience of international R&D over more than just the short term. This again provides a certain indication of some companies' opportunities and perspectives in this respect.

The sequence set out in Figure 20.2 is not necessarily generally applicable but one should note that it is not fortuitous that the companies concerned have followed this route. Some are companies which are currently well placed to internationalise their R&D or to improve existing internationalisation, and are aware of the strategic challenges which lie behind R&D globalisation/internationalisation. The problem is that the number of companies in this position is still far too low.

In SMEs, the decentralisation of R&D activities and the participation in international - not just European - networks for technological cooperation are still in their infancy in Spain. A few SMEs have embarked on such decentralisation or are beginning to do so. This stage seems to be most viable among those companies studied which have more than 100 employees and which belong to a group of leading companies occupying a particular market niche. In those companies where R&D internationalisation is already well established, the demand for public aid lies on what one might term a fourth level. The level of support needed for them to consolidate as small multinationals has already been mentioned. Without questioning the validity of this approach, one should note a few pertinent points. Support for modernisation, R&D, and innovation may not be sufficient if the aim is to defend national SMEs and ensure that most of the share capital remains in Spanish hands. The massive entry of foreign investors prepared to buy up competitive SMEs at any price disrupts industry and puts its future at risk. Should one place more emphasis on outstanding companies in particular strategic sectors of industry ? If so, what measures should be employed ? In the context of globalisation of markets and technologies, the frequent fear expressed by companies of losing their independence makes it clear that the bases of worldwide competitiveness are in a state of rapid flux.

At the beginning of 1992 the Spanish Ministry of Industry presented their Plan for Supporting the Internationalisation of Spanish Companies, which appeared to be no more than a first stab at the issue raised above. It is expected that over $200 million will be made available this year. The plan establishes various programmes on finance, commerce, information and training to help open up companies and attain and maintain their position in international markets. It is still too early to say what the plan's impact has been, to what extent SMEs have used it, and how effective the plan's measures are. In any event, beyond any criticism of particular government measures and government industrial and technology policy, it is clear that defending the international dimension of competitive SMEs deserves particular attention from Spanish policy-makers over the next few years.

Notes

1 In the case of Catalonia, the data (Escorsa *et al.*, 1987, 1990) reveals the trend of R&D expenditure against majority shareholding. Approximately 18 % of total R&D expenditure was made by companies with a foreign majority shareholding (1984), this figure rose to 32 % in 1987 and 36 % in 1990.

2 The OECD began two projects on SMEs in 1991. One was entitled "Technological resources and competitiveness strategies in SMEs", and the other "SME access to the research system". This paper is based on data collated on that project (Solé and Valls, 1991) and on a series of technological audits carried out under the pilot scheme run by EUROMANAGEMENT of the Commission of the European Communities, DG XXIII (Escorsa and Valls, 1992).

3 The criterion adopted was that R&D expenditure represented more than 3 % of the sales figure.

4 For the sake of brevity, methodological aspects are not detailed, the emphasis being on some of the results of the case studies conducted.

5 CDTI conceded subsidised loans amounting to 1,343 million Pesetas in 1987. In 1990 this figure had grown to 6,147 millions Pesetas.

6   Ms. Revilla, Director of Technological Policy of the Ministry of Industry commented to this effect (Barnatech seminar, Barcelona, June 1990). It should be noted that Spanish companies are represented in nearly 25 % of EUREKA projects.

7   For example, the Polytechnic University of Catalonia (UPC), (of which the authors are faculty members) received the following amounts for research and services: 1988 (927 m Pesetas), 1989 (1,533 m Pesetas), 1990 (1,993 m Pesetas), 1991 (2,500 m Pesetas).

8   This refers to Catalan universities.

9   Mr Josep Torrents, the managing director of one of the companies studied (Germans Boada), described his company as a "pocket multinational company". Torrents J. (1991), "Les enteprises catalanes face au défi 1992", DESS Innovation Management, BETA ULP, Mulhouse, June.

10 The methodology employed in the Euromanagement pilot scheme is based on these three elements. The methodology was produced by the French consultants, Technofi.

21 Networking strategies for small firms coping with globalisation

Colette Fourcade

I Introduction

The transformations of the productive system have resulted in a modification of the firms' environmental conditions ; and limiting the activities of smaller businesses to a regional or local scope while raising the strategy of bigger companies to a world level would represent a completely artificial separation. We can even say that smaller businesses are now drawn to globalisation. Hence the main problem : how can smaller businesses meet the requirements of globalisation ? How will they be able to overcome their handicap in terms of access to information about markets, technologies and innovation ? Our position is to underline that the small businesses should not try to find a solution alone. The answer lies in their joining an information network. So we can say that small business strategies facing globalisation need networking strategies. We intend to study the insertion of small businesses into networks, noting the objective sought by small firms as well as the expected results. But as a preamble, it is necessary to clarify the concept of "network".

II The network concept : a tool for analysis

The concept of network, first used by sociologists and political scientists, has been frequently applied for the last ten years to research in economics and management. A generic definition views the network as "an organised combination of relationships" [1], referring to "social relationships between individuals, as well as interactions among organised groups" [2]. More specifically towards the nature and content of networks Proulx (1991) differentiates **natural** networks, also called personal (Johannisson, 1987),

functional or exchange networks (Mitchell, 1973) ; and **utilitarian** networks, as a "combination of relational paths facilitating the flow of information between specific knots". They are at once a potential and a structure : one must make a distinction between network activity, that is a circulation of flows within a relational system or **networking** ; and the structure resulting from the density of interactions or **network** (Proulx, 1991). These utilitarian networks alone represent the network concept we are concerned with here. Three main characteristics of the network concept must be underlined.

First, the network is a sphere of relations. The **nature** of the relationships involved here is varied ; the relationships generated connections : common know-how and knowledge (Planque, 1991) ; as well as specific social relationships stemming from particular sets of values and rules accepted by the network actors in a context of "studied trust" (Sabel, 1990). Of the conjunction, even symbiosis of these relationships, is born a truly utilitarian network and not just a functional network as exposed by Proulx (1991). The **organisation** of the relationships has a multiplicity of patterns : they can be **contracts** with a limited objective, for example R&D partnerships associating firms which are competing in other respects and universities (Foray, 1990) ; or yet diffusion and marketing partnerships. An intensified form of organisation is the **convention** (Planque, 1991) or, in other words, a "system of reciprocal expectations based on competences and behaviours" (Salais, 1989). Interactions between social and economic positions is a characteristic of this type of relationship (Courlet, 1992). Contracts or conventions determine network regulation.

Second, the network is a sphere of innovation. Whether one considers innovation networks specifically [3] or the diffusion of innovation through the productive system, this dimension is apparent in all thorough analyses of the network concept. For clarity's sake we will adopt here Perrin's nomenclature (1990a) which distinguishes : (i) innovation networks **fostering technology** that utilise technologies while developing them. In this first case, one can find one-company networks as well as networks of firms as they appear in organised groups of small firms. Within this framework, the network appears as a by-product of innovation ; its role consists in spreading technologies and adapting them to the needs of the actors ; (ii) innovation networks **creating technology** ; in this case, the network, used to regroup collective procedures of associations, partnerships, synergies, is capable of producing innovation (Planque, 1991). This system presupposes a widespread relational network potential which causes "a self-sustaining dynamic effect of a reticular type" (Maillat *et al.*, 1991). The very dynamics of this environment generate innovation opportunities (Crevoisier *et al.*, 1991). The structure of the network sets itself up during the "ideation" phase (Maillat *et al.*, 1991), while the notion of a new product or a new process is being born.

Third, the network is a sphere of strategies. The network is a response to the complexity of the productive process, within an enlarged technological and geographical environment. Not only does the network help produce synergies, it also helps reduce costs : the cost of indecision, of appropriation, of transactions. Concerning strategies, the network is organised according to two types of logic : (i) **the logic of valorisation**, which seeks to reduce costs and to bring synergies into play by developing network activity. This logic comes foremost, for example, in the organisation of industrial districts as well as in local development policies applied to science and/or high-technology parks ; (ii) **the logic of intent**, which makes use of the dynamics within the network to produce synergies that will eventually generate technology out of the relational resources common to all actors. Innovation networks are organised according to this logic. As an analysis category used in studying small businesses, the network concept also constitutes a strategic tool for those companies which are striving to extend their geographic and technological environment.

III   Small businesses coping with globalisation : are networking strategies the answer ?

Access to information about markets, products and technologies have become vital for businesses as exchange and technological needs tend to function on a worldwide scale. For small companies the problem of access to information is all the more acute as their means are restricted ; to adapt to these changes, networking strategies must be privileged. Two types of strategies can be considered : insertion within territorial networks or insertion within innovation networks.

Territorial networks

The study of territorial networks made up of small businesses has been recently developed, particularly relative to the industrial district. The industrial district consists of the regrouping of small businesses specialising in the same industry - including so-called "auxiliary" activities such as machinery production - all located within limited boundaries. This concept is derived from Alfred Marshall's analysis which makes of this type of organisation a determining factor of external economies [4]. These are found in principally three main forms : specialisation economies, which stem from a task sharing between firms with complementary activities and production processes ; information and communication economies springing from the co-production of non-standardised products, which can be compared to the idea of transaction costs ; and economies built on labour demand, thanks to the existence of a large pool of specialised workers. These districts have been intensively studied in Italy (Becattini, 1987 ; Pyke *et al.*, 1990), in industrialised countries (Colletis *et al.*, 1990), and in developing countries (Courlet, 1990). Their major asset is the specificity of their organisation, supported by flexible specialisation (Piore, 1990 ; Capecchi, 1990 [5]), and simultaneous relations of cooperation and competition (Brusco, 1990 [6]). The interaction between the economic, social and cultural fields commands the operation of the whole district, resulting in a strong competitive capacity on national as well as international markets (Pyke *et al.*, 1990). If we refer to the three characteristic elements of the network as a sphere of relations, innovation and strategies, it is possible to define the **strategic lines** of the territorial network organisation using the industrial district as a working model of a localised system of small businesses.

Territorial networks constitute a **sphere of relations** of great diversity : intra-industrial relations between firms within the same industry, inter-industrial relations ; these relations also facilitate the flow of technical knowledge and know-how between firms by way of alternate subcontracting and labour exchanges. The organisation of relations depends entirely upon conventions (according to Salais' meaning, see above). This organisation represents a specific system of reference which permits the ordering and control of the social organisation of districts (Courlet, 1992).

Territorial networks constitute a **sphere of innovation**, structured to exploit technologies by developing and adapting them to the needs of the network actors. In fact, these networks find their place on the technological trajectory and spread innovation however without novation. The efficiency of these networks will improve if technology progresses step by step, whereas a sudden technological breakthrough might threaten their very existence.

Territorial networks constitute a **sphere of strategies** : they bring into operation the logic of valorisation of technical know-how and of the relational assets acquired through a long learning process (Maillat *et al.*, 1991). So territorial networks can be considered as multifunctional (Planque, 1991) ; but their structure and their workings necessitate two sets of conditions : (i) conditions for networking, namely territorial proximity, i.e. all the actors must be based in a single territorial ; and familiarity with environment, i.e. they must belong to a single cultural background ; (ii) conditions for structuring the network, namely economic coherence which necessarily implies sectorial specialisation and functional diversification of the network thus requiring a minimal size suitable for its activity or critical mass (Planque, 1991) ; and cultural coherence determined by a common technological culture and sets of values that can lead to the diversification of knowledge. These multifunctional networks offer a privileged strategic option to small businesses facing globalisation given that their efficiency is the result of the whole network and not the sum total of the actions of each individual firm. But such networks are bound to be limited in time, space and type of production as illustrated by the recurring examples of the Italian industrial districts (textile and mechanical industries), the Jura crescent (clock-making, then micro-mechanics), the French Cholet area (textile industries), and the Arve valley (screw-cutting). Access to this type of network is limited. Beyond these limits, we must seek out strategies a small company could contemplate in an expanded environment.

Innovation networks

Whereas territorialised networks are multifunctional, innovation networks can be said to be monofunctional, centred on a single function or step which constitutes the innovation process (Planque, 1991) ; the very synergies of these networks are a source of innovation. A small company will find it difficult to participate in such a network because of the required technological level - only small high-tech companies are able to - and because of its transnational scope, the reach of small firms often being limited to a specific sphere of influence. The small firm is faced with dimensional confinement which causes its isolation. A way out of this isolation might be found in local innovative networks instigated by territorial authorities (Perrin, 1990b). At first local authorities set up the framework for networking : substructure, technical guidance. Functional networks are then put together : telecommunications networks, business incubators and nurseries. Finally, the true local innovative networks or utilitarian networks, evolve into "technopolitan" organisations for the purpose of developing specific potential for technological innovation, endogenous to the territory.

As a **sphere of relations** the "technopolitan" networks are characterised by a great variety of relationships and actors with many different functions. They bring together businesses, universities, public and private research laboratories, banks and local financing establishments by means of ties either in or out of the market. The study of the Montpellier area and of the creation of the Montpellier Languedoc-Roussillon Technopolis network presents us with an example of this structure. This area comprises an economic fabric essentially made up of small businesses lacking specific industrial specialisation and a common "industrial history" side by side with an important source of innovation originating from universities and research institutes. But in the past these elements remained unrelated for two reasons : on the one hand, the firms were limited by their size which kept them from seeking information from organisations outside their scope of market ; on the other hand, most research laboratories were working on fundamental research programmes which hardly concerned business interests, certainly not smaller ones. Under these circumstances, small businesses were incapable of integrating a territorial network, further, more innovative networking was non-existent ; it did not then seem possible to consider the emergence of a networking strategy. It is the local authority, in other words the Montepellier district, which is going to give the initial impulse to the inception of a networking organisation by means of two types of proceedings ; first, facilitation of the flow of information by connecting the local actors to public or semi-public collective networks such as ANVAR, CRITT, ARIST ; then helping to create or strengthen small innovative companies by way of "stopgap actors" such as the European Centre for Business and Innovation or the Cap Alpha nursery.

As a **sphere of innovation**, the "technopolitan network" belongs to the category of networks that foster and develop technologies. Its aim is to make use of the innovating abilities of the network members, relying mostly on technology transfers. The Montpellier technopolis has thus decided to focus on five "spearheads of proficiency", commanding its "leading resources" (Marchesnay, 1991) : bio-medical and pharmaceutical research (Euromedicine), robotics and artificial intelligence (Informatique), tropical and Mediterranean agro-industry (Agropolis). Though their objective is the spread of innovation among local firms, principally the smaller ones, "technopolitan networks", it is to be noted, are not closed to outside influence and synergies are not restricted to only local actors. Members of the network, such as universities or research laboratories, already function within other innovation networks, monofunctional and international. The "technopolitan network" draws direct or indirect benefits from these connections through what one could call cross-networking synergies. The local innovative network thus enables small companies to come out of their isolation towards innovation, giving them access by way of inter-network connections, to a technological background far beyond the scope of their native territory.

As a **sphere of strategies**, such networks bring into operation a logic of valorisation and open the door to the integration and even creation - as in the Montpellier area - of the local socio-economic structure. They also express the logic of intent of local authorities to help develop a favourable environment, nurturing the growth of activity in the area : such is the aim of the "technopolitan" strategy. It is to be noted that within territorial networks like industrial districts, local authorities have also recently stepped in to help the connection between local networks and innovation networks. Their strategy is to connect local networks to larger extra-territorial innovation networks to ensure the permanence of the district and to avoid its eventual failure. Inversely economic and cultural coherence, which is a capital instrument for the integration of innovation when technology progresses step by step, can cause the collapse of the industrial district in the case of a major technological breakthrough, a risk not to be neglected. The logic of intent practised by local authorities also has its limits. It is quite possible to create a frame favourable to networking, though the territory has to be hand-picked ; it is conceivable to stimulate relations between actors by paving the way for contracts. But there is no way to impose conventions : here technopolitan policies find their limits. They can induce networking, but not the instantaneous creation of a network. A network is a construction that needs to be rooted in time. "Technopolitan networks", just like innovation networks or territorial networks are historical phenomena.

IV Conclusion

The network as an analysis concept is the key to the investigation into strategies of adaptation available to smaller firms confronted with the globalisation of their productive and marketing environment. The network is not only an analysis concept, it is also a strategic tool. As a matter of fact, a networking strategy is the only option for small units seeking to be competitive and well informed. But however necessary, the network system is not a universal remedy. Networks are always undergoing changes and if modification in one of their component parts or outside pressure may contribute to their evolution, there is always the possibility of their bringing about the failure of the networking structure. Finally, one must not forget the number of factors that determine the existence of a network and, more particularly the historical element, which limits the efficiency of support policies in setting up "technopolitan networks" : at twenty, a technopolis is barely of age ...

Notes

[1] Definition from Szarka, J. (1989), "Networking and Small Firms", *International Small Business Journal*, 8, 2.

[2] Definition from Melin, L. (1987), "The Field-of-Force Metaphor : a Study in Industrial Change", *International studies of Management and Organisation*, XVII, 1.

[3] Consideration widely adopted, for instance by Gordon, R. (1990), "Systèmes de production, réseaux industriels et régions : les transformations dans l'organisation sociale et spatiale de l'innovation", *Revue d'Economie Industrielle*, n° 51 ; or GREMI (1992), *Nouvelles formes d'organisation industrielle : réseaux d'innovation et milieux locaux*, Maillat, D. and Senn, L. (eds), EDES, Neuchâtel.

[4] See Zeitlin, J. (1990), *Industrial Districts and Local Economic Regeneration : Models, Institutions and Policies*, International Conference, IILS, Geneva, October.

5   Piore, M. (1990), "Work, Labour and Action : Work Experience in a System of Flexible Production", and Capecchi, V. (1990), "A History of Flexible Specialisation and Industrial Districts in Emilia Romagna", both in Pyke, F. *et al.* (eds) (1990).

6   Brusco, S. (1990), "The Idea of the Industrial District : its Genesis", in Pyke, F. *et al.* (eds) (1990).

22 Emerging global strategies in innovation management

Jeremy R. Howells

I   Introduction

This chapter focuses on how firms, particularly large firms, are seeking to deal with the innovation process in a global context. A major conceptual framework that has dominated conceptualisation of this process in the past has been the product life cycle model. The product life cycle model, stemming from the "law of industrial growth" and "filter-down" models, is associated with three stages of production, where manufacturing capacity will shift from innovating markets to foreign markets as products move into a "mature" phase of their life cycles (see for example Vernon, 1966). A number of studies have suggested that Research and Development (R&D ; or at least the development side of R&D) may follow this pattern of internationalisation, although lagging the production phase. However, leaving aside the considerable (if not insurmountable) inconsistencies and problems associated with the product life cycle model, the model itself provides an explanation of why multinationals do not shift their research abroad. As Vernon (1977, pp. 41-45) notes, the need in the early stages of the major technological work is to coordinate scientific, engineering planning, financial and marketing activities and to keep a close watch on expensive and high risk investments, this will induce both the R&D functional and its initial implementation in production to be kept at home. According to the model, by the time this phase is over and overseas production is planned, research and technology inputs associated with the product will have fallen to such a level that additional R&D capacity abroad will not be required. However, as Lall (1979, pp. 319-320) notes, the product life cycle model is concerned with national firms (a priori) starting out with a new product rather than (existing) multinationals (a posteriori) which have a stream of products being marketed abroad.

Whilst the product life cycle model may have been representative of what occurred in the innovation process in many large multinationals up to the mid-1960s, it has become increasingly less applicable thereafter. With the increased internationalisation of R&D during the 1970s and 1980s the assumption that all research is undertaken in the home market and that new technology and production is then gradually phased into overseas markets, is becoming less sustainable. This combined with the ever increasing pressure for shorter R&D development cycles, in turn associated with the shortening of product life spans, has meant the need for "telescoping" international innovation roll-out by multinational companies. Vernon (1979) himself suggests that there is a shortening of the product life cycle as all products move to a world market status. Telescoping the expected pattern of transnational R&D expansion in turn has implications for the flow of technology transfer overall as described above. If product markets move increasingly towards global status and the progression of R&D towards overseas operations is speeded up, the technological lag between the home market and foreign markets will increasingly disappear. As Vernon (1979, p. 259) notes "the interval of time between the introduction of any new product in the US and its first production in a foreign location has been rapidly shrinking". In a survey of 954 new products introduced in the US and transferred abroad, Vernon found that the number of products transferred abroad within one year rose from 8.1 % in 1946-50 to 35.4 % in 1971-75 (Vernon and Davidson, 1979). Vernon (1979, p. 259) concludes "as firms introduced one product after another into a given country, the lapse of time between the introduction of successive products in that country steadily declined". As Vernon suggests, the speeding up of technology transfer and the reduction in the hierarchical notion of superior home markets opposes inferior overseas research capability. Mansfield and Romeo (1984) moreover have raised the issue of reverse technology transfers from overseas subsidiaries to American firms. They found that far from overseas laboratories shifting little of their work back to the US, as much as 47 % of their 1979 R&D efforts were transferred to the US (Mansfield and Romeo 1984, p. 123 ; see also Pearce and Singh, 1992, pp. 144-145).

II   Global networking and coordination in innovation

For many large international companies introducing innovations onto a global market, the notion of the product life cycle with the innovation originating in the domestic market and gradually, over lengthy periods of time, being "rolled out" to overseas markets has become an increasingly inappropriate global innovation model. R&D and production for these companies involves a large number of individual sites spread across several continents, involving flows of research, technology and information in a highly complex and interrelated manner. These companies are increasingly facing two major interrelated challenges in their global innovation strategies (Howells and Wood, 1993). Firstly they are facing the challenges of **time-based competition** in the context of innovation (Keen, 1988 ; Stalk and Hout, 1990) where firms are under pressure to reduce R&D lead times as life spans of products are being shortened all the time. Secondly, there is the problem of the **geographical coordination and integration** on an increasingly global level of this complex innovation process involving key inputs from R&D, production and marketing. The management of overseas R&D in particular up to the late 1960s was at best "minimal" (or euphemistically described as "harmonised" management ; see Steele, 1975, p. 215) with little, if any, centralised control of overseas research operations. This did not matter in the past, when research and technical units, being small and involved in mainly adaptive work, did not affect the central thrust of R&D work undertaken in the home base. Hopefully duplication was minimal ; some good work overseas might develop which could be transferred back to the central domestic R&D laboratory ; whilst it would cause too many problems (and take up too many resources) to try and coordinate and integrate such work into the main body of research work run by the company. Firms now recognise that R&D has assumed too crucial a role for it to be left alone without proper coordination. However, it has also come at a time when firms have recognised that they should be implementing structures that allow considerable autonomy and flexibility on an international level so as not to stifle creativity and to achieve greater flexibility and competitiveness in world markets. In response to these pressures and challenges there has been a shift by at least some firms from what Kogut (1990, p. 58) terms "a dyadic relationship between headquarters and each subsidiary to the profile management of an international network". Hedlund (1986) similarly sees the internal hierarchy of the corporation being replaced by balanced interdependence or what he calls **heterarchy**, whilst Bartlett (1986) views the multinational corporation moving from a position of hierarchical control to a more cooperative relationship between headquarters (HQ) and subsidiaries. In terms of strategy, this is reflected by firms moving towards formulating strategies in the context of reciprocity between the HQ and subsidiaries (Prahalad and Doz, 1987).

Part of the drive towards some kind of networking formulae by firms has been the acknowledgement that for many of them, in terms of production, engineering and technical expertise, **overseas** facilities have become increasingly significant in terms of a multinational's technical and manufacturing capability. In addition many overseas facilities have gained increased responsibility for a company's worldwide production and technical competence, whilst domestic-based facilities (always seen as the pre-eminent leaders in a multinational's operations in the past) now often play a less significant role. Increasingly this may mean that domestic operations now may only have an equal or indeed subordinate role to their overseas subsidiaries (examples include ICI (UK) where overseas operations take a lead role in explosives (Canada) and polyurethenese (Belgium) ; similarly Du Pont (US) with agricultural products (Switzerland) ; IBM (US) with communication systems (UK) ; Roche (Switzerland) with pharmaceuticals (US) ; and Hoechst (Germany) with separation and photoresistant materials research (US)).

All this has meant that for most companies there has been a gradual shift away from hierarchical, top-down flows of commands and information from the parent to the subsidiaries. Instead a more open two-way flow between subsidiaries, and between subsidiaries and the parent organisation has been created (Bartlett, 1986). In an "integrated network" organisation, communication patterns become much more complex with considerable lateral contacts between subsidiaries (Hakansson, 1990, p. 270). However, the issue here is that although a centralised control system has been abandoned, an effective coordinating network structure has to be implemented which allows for differences in local capabilities and strategic importance but enables multinational integration (Bartlett and Ghoshal, 1986 ; Doz, 1986). As Hakansson (1990, p. 272) notes the purpose of coordination in a transnational organisation is two-fold : (i) to avoid unnecessary duplication of effort ; and (ii) to ensure that available capabilities and locally developed initiatives are efficiently exploited. One development which has helped facilitate this coordinating function in a network organisation is the spread and use of global corporate computer-communication networks. The availability of corporate-wide electronic mail and database systems, the development of computer-aided methods which allow designs to be transferred between sites and the increasing use of video-conferencing all have supported more effective inter-site coordination (Howells, 1992). However corporate-wide information and communication networks can only provide a facilitating role in this coordination effort and take considerable lengths of time to properly implement.

The role of global networking in the context of international innovation management is important but a growing number of companies have sought to develop more specific strategies for international innovation under the increasing pressure of "space-time compression". Two strategy-sets are outlined here which appear to be emerging amongst key international corporate players. They attempt to resolve the problem of introducing cost-effective, world beating innovations as rapidly as possible so as to amortize the ever increasing costs of R&D and technical development but on as wide a geographical area as possible. These strategies are termed here as "global switching" and "global focusing". Both attempt to realise, in different ways, the **internal** benefits of close integration of research, technical and manufacturing functions whilst tapping into, or optimising, the benefits of the **external** "task environment" by exploiting geographic-specific innovation pools including subcontractors and suppliers, research and technical infrastructure and key customers operating at a local, regional or sometimes national level. This latter, external element links in with Porter's (1990, pp. 41-43 and pp. 58-61) location-based competitive advantage (and the competitive advantage of nations) concept.

III Global switching

The trend towards the decentralisation of production overseas and shifts towards a dispersal of research and technology related to the production process has led companies to start developing strategies that can deal with the space-time compression outlined above ; one such being "global switching". The essence of global switching is the ability of companies to coordinate their different functional operations (i.e. research, development, manufacture, marketing, sales, administration) in an integrated fashion on a global scale. The ability to geographically "switch" between sites in terms of functional sequencing and link-ups ("vertical" global switching) is best exemplified and most impressive with the development cycle of a new product from initial discovery and invention through to first market launch. However, it can also occur on an intra-functional level ("horizontal" global switching), where the manufacture of certain specific products can be transferred or switched from one plant to another plant located right across the other side of the world. There are therefore basically two types of global switching : horizontal and vertical. The focus of this chapter, given its focus on technological innovation, will be on vertical global switching covering vertical functional integration on a worldwide basis in connection with new product development (from discovery through to final market launch).

The simplist vertical global switching involves a R&D-production-marketing-sales sequence of inter-functional linkages. Traditionally this vertical sequencing was undertaken mainly on one site or sets of closely inter-linked sites within a national territory. However, increasingly large multinationals with functions spread across the world have had the ability to switch such sequencing across national boundaries. R&D, or indeed one part of R&D, may be undertaken in one country, initial production scale-up in another, full production and related component production in other sets of countries and first market launch in a completely different country. The coordination and integration of these different (within and between) function interfacing is at the best of times extremely difficult and such problems are heightened if this occurs on a global basis. However, it provides considerable economic and technical benefits for corporations which have been able to exploit the different technical, manufacturing and marketing skills of the various sites, as well as to ease international compatibilities.

The ability to geographically "switch" between sites in terms of functional sequencing and link-ups is best exemplified and most impressive with the development cycle of new product from initial discovery and invention through to first market launch. Information relating to the exact sequencing of the locational switching is difficult to come by, but Figure 22.1 illustrates one example of a new beta-agonist, anti-asthma drug salmeterol ("Severent") developed by Glaxo. The product, salmeterol, involved R&D at its site at Ware in the UK, followed by extensive clinical trial studies across Europe. The scale-up of production for the active ingredients in the drug was transferred to Montrose in Scotland, which then moved into full-scale primary production. Another primary production site in Singapore factories is to supply secondary production and packaging operators in Evreux in France and Ware in the UK. The first market launch for the product in 1990 was actually the UK, although other European countries became also, soon afterwards, product launch sites. In a similar context Hewlett Packard also displays the phenomenon of global switching in global product development and production. Figure 22.2 provides an example of one new product introduction, relating to office systems, covering a span of countries. This has been facilitated by a more formalised life cycle for new product development and more attention paid to critical "hand over" periods, such as "manufacturing release" where responsibility for a new product has been moved from R&D to that of manufacturing.

The concept of vertical global switching involves functional integration on a worldwide scale which is far removed from the hierarchical and lagged notions of the product life cycle model noted earlier. The notion of vertical global switching sees a set of global linkages and interactions between functions which have increasingly less to do with a domestic-oriented, hierarchical structure associated with a "filtering down" of technical expertise from home base to overseas units. Instead it involves a more closely integrated international federated structure, with increased expertise and "lead role" functions situated in overseas affiliates.

IV   Global focusing

Global focusing relates to the spatial concentration of research, production and other key facilities specialising in a particular product, product group or related technologies on a single or closely related set of sites in selected locations across the world. The origins of this phenomenon can often be traced to the establishment of particular product mandates for manufacturing plants, but also links in with more recent issues to do with developing closer links with key suppliers and customers. The main advantages of global focusing stem from its basic simplicity (Table 22.1). By allowing cross-functional specialism to develop around a particular product group or

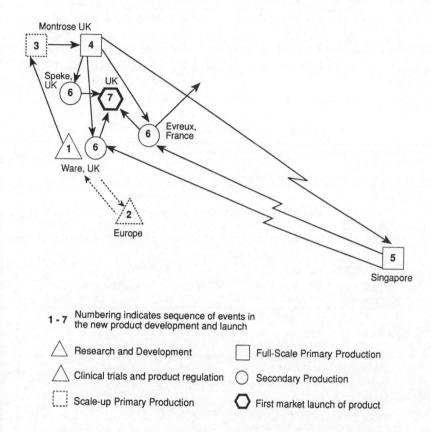

Figure 22.1   The global switching in new product development and
launch : the case of Glaxo's salmeterol

Basic Research	Applied / Development	Manufacture	Market Launch
HP Laboratory	HP Division	Plant	
Country (1)	Country (2)	Country (3)	Country (5)
		Country (4)	

Figure 22.2   Global switching - new product development :
Hewlett Packard

technology, all the necessary expertise and intra- and inter-firm linkages can be centred on a particular site, or set of closely interrelated sites. As such problems about inter-functional linkages within the firm, which are particularly important when developing new products, are reduced. In addition the facility may be sited near, or can build up, a set of key local suppliers.

Table 22.1   Global focusing - competitive advantages and disadvantages

Advantages
1. Intra-firm : Good inter-functional linkages within the firm.
2. Intra-firm : Good co-ordination of new product developments.
3. Inter-firm : Ability to develop localised links with suppliers (backward linkages).
4. Inter-firm : Potential for good contacts with lead, innovative customers (forward linkages).
5. Potential to tap into international centres of excellence for particular products/technologies.

Disadvantages
1. Problems of centric views/links.
2. Associated with this, danger of missing new developments occurring elsewhere in the world.
3. Susceptible to decline in specialist advantage due to decline in :   (i) internal competences   (ii) external competences - loss of inter-firm, agglomerative advantages   (iii) general long-term decline in product/technology specialism.
4. "Lumpy" nature of innovation and development
5. Danger of competition in resources from other companies seeking to locate in same.

Similarly it can gain benefits from good forward linkages with location at, or near to, "lead" innovative customers. These inter-firm benefits of global focusing can be gained by locating production in an existing international centre of excellence for that particular sector or technology group, such as in advanced materials. This localisation strategy for products and technologies therefore overcomes many of the problems of distance associated with poor communication, interfacing and coordination. Overall interaction on a formal and informal basis is much greater, both on an intra- and inter-organisational basis. More specifically here, in the context of inter-firm information flows, a study by Fredriksson and Lindmark (1979) on production systems in Sweden has stressed the issue of distance-sensitive contacts, particularly in the field of new product development.

However, although this obviously makes a highly desirable pattern of localised and specialised supplier/subcontractor networks it often cannot be obtained. A surprisingly large number of key suppliers are only effectively available from a highly restricted set of locations worldwide and on this basis would reduce the benefits, and ability to establish, local specialist subcontractor clusters. The build up of global focusing by firms, allowing an international network of units to take on responsibility for the development of particular products/technologies, represents a move towards a more decentralised, "networking" arrangement and away from a centralised, "home-based" orientation. However, in a sense, although it overcomes some of the problems of a centralised coordination system focused on the parent company's home base, there are still some certain dangers. The most obvious is that it still retains a centralised vision, even if it is transposed out of the company's home market. The dangers of missing key signals from other markets elsewhere in the world and the centre becoming too inward-looking and complacent are still there.   In addition, concentrating all the expertise in one main locale exposes the company to risks of putting "all its eggs in one basket" if the creative expertise built up within the single company unit does not remain effective.

More generally focusing a particular unit on one product group or technology exposes that establishment to downturns or fluctuations in demand which over the longer term would lead to closure as the markets or technologies move on. For the firm it also reduces its flexibility in allocating spare productive capacity. This would lead to a sub-optimal allocation of the company's total resources and reduction in flexibility in terms of being able to move products and production runs between plants (Cordell, 1971, p. 58). A further potential problem for global focusing may occur via its very success. When certain clusters become targeted by competitor firms because of their perceived excellence in certain sectors or technologies, it can lead to increased competition for resources, particularly in relation to skilled scientific and technical manpower. Problems of staff poaching and high labour-turnover may result, creating the additional problem of research confidentiality and appropriability. It should be noted here also that the reason for opting for a global focusing strategy may only be due to perceived benefit from only one or two factors noted above, and it is unlikely that companies will be able to gain or develop all the advantages listed in Table 22.1.

In addition companies may opt for global focusing in a more limited fashion. The strategy may be only partially implemented at least initially, focusing, for example, on specialist products/technologies where the expertise clearly lies outside the parent company's home base. Associated with this, the move to global focusing may have much to do with informal and evolutionary developments based on earlier designations of manufacturing plants to particular product mandates. The initial mandating of a factory to manufacture a particular product or family of products on a worldwide (or continental region) basis, often leads on to that unit building up expertise in other key functions, most notably R&D (Cordell, 1971 ; Haug *et al.*, 1983) general design/engineering and marketing. Over time therefore plants associated with world product mandates have taken international responsibility for these functions (Hakansson, 1990, p. 257) to form the basis for global focusing by firms. Lastly global focusing may arise via merger and acquisition activity. A company may acquire an overseas firm which has a particular strength in a product range/technology compared with its existing operations. This strength may only reside in basic R&D or close contact with the customers, but the acquiring company must decide to focus long-term investment in the overseas site rather than transfer it to its existing operations. The parent company, therefore, in rationalising its activity in this particular sector or division will often reverse its existing operations into the newly acquired firm's operations, often leading to the closure or downgrading of its domestic and/or existing facilities elsewhere. As such, this move towards global focusing is in direct contrast to a more evolutionary product mandate process, which builds upon initial manufacturing capabilities.

V   Conclusion

This chapter has briefly attempted to outline two key emerging strategies that a number of major global corporations have sought to establish to meet the pressures in technological innovation associated with globalisation. A key challenge within this overall globalisation process which confronts major corporations can be expressed as "space-time compression", namely the need to coordinate dispersed operations on a global basis in an effective and timely fashion. However it is the issue of time-based performance in combination with global coordination and control of operations on a widely dispersed geographical basis, that presents such a challenge to modern international corporations. Global switching and global focusing centre on these coordination aspects but within the context of timely and effective management.

23 Searching for a global management model : the case of Japanese multinationals

Susumu Watanabe

I Introduction

Japanese overseas direct investment (ODI) expanded dramatically after 1980 and 1985 in particular. Its motivation is multiple : discriminative import barriers set by Western nations, the appreciation of the yen, the ever increasing labour shortage at home, and lastly abundant supplies of capital supported by a high savings rate and in part by "easy money" or "bubbles". In this process, Japanese multinationals' scope of business operations has "globalised" : they now need to plan and organise their business on the world map, not just on the basis of a one-sided view from Tokyo or Osaka (section II). As one may easily surmise from their motives above, however, the pace of this globalisation has turned out to be something these companies did not plan. It has been imposed upon them exogenously, and for most of them it was too fast : their business operations, notably production base, became globalised before the necessary managerial system and strategies had been prepared. One major problem concerns the localisation or globalisation of managerial personnel (section III). In order to cope with this problem Japanese multinationals are now working on what one might call "the Japanese management model of the global age" or "the global Japanese management model". This emerging model is also destined to accommodate new patterns of supply and behaviour of labour in their home country (section IV).

II   Trend of Japanese ODI and business globalisation

After World War II, Japan resumed its ODI in 1951. It grew slowly until the late 1970s, when it began to accelerate. After exceeding US$10,000 million in 1984, its annual rate skyrocketed to reach a peak of US$67,540 million in 1989 as the value of the yen rose from about 42 cents in 1983-85 to 78 cents in 1988. The cumulative amount as reported (in advance) to the Ministry of Finance stood at US$310.8 billion (81.6 billion in the manufacturing sector) at the end of March 1991. Of this total 73 per cent was reported in 1986-90 and another 15 per cent in 1981-85, the corresponding figures for the manufacturing sector being 70 per cent and 14 per cent. This implies that a large majority of Japanese firms' affiliates abroad are very new. In MITI's survey of March 1990, affiliates established between FY [1] 1984 and 1989 accounted for 50 per cent of the total in the manufacturing sector (57 per cent in the industrialised regions and 14 per cent in the developing regions), while those established in or before FY 1977 accounted for just one-third of the total (23 per cent and 40 per cent, respectively).

Many of these new affiliates are still in the preparatory or initial stages of operation, but the rapid growth of ODI has entailed investing firms' "globalisation" in many respects. In a recent survey of major manufacturing companies over three-quarters out of 247 respondents were working in an internationally consolidated accounting system (EIBJ, 1990). Firms now raise funds for their overseas operations in the host country or in a third country. In automobile and other industries where economies of scale are substantial, a company's affiliates in different parts of the world specialise in the production of different products (e.g. car models) which are distributed throughout the world. Technological innovations are sometimes introduced at their overseas plant even earlier than at home.

R&D is also becoming increasingly globalised. MITI (1991) identified 222 R&D centres set up by Japanese firms abroad. The most common motives are : to adapt their products to local supply conditions so that their local contents can be raised, and to develop products meeting local needs more fully. The "electronisation" of consumer durables tends to encourage localisation of R&D even in developing countries, because their software needs to be tailored to local needs. For example, Matsushita's subsidiaries in South-East Asia and Mexico became increasingly involved in the development of product design. More recently, Japanese firms' enthusiasm for overseas R&D grew : because of a mounting difficulty to meet their fast expanding manpower requirements in the home country ; in the hope of securing a more heterogeneous R&D staff ; and for fear of "technology frictions" with Western Nations.

Such a widening of the scope of business operations naturally calls for adjustments to the managerial system in individual companies. In this manner, the delegation of responsibilities to individual affiliates advances, while regional headquarters supervise and coordinate their activities. In the mean time, it has become an increasingly important task of the world head office to control and coordinate the latter's operation from a global perspective. Hence, two apparently contradictory trends have arisen, one towards greater decentralisation and the other towards greater centralisation. Reportedly, Mr A. Morita, Chairman of Sony, called this situation "global localisation" some time ago. Today, Japanese often use "glocal" and "glocalisation", amalgamating the two English words.

In theoretical literature, development of a multinational's management system is usually depicted in a three to five stage model. One of the best models is found in Kobayashi (1985) [2], where a firm's internationalisation or multinationalisation advances in five steps : 1) management by the head office ; 2) delegation of management to overseas operating units ; 3) regional coordination of overseas operating units (e.g. production of automobile based on division of labour among ASEAN countries) ; 4) management from a global perspective ; and 5) management combining a global perspective with the integration of the activities of overseas operating units into the logistics of the firm as a whole.

After having visited a dozen Japanese multinationals' head offices since Spring 1992, however, I have the impression that they are not following steps 3, 4 and 5 mentioned above, gradually and systematically. Theirs are compressed and mixed models, where the preparation of these steps takes place simultaneously. This is quite natural, because to most firms the recent pace of globalisation is not the result of something planned well in advance. It has been imposed upon them by external circumstances such as the unexpectedly rapid growth of the value of the yen and protectionism in Western countries. In a number of important cases, ODI's decision was made partly in response to host governments' requests for their investment and promise of various incentives, for which they were sometimes forced to pay after they had made their investment either by the federal government (in the United States) or by the EC Commission (in Europe). Manufacturing operations and plant construction started in different parts of the world almost simultaneously. Consequently, they are now struggling to consolidate their managerial strategies and systems at different levels (enterprise, regional and global).

There seems to be little difference between manufacturers and traders in this respect. Before World War II and for some time after the war, the former, with notable exceptions of Matsushita and Ajinomoto, relied on general trading companies for exporting their products and importing raw materials, partly because they did not have enough human resources and capital and partly because their products were relatively crude and did not require technical expertise for marketing. Therefore, trading companies as well as major banks have had more experience in international business. However, these companies were used to trading between Japan and foreign countries and catering to other Japanese firms operating abroad. Truly international operations involving a third country and non-Japanese firms began only recently as they started acquiring new businesses through M&A and as non-Japanese firms began to seek their collaboration. Such a shift in their operational pattern has been motivated in part by the fact that Japanese manufacturers no longer rely on them for their international operations.

The actual degree of globalisation in Japanese companies varies depending not only on the length of experience in overseas operations but also on the relative weight (actual and target) of such business in overall corporate activities. The overseas affiliates' share in overall turnover is still 20 per cent or so even among manufacturers of automobiles and electrical and electronic machinery. Notable exceptions are Sony (over 70 per cent) and Honda (approaching 70 per cent). These firms, as well as a limited number of smaller firms in different industries, virtually started their business with exports, more often than not due to entry barriers to home markets arising from their latecomer status. In consequence, they are among the most globalised of Japanese firms.

The strategy for preparing a global managerial structure also varies from one company to another. For example, companies like Sony and Nissan appear to have started with a global perspective. In contrast, Matsushita's approach has been to consolidate first regional systems and operations under each regional headquarters and then gradually develop a global network around them : a "multi-local global network" system (*DHB* [3], Aug.-Sept. 1991). Here again, multiple factors will explain such differences, e.g. the corporate history and philosophy and the product range. No matter what strategy may be adopted, there seems to be one common area of concern : the personnel policy regarding managerial staff.

III   The degree of localisation of managerial personnel

In so far as their general behaviour pattern is concerned, there seems to be a fair degree of consensus of opinion that no categorical differences exist between Japanese and Western multinationals, and that the differences observed are largely explained by differences in the length of experience or in the stage of multinationalisation and globalisation (cf. Dunning, 1986 ; Kujawa, 1986 ; Graham and Krugman, 1989). In a recent survey of 407 American chief executive officers (CEOs) nearly 60 per cent of the respondents felt there was little difference between Japanese investors' behaviour and US firms' investment behaviour abroad during the "strong dollar" period, while 30 per cent found some difference (*Nihon Keizai Shimbun*, 12 February 1990, morning). In this context, one probably needs to distinguish multinationals from a country with a large home market such as the United States from those of a small country like The Netherlands. The behaviour pattern of companies like Sony resembles that of the latter, who had to go out of the home country at an early period in their history. While these companies are more likely to appoint locals to top management posts, *inter alia*, due to internal human resource supply constraints which accrue from the small scale of domestic operations, larger firms may find it easier to rely on in-house personnel during earlier periods of overseas affiliates' operations. Major US multinationals reportedly localised top management posts in response to their "delay" in this respect, sometimes excessively so that they had to somewhat reverse their policy subsequently. Critics of Japanese firms compare them with today's Western multinationals, not yesterday's, and blame them for keeping their top posts for compatriots (another major criticism concerns limited local procurements, a subject I have dealt with in some detail elsewhere [4]).

Japanese firms used to be accused of bringing in too many nationals. Today, their expatriate-local ratio is not particularly high compared with those of firms from other countries (cf. Sibunruang and Brimble, 1988, for example). MITI's survey findings (MITI, 1989 and 1991) also suggest that the proportion of Japanese in the managerial staff has continued to decline in all regions since 1980. A number of factors contribute to this : 1) at relatively old affiliates, local workers have acquired sufficient experience to take up middle management posts ; 2) the cost of Japanese executives relative to that of locals has been rising rapidly even in Europe and North America ; 3) it is difficult to secure sufficient Japanese staff to many fast growing overseas operations ; and 4) Japanese firms are under pressure to promote locals.

In MITI (1991), the global average rate of localisation of directors' posts was 45 per cent in all sectors and 54 per cent in the manufacturing sector. It was highest in personnel and purchasing units (56 per cent each), followed by sales and R&D units (52 per cent), planning units (49 per cent) and accounting units (45 per cent). These findings support Dunning (1986), when he argues that Japanese firms tend to entrust to compatriots those units where close and accurate communication and understanding are required with the head office. British nationals usually head those units where a full understanding of the local language, culture, business customs and psychology, and commercial law is needed.

In the same survey, the proportion of Japanese at the highest corporate posts varied from one region to another, ranging from 82 per cent in North America to 63 per cent in Asia. It was much higher in the industrialised regions where most affiliates are wholly-owned and relatively new, than in the developing regions where the proportion of wholly- or majority-owned firms is low and that of relatively old firms is high.

The rates of localisation of top posts cited above are extremely low, compared with that among foreign-owned companies operating in Japan. In a survey conducted by the American Electronics Association (AEA) in 1989, for example, 71 per cent of a total of 361 US-owned electronics companies and plants had a Japanese at the top, as compared with only 2 per cent of 139 Japanese-owned electronics firms in the United States. As a means of explaining the difference, this report notes the following points : that Japanese firms have a good knowledge of the US market and their staff brought to the United States can communicate with local people in English, and that their top management needs to maintain close communication with their head office in Japan. In contrast, US firms need a Japanese at the top in order to effectively enter the Japanese market (*Nihon keizai Shimbun*, 22 December 1989). This need may arise partly from US managers' limited knowledge of the Japanese language, culture and market and partly from the peculiarly Japanese "human network" business system requiring extensive personal connections and communication, while the relatively high quality of average Japanese workers may reduce the need for direct control. It is, however, also clear that Western firms have incomparably greater experience in international business and that they are better prepared for managerial localisation. It has been suggested, for example, that American companies generally try to develop "a structure which functions sufficiently well irrespective of the personalities and attitudes of the work-force", while "the Japanese approach is to create the right people, who can work effectively irrespective of structure" (Takamiya, 1985, p. 193).

The pace of localisation of managerial posts could have been faster among relatively older affiliates, if they had been able to build up necessary local manpower. In a recent survey of 247 parent firms with a total of 1,677 manufacturing affiliates (EIJB, 1990), however, securing and training of local managerial staff and technical personnel was felt to be a problem by 96 per cent of the respondents with affiliates in the ASEAN-4 (Indonesia, Malaysia, Philippines and Thailand), 87 per cent in Europe, and about 80 per cent in the Asian NIEs (Hong Kong, Republic of Korea, Singapore and Taiwan) and in the United States. Recently, the local market for elite manpower (i.e. first-class university graduates and   competent professionals) has become more easily accessible for Japanese firms, as a result of the improvement of their international status. Still, they are handicapped by their affiliates' small size and latecomer status and by linguistic and cultural barriers. In the fast growing ASEAN economies the absolute shortage of qualified manpower adds to the problem.

One of the main features of the Japanese managerial style is its reliance on internally developed human resources. For Japanese firms, therefore, the high rate of turnover of elite manpower is a problem no less serious than the limited access to it. The high mobility of professionals seems to be part of the business culture in the West, especially in North America. To make the situation worse, Japanese firms abroad appear to have been less successful in managing professionals than in managing ordinary factory workers, as many studies suggest. Employees of the former category tend to get frustrated with Japanese practices such as collective responsibility and a slow and ambiguous career path. They are also likely to be unhappy, being left out of the decision-making process due to the linguistic barrier and lack of "human network".

IV   Japanese firms' attitudes and strategies

Japanese firms have confidence in their basic managerial strategy built on internally developed human resources. Even at Sony, which is known for an almost complete localisation of management staff at its overseas affiliates, in-house experience in diverse areas of business operations is highly valued in promotion and it is one of the manager's main duties to train younger people instead of just recruiting experienced people (*DHB*, June-July 1991, p. 24). They also believe in their "human network" managerial system and team work, which presupposes long-term (if not lifetime) employment, flexible job allocation and rotation, and peaceful labour-management relations. They do not discard these elements of the conventional Japanese management system, but are looking for ways to make them compatible with the new business climate. This cannot be but a process of trial and error : "there is no occidental model for us to copy", a number of company representatives mentioned to me during my visits.

The experience of a number of well-known companies, both Japanese and Western, have made Japanese firms more cautious in localising management and sometimes R&D. For example, Nissan Tennessee Plant's record is considered to be less impressive than Honda Ohio Plant's in terms of local assessment of product quality and plant operations, and the Japanese attribute this difference to Nissan's premature localisation of management and insufficient communication with the head office in Japan. From the beginning Nissan has entrusted plant operations to a local staff coming from Ford and other US firms. In contrast, in 1989, ten years after its entry, Honda's plant had over 400 Japanese preparing the "Honda Way" of management. In light of its experiences in the United States, Nissan opted for a somewhat different strategy in the UK and placed a larger number of Japanese managers including the president during the start-up period (*DHB*, Oct.-Nov. 1991, p. 70).

Honda, as well as other major Japanese firms, has taken Volkswagen's experience very seriously : the German company, who had once taught them the crucial importance of an extensive sales network, had to withdraw from the US market not just because they had failed in marketing and in product development, but more importantly because "the quality of the cars built in Pennsylvania wasn't up to the quality of the cars [built] in Germany", as the *Wall Street Journal* argued (Shook, 1988, p. 68). The Japanese attribute this failure to an excessive transfer of managerial responsibility to locals (Ishii, and Ishida & Shiroki).

In brief, Japanese multinationals believe that the transfer of managerial responsibility to non-Japanese can advance only gradually as required manpower is built up through in-house education and training. In order to accelerate this process, they are now making all kinds of efforts. Matsushita's approach is among the most systematic and comprehensive.

For the purpose of promoting managerial globalisation of overseas affiliates, Matsushita has started-up a Model Company Programme. Choosing one major regional affiliate each year (Matsushita Germany in 1991), personnel officers of the company, the regional headquarters and the head office in Japan get together to establish a model of personnel policy to be spread among other affiliates in the region with necessary modifications. Its ultimate objective is to systematise high-level managerial staff development in a global perspective, but it is also expected to help discover possible gaps among the three parties e.g. regarding the norm of evaluation of workers' abilities. Through interviews with the local staff of individual affiliates, the head office in Japan can also identify those who may be considered for promotion in the future.

This company is also experimenting with a "division company system", whereby each affiliate is divided into multiple small units which take responsibility for their own operations as a separate profit centre. Their management is entrusted to competent locals with a view to providing incentives.

In order to reduce communication problems with non-Japanese managerial staff, different companies have different schemes of "internal internationalisation", in addition to very common in-house language courses and overseas trainee/study programmes. For example, a trading company has made English its official language for in-house communication. Some other companies use English at in-house meetings and for presentation of R&D results. In order to improve understanding of Japanese culture and language, as well as corporate philosophy and systems, and to help develop a "human network" in Japan, an increasing number of companies are introducing a "reverse secondment system", whereby overseas affiliates' staff is sent to Japan for an extended period. These programmes also contribute to the "internal internationalisation" by familiarising Japanese workers with non-Japanese ways of thinking and business. They are supplemented with short-term training/study programmes for those high-level and middle-management staff who cannot be away from home for a long time. In the case of Matsushita training centres have been established in New Jersey, Singapore and Frankfurt, and its overseas training centre in Japan is becoming specialised in the training of core managerial staff.

Partly for the purpose of making it easier to recruit and keep those professional workers who are not interested in long-term job security but also in immediate remuneration for currently possessed capabilities, an increasing number of companies are introducing a contract work system as an alternative to the conventional (implicit) lifetime-employment cum seniority-pay-and-promotion system. This is meant to accommodate the diverse work attitudes of not only non-Japanese but also younger Japanese workers. It is also intended to meet high-tech industries' rapidly changing manpower requirements. A greater flexibility of the employment and pay system is also being sought by means of providing employees with a choice between different retirement ages and correspondingly varied pay-promotion paths. This is aimed at coping with the scarcity of promotion opportunities for the workers in the advanced age group, a group which is increasing as a result of the extension of the retirement age.

IV Conclusions

Localisation of high-level managerial posts at Japanese affiliates will be a slow process because most of these firms are opting for the development of necessary manpower in house. In view of the very short history of their overseas affiliates, it makes little sense to talk about Japanese firms' "notorious" delay in transferring top management posts to the non-Japanese, comparing them with well-established Western multinationals. Nor does it seem to be necessarily true that swift transfer of responsibilities to locals is a condition for their survival in international competition as some Western authors maintain (e.g. Reich, 1991b).

The "global management model", which Japanese firms are currently working out, is likely to retain the main features of their conventional management model. It will be made, however, sufficiently flexible to accommodate diverse values and work attitudes held by workers of different nationalities and generations.

Notes

1   FY = Fiscal Year.
2   Kobayashi, N. (1985), "The Patterns of Management Style Developing in Japanese Multinationals in the 1980s", in Takamiya, S., *et al.* (eds) (1985).
3   *DHB* -Diamond Harvard Business (in Japanese).
4   See Watanabe, forthcoming.

References

Alcouffe, A., and Gilly, J.P. (1991), *L'Europe industrielle horizon 93*, vol.1 : Les groupes et l'intégration européenne ; vol. 2 : Stratégies sectorielles des groupes, Paris : La Documentation Française.

Amin, A., and Dietrich, M. (eds) (1991), *Towards a New Europe : Structural Change in the European Economy*, London : Edward Elgar.

Andrews, M., and Hughes, K. (1992) "UK Productivity in the 1980s : Evidence from a Manufacturing 4-digit Panel", University of Manchester, mimeo.

Andrews, M., Hughes, K., Nicolitsas, D., and Woods, S. (1990), "A UK Manufacturing (4-digit) Industry Panel Database (1980-87)", University of Manchester, mimeo, June.

Antonelli, C. (1984), *Cambiamento tecnologico e impresa multinazionali : il ruolo deli reti telematiche nelle strategie globale*, Milan : Franco Angeli.

Antonelli, C. (1988), "The Emergence of the Network Firm", in Antonelli, C. (ed.), *New Information Technology and Industrial Change : The Italian Case*, Dordrecht : Kluwer Academic Publishers.

Antonelli, C., and Foray, D. (1992), "The Economics of Technological Clubs", *Economics of Innovation and New Technology*, vol. 2, pp. 37-47.

Aoki, M. (1984), *The Cooperative Game Theory of the Firm*, Oxford University Press.

Arcangeli, F. (1992), "Some Distinctive Features of Learning Information Technologies", in Mowery, D.C. , and Foray, D. (eds), Proceedings of the Colloquium : Management of Technology - Implications for Enterprise Management and Public Policy, Paris, 27-8 May 1991.

Arcangeli, F., and Camagni, R (1990), "The Programmable Automation Trajectory in Time and Space", in Nijkamp, P., and Cappellin, R (eds), *The Spatial Context of Technological Development*, Aldershot : Avesbury.

Arena, R., Ravix, J.T., Romani, P.M. (forthcoming), "Firm Cooperation and Subcontracting", *Metroeconomica*.

Arrow, K. (1962), "Economic Welfare and the Allocation of Resources to Invention", in *The Rate and Direction of Inventive Activity : Economic and Social Factors*, Princeton : NBER.

Arthur, W.B. (1988), "Competing Technologies : an Overview", in Dosi, G., *et al.* (eds), op. cit.

Bailey, E., Friedlaender, A. (1982), "Market Structure and Multiproduct Industries: A Review Article", *Journal of Economic Literature*, vol. 20 (Sept.)

Bain, J.S. (1968), *Industrial Organisation*, New York. : J. Wiley and Sons.

Baldwin, R., and Krugman, P. (1988a), "Industrial Policy and International Competition in Wide-Bodied Jet Aircraft," in Baldwin, R.E. (ed.), *Trade Policy Issues and Empirical Analysis*, Chicago : University of Chicago Press.

Baldwin, R., and Krugman, P. (1988b), "Market access and International Competition", in Feenstra, E., *Empirical Methods in International Economics*, MIT, pp. 171-201.

Ballance, R. (1987), *International Industry and Business*, London : Allen & Unwin.

Banville, E. de, Chanaron, J.J. (1991), *Vers un système automobile européen*, Paris : CPE-Economica.

Bartlett, C.A. (1986), "Building and Managing the Transnational : the New Organisational Challenge", in Porter, M. (ed.), op. cit.

Bartlett, C.A., and Ghoshal (1986), "Tap your Subsidiaries for Global Research", *Harvard Business Review*, 64;6, pp. 87-94.

Bartlett, C., Doz, Y., and Helund, G. (eds) (1990), *Managing the Global Firm*, London : Routledge.

Becattini, G. (ed.) (1987), *Mercato e forze locali : il distretto industriale*, Bologne : Il Mulino.

Belderbos, R. (1991), "Tariff Jumping DFI and Welfare Under Cournot Duopoly", Erasmus University.

Besen, S., and Raskind, L. (1991), "An Introduction to the Law and Economics of Intellectual Property", *Journal of Economic Perspectives*, vol. 5, 1.

BEUC (European Bureau of Consumer Unions) (1991), Complaint to DG-IV against UK-Japan Car VER. Brussels.

Blair, J. (1972), *Economic Concentration - Structure, Behavior & Public Policy*, New York : Harcourt Brace Jovanovich.

Blair, R., *et al.* (1991), "An Economic Analysis of Matsushita", *Anti Trust Bulletin*, Summer, pp. 355-381.

BMFT (1990), *Faktenbericht 1990 zum bundesbericht Forschung*, Bonn : Bundesminister für Forschung und Technologie, April.

Borrus, M. (1990), "Chips of State", *Issues in Science and Technology*, vol. 7, no. 1, Fall.

Boston Consulting Group (1990), *The EC Automotive Components Sector in the Context of the Single Market*, vol. 1 and 2, Commission of the European Communities.

Bouju, A. (1978), "L'incidence de la protection juridique d'une invention sur les modalités d'une licence", Le Progrès Technique.

Bourgeois, J. (1989), "Anti-trust and Economic Policy: A Peaceful Coexistence ?, *International Business Lawyer*, Feb., Mar., pp. 58-67, 115-122.

Bresnahan, T.F. (1986), "Measuring the Spillovers from Technical Advance : Mainframe Computers in Financial Services," *American Economic Review*, 76, pp. 742-755.

BRIE (1992), *The Highest Stake : the Economic Foundation of the New Security System*, Oxford : Oxford University Press.

Brock, G. (1975), *The US Computer Industry. A study of Market Power*, Cambridge, Mass. : Ballinger.

Buckley, P. (1989), "Foreign Direct Investment by Small and Medium Sized Enterprises : The Theoretical Background", *Small Business Economics*, vol. 1.

Buigues, P., Ilzkovitz, F., and Lebrun, J.J. (1990), "The Impact of the Internal Market by Industrial Sectors : The Challenge for the Member States", *European Economy*, Special Edition, November.

Bürgenmeier, B., and Mucchielli, J.L. (1991), *Multinationals and Europe 1992, Strategies for the Future*, London : Routledge.

Cabre, J., Valls, J. (1991). "An Evaluation of Technology Policies. Towards an Analytical Framework at the Regional Level", EARIE Annual Conference, Ferrara, September.

Caicarna, G., Colombo, M., and Mariotti, S. (1989), *Tecnologie dell'informazione e accorditra imprese*, Milan : Edizioni Comunita.

Caldwell Harris, M., and Moore, G. (eds) (1992), *Linking Trade and Technology Policies*, Washington, DC : National Academy Press.

Camagni, R.P. (1991), "Networks of Innovators", in *Innovation Networks : the Spatial Perspective*, London : Belhaven-Pinter.

Cantwell, J. (1989), *Technological Innovation and Multinational Corporations*, Oxford : Blackwell.

Cantwell, J. (ed.) (1992), *Multinational Investment in Modern Europe - Strategic Interaction in the Integrated Community*, Aldershot : Edward Elgar.

Carlson, B. (1989), "Flexibility and the Theory of the Firm", *International Journal of Industrial Organization*, vol. 7.

Casson, M. (ed.) (1991), *Global Research Strategy and International Competitiveness*, Oxford : Blackwell.

Caves, R.E. (1974), *Industrial Corporations : The Industrial Economics of Foreign Investment*, Paris : Economica (August).

Cecchini, P., *et al.* (1992), *The European Challenge*, Gower, [1988].

CEPII (1992), *Economie mondiale 1990-2000 : l'impératif de croissance*, Paris : Economica.

Charbit, C., *et al.* (1991), *Coherence and Diversity of Systems of Innovation : the Study of Local Systems of Innovation in Europe*, Sophia Antipolis : Latapses.

Chesnais, F. (1982), "Schumpeterian Recovery and the Schumpeterian perspective - Some Unsettled Issues and Alternative Interpretation", in Giersch, H., proceedings of the 1981 Kiel Symposium on Emerging Technology, *Consequences for Economic Growth, Structural Change and Employment in Advanced Open Economies*, Tübingen, J.C.B. Mohr.

Chesnais, F. (1986), "Some Notes on Technical Cumulativeness, the Appropriation of Technology and Technical Progressiveness in Concentrated Market Structures", paper presented to the conference on Innovation Diffusion, Venice, March.

Chesnais, F. (1988a), "Multinational Enterprises and the International Diffusion of Technology", in Dosi, *et al.* (1988), op. cit.

Chesnais, F. (1988b), "Technological Co-operation Agreements between Firms" *STI Review*, no. 4, December, pp. 52-119.

Chesnais, F. (1990a), "Present International Patterns of FDI : Underlying Causes and some Policy Implications for Brasil", paper submitted at the Seminar on "The international Standing of Brazil in the 1990s", Sao Paulo, 26-30 March.

Chesnais, F. (1990b), "Accords de coopération interfirmes, dynamiques de l'économie mondiale et théorie de l'entreprise", in Humbert, M. (1990), op. cit.

Chesnais, F. (1992), "National Systems of Innovation, Foreign Direct Investment and the Operations of Multinational Enterprises", in Lundvall, B.A. (ed.), *National Systems of Innovation - Towards a Theory of Innovation and Interactive Learning*, London : Pinter Publishers.

Cohen, L., and Noll, R. (1991), *The Technology Pork Barrel*, Washington, DC : Brookings Institution.

Cohendet, P., Llerena, P., Sorge, A. (eds) (1990), "Modes of Usage and Diffusion of New Technology and New Knowledge : The MUST project - Overall Synthesis Report", CEC, FAST/MONITOR. FOP. 227.

Cohendet, P., Llerena, P., and Sorge, A. (1992), "Technological Diversity and Coherence in Europe : an Analytical Overview", *Revue d'Economie Industrielle*, 59.

Colletis, G., Courlet, C. and Pecqueur, B. (1990), *Les systèmes industriels localisés en Europe*, IREP/D, Grenoble.

Commission des Communautés Européennes, DGXIII (1991), "L'Industrie Européenne de l'Electronique et de l'Informatique", *Futuribles*, n° 161, déc.

Commission of the European Communities (1989, 1990), *ESPRIT project synopses*,Volumes 1-8, [Sept.].

Commission of the European Communities (1989-1991), *ESPRIT Annual Report*, Brussels : Commission of the European Communities, DGXIII.

Commission of the European Communities (1990a), *A Competitive European Aeronautical Industry*, Brussels : EC Commission.

Commission of the European Communities (1990b), "Industrial Policy in an Open and Competitive Environment" (COM(90)556, Nov.).

Commission of the European Communities (1991a) "Annual Report on Anti Subsidy and Antidumping Activities, 1990", May.

Commission of the European Communities (1991b), "The European Electronics and Information Technology industry" (SEC (91)565), April.

Congressional Research Service (1992), *Airbus Industrie : An Economic and Trade Perspective*, Washington, DC : US Library of Congress.

Coombs, R., Saviotti, P., and Walsh, V. (eds) (1992), *Technological Change and Company Strategies : Economic & Sociological Perspectives*, London : Academic Press.

Cordell, A.J. (1971), *The Multinational Firm, Foreign Direct Investment and Canadian Science Policy*, Special Study 22, Science Council of Canada, Ottawa.

Council of the European Communities (1991), Resolution Concerning Electronics, Information and Communication Technologies, 18 November.

Courlet, C. (1990), *Les industrialisations du Tiers-Monde*, Paris : Syros.

Courlet, C. (1992), "Le district industriel de la Vallée de l'Arve : origine, fonctionnement et évolution récente", in *Développement local et ensembles de PME*, rapport PIRTTEM, Lyon.

Crevoisier, O., Maillat, D., and Vasserot, J.Y. (1992), "L'apport du milieu dans le processus d'innovation : le cas de l'arc jurassien", in Maillat, D., and Perrin, J.C. (eds), *Entreprises innovantes et développement territorial*, Neuchâtel : EDES.

Cypher, J. (1979), "The Transnational Challenge to the Corporate State, *Journal of Economic Issues*, vol. 13, no. 2, pp. 513-542.

D'Andrea Tyson, L. (1992), *Who's Bashing whom : Trade Conflict in High Technology Industries*, Washington, DC : Institute for International Economics.

Daly, P. (1985), *The Biotechnology Business - A Strategic Analysis*, London : Frances Pinter.

DATAR (1990), *Les investissements japonais de production dans 17 pays d'Europe occidentale*, Paris.

David, P. (1992), "Knowledge, Property and the System Dynamics of Technological Change", World Bank Annual Conference on Development Economics, Washington DC.

Delapierre, M., Lemettre, J.F., Mytelka, L.K., Zimmermann, J.B., Vavakova, B. (1988), *Cooperation between Firms and Research Institutes : The French Case*, prepared for the EUREKA Programme conference, Milan, Bocconi University.

Delapierre, M., and Mytelka, L.K. (1988), "Décomposition, Recomposition des Oligopoles", *Cahiers de l'ISMEA, Economie et Société*, n° 11-12, pp. 57-86.

Delapierre, M., and Zimmermann, J.B. (1991a), "La Globalisation de l'Industrie des Ordinateurs", EEC, MONITOR/FAST report, FOP 283, July.

Delapierre, M., and Zimmermann, J.B. (1991b), "Toward a New Europeanism, French Firms in Strategic Partnerships", in Mytelka, L.K. (ed.), op. cit.

Delmas, P. (1891), *Le Maître des Horloges. Modernité de l'Action Publique*, Paris : Odile Jacob.

Dick, A. (1991), "Learning by Doing and Dumping in the Semi-conductor Industry", *Journal of Law and Economics*, Vol. XXXIV, April, pp. 133-159.

Dicken, P. (1986), *Global Shift : Industrial Change in a Turbulent World*, London : P. Chapman Publishing.

Dodgson, M. (1991), *The Management of Technological Learning : lessons from a biotechnology company*, Berlin : De Gruyter.

Dorado, R., *et al.* (ed.) (1991), *Ciencia, tecnología e industría en España*, Madrid : Fundesco.

Dosi, G. (1982), "Technological Paradigms and Technological Trajectories", *Research Policy*, 11, pp. 147-162.

Dosi, G., Freeman, C., Nelson, R., Silverberg, G., and Soete, L. (eds) (1988), *Technical Change and Economic Theory*, London : Pinter Publishers.

Doz, Y. (1986), *Strategic Management in Multinational Companies*, Oxford : Pergamon Press.

Doz, Y. (1987), "International : Industries : Fragmentation versus Globalisation", in Guile, B.R., and Brooks, M. (eds), op. cit.

Dunning, J.H. (1981), *International Production and the Multinational Enterprise*, London : Allen and Unwin.

Dunning, J.H. (1986), "Decision-making Structures in US and Japanese Manufacturing Affiliates in the U.K. : some Similarities and Contrasts", Multinational Enterprises Programme, Working paper no. 41, Geneva, ILO.

Dunning, J.H. (1988a), *Multinationals, Technology and Competitiveness*, London : Unwin Hyman.

Dunning, J.H. (ed.) (1988b), *Explaining International Production*, London : Unwin Hyman.

Dunning, J.H. (1990), "Discurso de Investidura de Doctor Honoris Causa", Madrid, Universidad Autónoma, December.

Dunning, J.H. (1992), "Mutinational Investment in the EC : Some Policy Implications", in Cantwell, J. (ed.), op. cit.

Dunning, J.H., and Cantwell, J. (1991), "MNEs, Technology and Competitiveness of European Industries", *Aussenwirtschaft*, vol. 1, no. 46.

Dupuy, C., Milelli, C., and Savary, J. (1991), *Stratégies des Multinationales*, Paris : Reclus-La Documentation Française.

Eads, G., and Nelson, R.R. (1971) "Governmental Support of Advanced Civilian Technology : Power Reactors and the Supersonic Transport," *Public Policy*.

Economist Intelligence Unit (1990), *Japanese Motor Business*, September.

European Court of Justice Judgement in AKZO case, June [1991].

EIBJ (1990), "Kaigai Tôshi no Kyû-kakudai to Global Keiei no Shinten (Rapid Growth of Overseas Investment and the Development of Global Management : a survey report), *Kaigai Tôshi Kenkyûjo-hô* (Bulletin of the Research Institute), Export and Import Bank of Japan, January.

Emerson, M., *et al.* (1988), "The Economics of 1992", Oxford : Oxford University Press.

Ergas, H. (1986), "Does Technology Policy Matter ?", Ceps papers no. 29, Centre For European Policy Studies. Brussels.

Ernst, D., and O'Connor, D. (1989), *Technology and Global Competition : the Challenge for Newly Industrialising Economies*, Paris : OECD Development Centre Studies.

Escorsa, P., Valls, J. (1992), "Recerca i tecnologia ...", Colecció Quaderns de competitivitat, vol. 7, Generalitat de Catalunya, Departament d'Industria, Barcelona.

Escorsa, P., Sole, F., Valls, J., *et al.* (1990), "R+D a Catalunya. Determinació de les despeses globals - 1987", CIRIT, Generalitat de Catalunya, Col. Informes, Num. 7, Barcelona.

Fagerberg, J. (1988a) "Why Growth Rates Differ", in Dosi, G., *et al.* (eds), op. cit., pp. 432-457.

Fagerberg, J. (1988b), "International Competitiveness", *The Economic Journal*, 98, June, pp. 355-374.

Faulkner, W. (1989), "The New Firm Phenomenon in Biotechnology", in Rosa, P., Burley, S., Cannon, T., and O'Neil, K. (eds), *The Role and Contribution of Small Business Research*, Aldershot : Gower.

Ferguson, C. (1990), "The Coming US Keiretsu", in *Harvard Business Review*.

Financial Times Survey (1990), *Japanese Automotive Industry*, 20 December, p. 5.

Fitzpatrick Associates (1990), *Review of the E.C. R & D Framework Programme in Ireland, 1984-88*, Dublin.

Flamm, K. (1987), *Targeting the Computer*, Washington : The Brookings Institution.

Flamm, K. (1990), "Semiconductors", in Hufbauer, G. (ed.), op. cit., pp. 225-292.

Foray, D. (1990), "The Secrets of Industry are in the Air, Industrial Cooperation and the Innovative's Firm Organizational Equilibrium", paper presented at the workshop on Networks of Innovators, HEC Montreal, May.

Foray, D. (1991a), "Economie et politique de la science: les développements théoriques récents", *Revue Française d'Economie*.

Foray, D. (1991b), "Repères pour une économie des organisations de recherche-développement", *Revue d'Economie Politique*.

Foray, D. (1992), Toward a Single Patent Community ? Quandaries in the Economics of Invention Incentives, Planning Workshop, Bocconi University, Milan, 1992.

Foray, D., and Mowery, D. (1990), "L'intégration de la recherche industrielle", *Revue Economique*.

Freeman, C. (1982) "Innovation as an Engine of Economic Growth", in Giersch, H. (ed.), *Emerging Technologies : Consequences for Economic Growth, Structural Change and Employment*, Tübingen : J.C. B. Bohr, pp. 1-27.

Freeman, C., and Soete, L. (eds) (1990), *New Explorations in the Economics of Technical Change*, London : Pinter Publishers.

Freeman, C., Sharp, M., and Walker, W. (eds) (1991), *Technology and the Future of Europe*, London : Pinter Publishers.

Friedlaender, A., Winston, C., and Wang, D. (1982), "Cost, Technology and Productivity in the *US* Automobile Industry", Dpt. of Economics Working Paper 294, MIT (Jan.).

Friedman, J. (1983), *Oligopoly Theory*, Cambridge, UK : Cambridge University Press.

Friedrikson, C.G., and Lindmark, L.G. (1979), "From Firms to Systems of Firms", in Hamilton, F.E.I., and Hinge, G.J.R. (eds), *Spatial Analysis, Industry and the Industrial Environment - Progress in Research and Application :* Volume 1 - *Industrial Systems,* Chichester : Wiley, pp. 155-186.

Fröbel, F., Heinrichs, J., Kreye, O. (1977), *Die neue internationale Arbeitsteilung,* Reinbek bei Hamburg : Rowohlt.

Gasiorek, M., Smith, A., and Venables, A. (1989), "Tariffs Subsidies and Retaliation", *European Economic Review*.

GATT (1990), *Trade Policy Review of Japan*, Geneva : GATT.

GATT (1991), *Trade Policy Review of the European Communities*, Geneva : GATT, Vols. 1 & 2.

Gellman Research Associates (1990), "An Economic and Financial Review of Airbus Industrie", prepared for the International Trade Administration, US Commerce Department (Jenkintown, PA : Gellman Research Associates).

Ghemawat, P., Nalebuff, B. (1990), "The Devolution of Declining Industries, *Quarterly Journal of Economics*, no. 1, pp. 167-186.

Giannitsis, T. (1991), "Globalisation of Economy and the Small less Advanced Countries : the Case of Greece", Brussels : Report to FAST/MONITOR, FOP 293, vol. 21

Gille, B. (1978), *Histoire des Techniques*, Paris : Gallimard, nrf.

Gonçalves, F., and Caraça, J.M.G. (1990), "Globalisation, Competitiveness and the Role of Small Countries", paper presented at the OECD Symposium on "Towards Technoglobalisation", Tokyo, March.

Graham, E. (1985), "Intra-industry Direct Foreign Investment, Market Structure, Firm Rivalry and Technological Performance", in Erdilek, A., (ed.), *Multinationals as Mutual Invaders : Intra-Industry Direct Foreign Investment*, London : Croom Helm.

Graham, E. (1991), "Foreign Direct Investment in the United States and US Interests", *Science*, vol. 253, December.

Graham, E., and Krugman, P. (1989), *Foreign Direct Investment in the United States*, Washington, DC : Institute for International Economics.

Gual, J., Sola, J., Fluvia, M. (1991), *La indústria catalana en els anys noranta*, Barcelona : Ariel/CIDEM.

Guelle, F. (1989), Les effets des investissements industriels japonais : le cas de la bureautique en France, *Japon In Extenso*, n° 14, décembre, pp. 2-10.

Guelle, F. (1990), Quelles politiques pour une présence industrielle japonaise en France ?, *France Japon Eco*, n° 45, décembre, CCIFJ, Tôkyô, pp. 16-26.

Gugler, P. (1992), Building Transnational Alliances to Create Competitive Advantage, *Long Range Planning*, vol. 25, no. 1, pp. 90-99

Guile, B.R., and Brooks, M. (eds) (1987), *Technology and Global Industry*, Washington : National Academy Press.

Hagedoorn, J., and Schakenraad, J. (1990a), "Strategic Partnering and Technological Co-operation", in Freeman, C., and Soete, L. (eds), op. cit.

Hagedoorn, J., and Schakenraad, J. (1990b), "Technology Cooperation, Strategic Alliances and their Motives : Brother, can you Spare a Dime, or do you have a Light ?", Maastricht : MERIT Working Paper.

Hagedoorn, J., and Schakenraad, J. (1991), "The Role of Interfirm Cooperation Agreements in the Globalisation of the Economy and Technology", Brussels : EC MONITOR/ FAST Programme.

Hakansson, L. (1990), "International Decentralisation of R&D - the Organisational Challenge", in Bartlett, C.A., Doz, Y., and Helund, G. (eds), op. cit., pp. 256-278.

Hamill, J., and Crosbie, J. (1989), "Acquiring in the US Food and Drink Industry", *Acquisitions Monthly*, May, p. 51.

Haug, P., Hood, M., and Young, S. (1983), "R&D Intensity in the Affiliates of US Owned Electronics Manufacturing in Scotland", *Regional Studies*, 17, pp. 383-392.

Hawk, B. (1988), "The US (anti-trust) Revolution : Lessons for the EC", *European Competition Law Review*, vol. 9, no. 1, pp. 53-87.

Hayward, K. (1986), *International Collaboration in Civil Aerospace*, London : Routledge & Kegan Paul.

Hedlund, G. (1986), "The Hypermodern MNC - a Heterarchy", *Human Resource Management*, 25.

Hindley, B. (1989) "Dumping and the Far East Trade of the EC", *World Economy*, Sept.

Hirshleifer, J., and Riley, J. (1979), "The Analytics of Uncertainty and Information - an Expository Survey", *Journal of Economic Literature*, vol. XVII.

Hobday, M. (1992), "External Operations in the European Semiconductor Industry : Corporate Strategies, Government Policies and Competitiveness", paper prepared for a conference at IFRI, Paris [January].

Holmes, P. (1991), "Trade and Competition Policy : the Consumer Interest", Working Paper 6, National Consumer Council, London.

Holmes, P., Smith, A., and Belderbos, R. (1992), "Strategic Trade and 'Unfair' Business Practices : Problems and Policy Responses in the IT&T and Electronics Sector", Report for DG-XIII-1, June.

Howells, J. (1992), "Going Global : the Use of ICT Networks in Research and Development", *Working Paper* no. 6, Newcastle PICT Centre, CURDS, University of Newcastle upon Tyne.

Howells, J., and Wood, M. (forthcoming), *The Globalisation of Production and Technology*, London : Pinter Publishers.

Hufbauer, G.C. (ed.) (1990), *Europe 1992 : An American Perspective*, Washington DC : The Brookings Institution.

Hughes, K. (1986), *Exports and Technology*, Cambridge University Press.

Hughes, K., and Oughton, C. (1991), "Diversification, Multi-market Contact and Profitability", University of Glasgow, discussion paper no. 9101.

Hughes, K., and Oughton, C. (forthcoming), "Foreign and Domestic Multinational Presence in the UK", *Applied Economics*.

Humbert, M. (1988), "De l'oligopole à la concurrence systémique", *Economies et Sociétés*, n° 11-12, pp. 241-258.

Humbert, M. (ed.) (1990), *Investissement international et dynamique de l'économie mondiale*, Paris : Economica.

Humbert, M. (1992), "Strategic Industrial Policies in a Global Industrial System", paper presented at the EAEPE conference, Paris : November, 1992.

Humbert, M. (forthcoming), *Le Système Industriel Mondial*, Paris : Economica.

Hymer, S. (1960), *The International Operations of National Firms*, Cambridge, Mass. : MIT Press.

Hymer, S., and Rowthorn, R. (1970), "Multinational Corporations and International Oligopoly : the Non-American Challenge", in Kindleberger, C.P. (ed.), *The International Corporation : A symposium*, Cambridge, Mass. : MIT Press.

Imai, K. (1988), "International Corporate Networks : A Japanese Perspective", Project Prométhée Perspectives, June.

Imai, K. (1990), "The Japan's National System of Innovation", Mimeo, Hitotsubashi University, Tokyo, January.

Imai, K.J. (1991), "Globalization and Cross-border Networks of Japanese Firms", paper presented at the conference "Japan in a Global Economy", the Stockholm School of Economics, September.

Ishida, H., and Shiraki, M. (eds) (1990), *Kigyô Global-ka no Jinzai Senryaku* (Strategies for Business Globalisation), Tokyo : Nikkan Shimbunsha.

Ishii, S. (1990), "Hokubei ni okeru Nikkei Jidôsha Sangyô no Genchika Senryaku (Localisation Strategies of Japanese-owned Automobile Manufacturers in North-America)", *Kaigai Tôshi Kenkyûjo-hô* (Japan Export-Import Bank), February.

Jacquemin, A. (1987), The New Industrial Organisation, Oxford : Oxford University Press.

Jacquemin, A., and Marchipont, J.F. (1992), "De Nouveaux Enjeux pour la Politique Industrielle de la Communauté", *Revue d'Economie Politique*, jan.-fév.

Japan Motor Industrial Federation, INC (ed.) (1989), *Future of the Japanese Automotive Industry*, a Report of the Consultative Committee on the Automobile Industry, Tokyo, 82 pp.

Jessop, B. (1992), "Changing Forms and Functions of the State in an Era of Globalization and Regionalization", paper presented to EAEPE conference, Paris, 4-7 November 1992.

Johannisson, B. (1987), "Beyond Process and Structure : Social Exchange Networks", *International Studies of Management and Organisation*, XVII, 1.

Julius, D. (1990), Global Companies and Public Policy, London : RIIA/Pinter Publishers.

Junne, G. (1987), "Automation in the North : Consequences for Developing Countries' exports", in Caporaso, J. (ed.) (1987), *A Changing International Division of Labour*, London : F. Pinter.

Katz, M., and Ordover, J. (1990), "R & D Co-operation and Competition", in Baily and Winston (eds), *Brookings Papers on Economic Activity*, pp. 137-203.

Keen, P.W.G. (1988), *Competing in Time : Using Telecommunications for Competitive Advantage*, Cambridge, Mass. : Ballinger.

Kitch, E. (1977), "The Nature and Function of the Patent System", *Journal of law and economics*, 20.

Kline, S.J., and Rosenberg, N. (1986) "An Overview of Innovation", in *The Positive Sum Strategy*, Washington : National Academy Press.

Knickerbocker, F.T. (1973), *Oligopolistic Reaction and Multinational Enterprises*, Boston, Mass. : Harvard University Press.

Kogut, B. (1990), "International Sequential Advantages and Network Flexibility", in Bartlett, C.A., *et al.* (eds), op. cit., pp. 47-68.

Krugman, P. (ed.) (1986), *Strategic Trade Policy and the New International Economics*, Cambridge, Mass. : MIT Press.

Krugman, P. (1987), "Is Free Trade Passé ?", *Journal of Economic Perspectives*, Fall.

Kujawa, D. (1986), *Japanese Multinationals in the United States : Case Studies*, New-York : Praeger.

Kuttner, R. (1989), *Managed Trade and Economic Sovereignty*, Economic Policy Institute.

Lall, S. (1979) "The International Allocation of Research Activity by U.S. Multinationals", *Oxford Bulletin of Economics and Statistics*, 41, pp. 313-333.

Lanvin, B. (1990), "Technology-based Competition : Globalisation vs. Fragmentation ?", paper presented at the Tokyo TEP Conference on Techno-globalism, February, p. 1.

Lemettre, J.F. (1988), "Les oligopoles technologiques, quelques hypothèses sur les oligopoles de ressources", *Economies et Sociétés*, n° 11-12, pp. 201-220.

Long, P. (1991), "Invention, Autorship, 'Intellectual Property', and the Origin of Patents : Notes toward a Conceptual History", *Technology and Culture*.

MacLeod, C. (1991), "The Paradoxes of Patenting : Invention and its Diffusion in 18th- and 19th-Century Britain, France, and North America", *Technology and Culture*.

MacLuhan, M. (1960), *Explorations in Communication*, Boston : Beacon Press.

Maillat, D., Crevoisier, O., and Lecoq, B. (1991), "Réseau d'innovation et dynamique territoriale : essai de typologie", *Revue d'Economie Régionale et Urbaine*, n° 3/4.

Mansfield, E. and Romeo, A. (1984), "Reverse Transfers of Technology from Overseas Subsidiaries to American Firms", *IEEE Transactions on Engineering Management*, EM-31, pp. 122-127.

Marchesnay, M. (1991), "Les transferts de technologie de la région vers les PME : le cas du Languedoc-Roussillon", *Economies et Sociétés*, F, n° 32.

Mariti, P. (1990), "Constructive Cooperation between Smaller Firms for Efficiency, Quality and Product Changes", in O'Doherty, D. (ed.), op. cit.

Mariti, P., Smiley, R. (1983), "Co-operative Agreements and the Organization of Industry", *Journal of Industrial Economics*, vol. 21, June.

Marquez Mendes, M. (1991), *Antitrust in a World of Interrelated Economies*, Editions Université de Bruxelles.

Mattson, L., and Stymne, B. (eds) (1991), *Corporate and Industry Strategies for Europe*, Amsterdam : North Holland.

Mayes, D. (ed.) (1991), *The European Challenge : Industry's response to the 1992 programme*, Hemel Hempstead : Harvester Wheatsheaf.

Metcalfe, S. (1991), "Competition and Collaboration in the Innovation Process", Discussion Paper no. 79, University of Manchester.

Metcalfe, J.S., and Boden, M. (1992), "Evolutionary Epistemology and the Nature of Technology Strategy", in Coombs, *et al.* (eds), op. cit.

Michalet, C.A. (1985), *Le Capitalisme Mondial*, Paris : PUF, 2e ed.

Michalet, C.A. (1990), "Où en est la notion d'économie mondiale ?", in Humbert, M., (ed.), op. cit.

Mitchell, J.C. (1973), "Networks, Norms and Institutions", in Boissevain, J., and Mitchell, J.C. (eds), *Network Analysis. Studies in Human Interactions*, The Hague : Mouton.

Ministry of Finance (annual), Government of Japan, *Kaigai Chokusetsu Tôshi (Todokeide Bêsu)* (Overseas Direct Investment Statistics on the Reporting Basis).

MITI (1989), *Daisankai Kaigai Jigyô Katsudô Kihon Chôsa : Kaigai Tôshi Tôkei Sôran* (The 3rd Basic Survey on Japanese Firms' Overseas Business Activities : Comprehensive Statistics on Overseas Investment), Tokyo : Keibun Shuppan.

MITI (1991), *Daiyonkai Kaigai Jigyô Katsudô Kihon Chôsa* (The 4th Basic Survey), Tokyo : Keibun Shuppan.

Moran, T.H., and Mowery, D.C. (1991), "Aerospace," *Daedalus*.

Mowery, D. (1983), "The Relationship between Contractual and Intra-Firm Forms of Industrial Research in American Manufacturing 1900-1940", *Explorations in Economic History*, October, pp. 351-374.

Mowery, D.C. (1987), *Alliance Politics and Economics : International Joint Ventures in Commercial Aircraft*, Cambridge, Mass. : Ballinger Publishers.

Mowery, D. (1989), "Collaborative Ventures Between US & Foreign Manufacturing Firms", *Research Policy*, 18, pp. 19-32.

Mowery, D.C. (1991), "International Collaboration in the Commercial Aircraft Industry", in Mytelka, L. (ed.), op. cit.

Mowery, D.C. (1992a), "Congressional Decisionmaking in Science and Technology Programs : Three Case Studies", prepared for the Carnegie Commission on Science, Technology and Government, Washington, DC.

Mowery D. (1992b), "The U.S. National Innovation System : Origins and Prospects for Change", *Research Policy*, 21.

Muellabauer, J. (1986), "Productivity and Competitiveness in British Manufacturing", *Oxford Review of Economic Policy*, no. 20, pp. 1-25.

Mytelka, L.K. (ed.) (1991a), *Strategic Partnerships. States, Firms and International Competition*, London : Pinter Publishers.

Mytelka, L.K. (1991b), "States, Strategic Alliances and International Oligopolies : The European ESPRIT Programme", in Mytelka, L.K. (ed.), op. cit.

Mytelka, L.K. (1992), "Diffusing the Results of Transnational Research Programmes to European Industry. The IT Case", paper presented at the European Communities Conference on Innovation in the Nineties [Brussels : 22-23 June].

Nelson, R. (1981), "Research on Productivity Growth and Productivity Differences : Dead Ends and New Departures", *Journal of Economic Literature*, Vol. XIX [Sept.], pp. 1029-1064.

Nelson, R. (ed.) (1982), *Government and Technical Progress : A Cross-Industry Comparison*, New York : Pergamon Press.

Nelson, R. (ed.) (1984), *High-Technology Policies : A Five-Nation Comparison*, Washington, DC : American Enterprise Institute.

Nelson, R. (1987), *Understanding Technical Change as an Evolutionary Process*, North Holland.

Newfarmer, R.S. (1978), *The International Market Power of Transnational Corporations : A Case Study of the Electrical Industry*, Geneva : United Nations.

Newfarmer, R.S. (1985), "International Industrial Organisation and Development : A Survey", in Newfarmer, R.S., *Profits, Progress and Power : Case Studies of International Industries in Latin America*, Indiana : University of Notre Dame Press.

Nguyen, S., Reznek, A. (1991), "Returns to Scale in Small and Large US Manufacturing Establishments", *Small Business Economics*, vol. 3, September.

Oakey, R., Rothwell, R., and Cooper, S. (1988), *The Management of Innovation in High Technology Small Firms*, London : Pinter Publishers.

Oakey, R., Faulkner, W., Cooper, S., and Walsh, V. (1990), *New Firms in the Biotechnology Industry - Their Contribution to Innovation and Growth*, London : Frances Pinter.

O'Doherty, D. (ed.) (1990), *The Cooperation Phenomenon. Prospects for Small Firms and the Small Economies*, London : Graham & Trotman.

O'Doherty, D., and McDevitt, J. (1991), "Globalisation and the Small Less Advanced Member States - Synthesis Report", Brussels : Report to FAST/MONITOR, FOT 291, Vol. 19.

OECD (1979a), *The Impact of the Newly Industrialisating Countries on Production and Trade in Manufactures*, Paris : Organisation for Economic Cooperation and Development.

OECD (1979b), *Facing the Future Mastering the probable and Managing the unpredictable*, Paris : Organisation for Economic Cooperation and Development.

OECD (1981), *Technology and Productivity : The Challenge for Economic Policy*, Paris.

OECD (1992a), "Globalisation of the Semiconductor Industry : Trends and Issues", Working Paper, DSTI/IND(92)29.

OECD (1992b), *Technology and the Economy : The Key Relationships*, Paris : Organisation for Economic Cooperation and Development.

O'Farrell, P.N., and Hitchens, D. (1989), *Small Firm Competitiveness and Performance*, Dublin : Gill & MacMillan.

Ohmae, K. (1985), *Triad Power*, New York : The Free Press.

Ordover, J. (1991), "A Patent System for Both Diffusion and Exclusion", *Journal of Economic Perspectives*, vol. 5, no. 1.

Orsenigo, L. (1989), *The Emergence of Biotechnology*, London : Frances Pinter.

Ostry, S. (1990), *Governments and Corporations in a Shrinking World*, New York : Council on Foreign Relations.

OTA (Office of Technology Assessment) (1984), *Commercial Biotechnology*, Washington DC : Government Printing Office.

OTA (1988), *New Developments in Biotechnology : US Investment in Biotechnology*, Washington DC : Government Printing Office.

Panic, M., and Joyce, P. (1980), "UK Manufacturing Industry : International Integration and Trade Performance", Bank of England Quarterly Bulletin, vol. 20, June, pp. 42-55.

Patel, P., and Pavitt, K. (1991), "Large Firms in the Production of the World's Technology : An Important Case of Non-Globalisation", *Journal of International Business Studies*, 22, (1) pp. 1-21.

Pavitt, K. (1984), "Sectoral Patterns of Technical Change : Towards a Taxonomy and a Theory", *Research Policy*, 13, p. 343.

Pavitt, K. (1991), "Key Characteristics of the Large Innovating Firm", *British Journal of Management*, 2, pp. 41-50.

Pearce, R.D., and Singh, S. (1992), *Globalising Research and Development*, London : Macmillan.

Perrault, J.L. (1984), "Les Réorientations Récentes dans la Stratégie d'International Business Machines", Université de Rennes, Centre de Développement, Cahiers n° 1.

Perez, L.H. (1991), "Invention and the State in 18th-Century France", *Technology and Culture*.

Perrin, J.C. (1990a), "Réseau d'innovation : contribution à une typologie", networks of innovators workshop, HEC Montreal, May.

Perrin, J.C. (1990b), "Organisation industrielle : la composante territoriale", *Revue d'Economie Industrielle*, n° 51.

Petrella, R. (1989a), "Globalisation of Technological Innovation", *Technology Analysis and Strategic Management*, vol. 1, no. 4.

Petrella, R. (1989b), "La Mondialisation de la Technologie et de l'Economie. Une (Hypo)thèse Prospective", *Futuribles*, sept.

Petrella, R. (1990), "Technology and the Firm", *Technology Analysis and Strategic Management*, vol. 2, no. 2.

Piacentini, P. (1990), "Note sullo stato e le prospettive di sviluppo dell'automazione flessibile nell'industria manufatturiera giapponese", in Amendola, M., Ingrao, B., Piacentini, P., Poti, B. (eds), *L'Automazione flessibile - Analisi ed interpretazione delle tendenze a livello internazionale*, Milano : F. Angeli.

Pickering, J.F. (1972), *Industrial Structure and Market Conduct*, Oxford : Martin Robertson.

Pisano, G. (1990), "The R & D Boundaries of the Firm : an Empirical Analysis", *Administrative Science Quarterly*, 35, pp. 153-176.

Planque, B. (1991), "Note sur la notion de réseau d'innovation : réseaux contractuels et réseaux conventionnels", *Revue d'Economie Régionale et Urbaine*, n° 3/4.

Porter, M. (ed.) (1986a), *Competition in Global Industries*, Boston : Harvard Business School Press.

Porter, M. (1986b), "Changing Patterns of International Competition", *California Management Review*, 28, no. 2.

Porter, M. (1990), *The Competitive Advantage of Nations*, London : Macmillan.

Porter, M., and Fuller, M. (1986), "Coalitions and Global Strategy", in Porter, M. (ed.), op. cit.

Prahalad, L., and Doz, Y. (1987), *The Multinational Mission : Balancing Local Demands and Global Vision*, New York : The Free Press.

Pratten, C. (1991), *The Competitiveness of Small Firms*, Cambridge : Cambridge University Press.

Proulx, M.U. (1991), "Réseaux utilitaires spatialisés et dynamique économique", Revue Canadienne de Science Régionale.

Pyke, F., Becattini, G., and Sengenberger, W. (eds) (1990), *Industrial Districts and Inter-firms Co-operation in Italy*, Geneva : IILS.

Reich, R. (1990), "Who Is Us ?", *Harvard Business Review*, January-February.

Reich, R. (1991a), "Does Corporate Nationality Matter ?", Issues in Science and Technology, Winter 1990-1991.

Reich, R. (1991b), "Who Is Them ?", *Harvard Business Review*, March-April.

Reich, R. (1991c), *The Work of Nations, Preparing Ourselves For 21st Century Capitalism*, New York and London : Alfred Knopf and Simon & Schuster.

Reidenberg J. (1988), "Information Property : Some Intellectual Property Aspects of the Global Information Economy", *Information Age*.

Rosenberg, N. (1976), *Perspectives on Technology*, Cambridge : Cambridge University Press.

Rosenberg, N. (1982), *Inside the Black Box : Technology and Economics*, Cambridge : Cambridge University Press.

Rosenberg, N. (1990) "Why Do Firms Do Basic Research (with their Own Money) ?", *Research Policy*, vol. 19, pp. 165-174.

Rosenberg, N. (1992), "Economic Experiments", *Industrial and Corporate Change*, vol. 1.

Rothwell, R. (1989), "SMFs, Interfirm Relationships and Technological Change", in *Entrepreneurship and Regional Development*, Vol. 1, Dublin, pp. 275-291.

Ruigrok, W., and Tulder, R. van (1991), "Cars and Complexes : Globalisation versus Global Localisation Strategies in the World Car Industry", FAST-programme, Commission of the European Communities.

Sabel, C.F. (1990), "Studied Trust : Building New Forms of Cooperation in a Volatile Economy", International Conference, IILS, Geneva, October.

Salais, R. (1989), "L'Analyse économique des conventions du travail", *Revue Economique*, vol. 40, n° 2.

Santucci, G. (1991), "The European Semiconductor Industry : Learning from the Past 40 Years", *XIII Magazine*, Issue no. 3, October.

Savary, J. (1989), "Des stratégies multinationales aux stratégies globales des groupes en Europe", Colloque international, LEREP, Toulouse.

Scherer, F.M., and Ross, D. (1990), *Industrial Market Structure and Economic Performance*, Houghton Mifflin.

Servan-Schreiber, J.J. (1967), *Le défi américain*, Paris : Denoël.

Sharp, M. (1989), "Collaboration in the Pharmaceutical Industry - Is it the Way Forward ?", DRC Discussion Paper 71, Science Policy Research Unit, Sussex University (mimeo).

Sharp, M. (1991), "The Single Market and European Policies for Advanced Technologies,", in Freeman, *et al.* (eds), op. cit.

Sharp, M., and Pavitt, K. (1992), "Key Technologies and New Industrial Policies", University of Sussex.

Sharp, M., and Shearman, C. (1987), *European Technological CollaborationI*, London : Royal Institute of International Affairs.

Shook, R.L. (1988), *Honda : an American Success Story*, New York : Prentice Hall Press.

SIA-Semiconductor Industry Association (1992), *The 1991 U.S.-Japan Semiconductor Agreement : Heading Towards Crisis*, March.

Sibunruang, A., and Brimble, P. (1988), "The Employment Effects of Manufacturing Multinational Enterprises in Thaïland", Multinational Enterprises Programmes, Working paper no. 54, Geneva, ILO.

Simões, V.C. (1991), "Globalisation and the Small Less Advanced Countries : The Case of Portugal", Brussels : Report to FAST/MONITOR, FOP 294, vol. 22.

Simões, V.C. (1992), "European Integration and the Pattern of FDI Inflow in Portugal", in Cantwell, J. (ed.), op. cit.

Smith, A. (1987), "Strategic Investment, Multinational Corporations and Trade Policy", *European Economic Review*.

Soete, L. (1991), "Technology in a changing world", Limburg : MERIT.

Sole, F., Valls, J. (1991). "La política tecnólogica de cataluña", *Economistas*, Num 45-46, Madrid, pp. 170-177.

Sole, F., Valls, J., *et al.* (1991), *Transfert de technologie PME/Universités. Etudes de cas*, Paris : OCDE, DSTI/IND/RD(91).

Stalk, G., and Hout, T.M. (1990), *Competing Against Time : How Time-Based Competition is Re-shaping Global Markets*, New York : The Free Press.

Steele, L.W. (1975), *Innovation in Big Business*, New York : Elsener.

Stiglitz, J. (1987), "Learning to Learn, Localized Learning and Technological Progress", in Dasgupta, P., and Stoneman, P. (eds), *Economic Policy and Technological Performance*, Cambridge, Mass. : Cambridge University Press, pp. 125-154.

256

Stopford, J., and Strange, S. (eds) (1992), *Rival States, Rival Firms : Competition for World Market Shares*, Cambridge, UK : Cambridge University Press.

Suris, J.M. (1988), "Què fa l'empresa catalana en matèria d'innovació tecnològica ?", *Tecno 2000*, April.

Szarka, J. (1989), "Networking and small firms", *International Small Business Journal*, 8, 2.

Takamiya, M. (1985), "Conclusions and Policy Implications", in Takamiya and Thurley, op. cit.

Takamiya, S., and Thurley, K. (eds) (1985), *Japan's Emerging Multinationals*, Tokyo : Tokyo University Press.

Teece, D.J. (1986), "Profiting from Technological Innovation : Implications for International Collaboration, Licensing & Public Policy", *Research Policy*, 15, pp. 285-305.

Teece, D.J. (1988), "Technological Change and the Nature of the Firm", in Dosi, G., _et al._ (eds) op. cit., pp. 256-281.

Teece, D.J., Pisano, G., and Shuen, A. (1990), "Firm Capabilities, Resources, and the Concept of Strategy", CCC Working Paper no. 90-8 (mimeo), Consortium on Competitiveness and Co-operation, University of California at Berkeley.

Tilton, J. (1971), *International Diffusion of Technology*, Washington : Brookings Institution.

UNCTC (1991), "World Investment Report 1991, the Triad in Foreign Direct Investment", New York : ONU, ST/CTC/118.

US Supreme Court (1986), Judgment in Matsushita vs Zenith Case, 26 March, Lexis.

Valls, J., Escorsa, P., Martinez, C. (1991), "Technological Audits to SMEs, Final Report, Catalonia", Euromanagement Pilot Scheme, DG XXIII, Commission of European Communities, Brussels

Valls, J., Martinez, C. (1992), "Institutional Diversity, Cohesion and Technological Policies at a Regional Level. Some Lessons from the Spanish Experience", *Revue d'Economie Industrielle*, April.

Vernon, R. (1966), "International Investment and International Trade in the Product Cycle", *Quarterly Journal of Economics*, 80, pp. 190-207.

Vernon, R. (1971), *Sovereignty at Bay : the Multinational Spread of US Enterprises*, New York : Basic Books.

Vernon, R. (1977), *Storm over the Multinationals : The Real Issues*, London : Macmillan.

Vernon, R. (1979), "The Product Cycle Hypothesis in a New International Environment", *Bulletin of Economic and Social Statistics*, 41, pp. 255-267.

Vernon, J., and Graham, D. (1971), "Profitability of Monopolization by Vertical Integration", *Journal of Political Economy*, vol. 79, July-August, pp. 924-925.

Vernon, R., and Davidson, W. (1979), "Foreign Production of Technology-Intensive Products by US-based Multinational Enterprises", Working Paper no. 79-5, Division of Research, Graduate School of Business Administration, Harvard University.

Von Hippel, E. (1988), "Trading Trade Secrets", *Technology Review*.

Walsh, V. (1984), "Invention and Innovation in the Chemical Industry : Demand Pull or Discovery Push ?", *Research Policy*, 13, pp. 211-234.

Walsh, V. (forthcoming), "Demand, Public Markets and Innovation in Biotechnology", *Science and Public Policy*.

Walsh, V., Galimberti, I., Gill, J., Richards, A., and Sharma, Y. (1991), "Globalisation of Technology and the Economy : The Case of Biotechnology", Report to EC/FAST Programme DP 2/13.

Watanabe, S. (forthcoming), "Growth and Structural Changes of */ ?.Japanese Overseas Direct Investment : Implications for Labour and Management in Host Economies", in Renshaw, G. (ed.), *Employment and multinationals in the 1990s*, Geneva : ILO.

Weber, A. (1909), *Über den Standort der Industrien,* Tübingen : Mohr (English translation by C. Friedrich, 1929).

Weber, A. (1911), Die Standortslehre und die Handelspolitik. Archiv für Wissenschaft und Sozialpolitik, XXXII, pp. 667-88 (English version in International Economic Papers, vol. 8, 1958, pp. 133-46).

Williamson, O. (1975), *Markets and Hierarchies : Analysis and Anti-Trust Implications*, New York : The Free Press.

Williamson, O. (1985), *The Economic Institutions of Capitalism*, New York : The Free Press.

Womack, J., Jones, D., and Roos, D. (1990), *The Machine that Changed the World*, New York : Rawson Associates/ Macmillan.

Wright, B. (1983), "The Economics of Invention Incentives : Patents, Prizes and Research Contracts", *American Economic Review*, September.

Yamamura, K. (1986), "'Caveat Emptor'. The Industrial Policy of Japan", in Krugman (ed.), op. cit., pp. 169-210.

Yoshitomi, M. (1992), "Corporate Society-Keiretsu", *Look Japan*, March.

Young, A. (1991), "Learning by Doing and the Dynamic Effects of International Trade", *Quarterly Journal of Economics*, May.

Yoxen, E., and Green, K. (1990), *Scenarios for Biotechnology in Europe : A Research Agenda,* Luxembourg : Office for Official Publications of the European Communities (European Foundation for the Improvement of Living and Working Conditions).

Zimmermann, J.B. (1988), "L'équilibre oligopolistique face à la transformation des modes d'organisation industrielle et de la concurrence", *Economies et Sociétés*, n° 11-12, pp. 221-240.

Zimmermann, J.B. (1991), "Destabilisation des oligopoles et nouvelles formes d'organisation industrielle. Le cas d'IBM et de l'industrie informatique", Working Paper 91B01, mimeo, Marseille, GREQE.

Index